To Maggie

Contents

Illustrations

Foreword

Quintin Gilbey has a big advantage over most historians in that he is acquainted with all the characters of whom he writes, and many of them were, and are, his personal friends.

Quinny and I have been friends for nearly forty-five years, and we have had some grand times together. I know that throughout his long career in Fleet Street nothing gave him more pleasure than to write a glowing report of some race in which he thought that one or perhaps two of us had excelled ourselves.

He hated to accuse a jockey of riding a bad race, and when he did so you can bet your life the man had ridden a shocker.

Quinny's story begins a few months before I joined Mr. Martin Hartigan's stable as a fifteen-year-old apprentice, and ends with Nijinsky's Triple Crown. He was an eyewitness of all the great races he describes, and I am not ashamed to admit that my eyes became misty as I read his tales of lovable Steve from whom I learnt so much when I was a kid at Foxhill, of Brownie Carslake, old Joe Childs, Freddy Fox, Michael Beary and Frank Bullock. Alas, they are no longer with us, but they live again in Quinny's stories of their deeds, in what he describes as the golden age of jockeyship.

The past, however, is not glorified at the expense of the present, and Quinny is firmly of the opinion that never in the history of racing has there been a better jockey than Lester. I couldn't agree with him more.

GORDON RICHARDS

1 Peace of a kind

The war was over and the fortunate survivors were determined to extract every ounce of fun from the lives which they had risked, day by day, for what seemed an eternity. Thankful that they had not stopped one in a place that really mattered, the returning soldiers were intoxicated by the knowledge that never again would they stand knee deep in mud or be required to offer their bodies to the enemy to satisfy the vanity of some general miles behind the front line.

The only thing to be said in favour of the trenches was that you couldn't spend money in them, so on Armistice Day 1918 every soldier in the British Army, unless he had recently returned from leave, had a few quid in his pocket and the prospect of a gratuity.

We all know that a fool and his money are soon parted, but the British Army at the end of 1918 was not composed of fools, but of men and boys who were thankful to be alive in a world in which death was no longer a constant companion. The top brass and the regimental sergeant-majors may have been content to put their feet up, but for 90 per cent of the rest the prospect of Civvy Street was the be-all and end-all of their young lives. They craved excitement, and where better to find it than on the racecourse?

'Oh to be a bookmaker, now that peace is here!' an elderly racegoer remarked to me shortly after I had been gazetted in December 1918, having missed the slaughter by a very short head and being unashamedly thankful to have done so. Although these deliriously happy soldiers, soon to be civilians, were not fools, they were, of course, mugs, and mugs with money in their pockets are the answer to a bookmaker's prayer.

Racing had been my hobby from the time I had learned to read, and I was fortunate to have it impressed on me in my extreme youth that the bookmakers knew far more about the game than I did. But the men who had spent their formative years trying to kill, while avoiding being killed themselves, just betted for the hell of it. In consequence, every layabout became a tipster, with long-priced winners which couldn't get beaten, and S.P. bookmakers sprang up like mushrooms. The bookmakers and the spivs cleaned up, and it was a tragedy that those who had gone through hell should derive so little pleasure from the money they had risked their lives to earn.

Neither the Jockey Club nor the National Hunt Committee was renowned for the speed at which it operated, but in 1919 they got a move on to cater for the post-war racing boom, and, against all the odds, the Grand National was run at Liverpool in the spring for the first time for four years.

Major Hugh Peel's Poethlyn had won a substitute National the previous year, and though he had 12 stone 7 lb to carry he was installed a hot favourite. This was a cruel weight to ask a horse to carry round 4 miles 856 yards and over thirty of the biggest fences in the world, and only four horses have ever carried it successfully. But Poethlyn, ridden by Lester Piggott's grandfather Ernie, triumphed under it and was the last horse to do so. In the following year he fell at the first fence, and I can sympathise with his resolution never to tackle the course again. Very little steeplechasing had been permitted during the war, and the opposition to Poethlyn was substandard, but by this feat he assured himself a place among the immortals.

A day's racing was quite an adventure till well into the twenties, and thousands who set off for the 1919 Derby never got there. No private cars had been built since 1914, at which time they were still primitive contraptions.

Immediately petrol was available, old crocks, which had been rusting for years in backyards, were recalled to duty and sold at two and three times their original price. My racing took place in the Home Counties, where on roads constructed for horse traffic, ankle deep in dust, traffic jams were worse than anything we experience today.

The breakdown of only one of these old crocks in some lane which went by the name of a highway could immobilise hundreds of vehicles. A car had only to remain stationary on a hot summer's day for more than a few minutes, with the engine running, for it to boil over.

Only one car in ten had a self-starter which worked, and if you stalled the engine you could consider yourself lucky if it re-started with less than a dozen turns of the starting handle.

Sensible people went racing by train whenever they could, but even this traditional means of transport was not without its hazards. Although crime was not as sophisticated as it is today, there were more petty crooks around then than at any time in our history. Back pay and war gratuities were their main objectives, and what the demobbed, and those waiting to be demobbed, did not lose to the bookmakers on the course they lost to the cardsharpers on the trains.

Sometimes they lost the lot on the way, and hadn't even got the entrance money to the silver ring when they arrived at the course. 'Spot the lady' (the three-card trick) was the usual game. The number I spiv would start the game with a couple of accomplices, who pretended to be mugs. The corner of the Queen was turned up, one of the 'mugs' would back it, and, of course, he won.

This appeared to be money for jam; the corner of the Queen was still turned up, and the real mugs fell over themselves to back it. Number I spiv would appear reluctant to let them join in, saying it was a private game, but, after all, they looked good sports, and he had a soft spot for soldiers. The card was still turned up at the corner, but when it was turned face upwards it had become any other card in the pack except the Queen.

Provided there were plenty of mugs in the carriage the card-sharpers would leave the ordinary racegoer alone, but if there were not enough people willing to play with them they could turn very nasty indeed if one declined to participate in what they described as their harmless bit of fun. When the train arrived at its destination a large man would bar the carriage door till all his mates were haring along the platform in case one of their victims complained to the police, who were on every racecourse station.

The cardsharpers' victims had really only themselves to blame as police paraded the platforms at all the London stations warning passengers not to play cards with strangers.

More sinister were 'the boys', though apart from the pocket-picking they did not bother the punters, their objective being the bookmakers' satchels. They were a desperate lot of criminals, but their most sensational affray was between rival gangs. It took place on Lewes racecourse, and one man was killed while a number of others received severe knife wounds. As far as I can remember, none carried guns, but a fearful array of knives of all sorts and other lethal weapons was seized by the police.

Scotland Yard and the police did a great job in stamping out racecourse hooliganism by the middle twenties.

2 Getting back to normal

Steve Donoghue—most popular jockey since Fred Archer – Grand Parade, whose mother pulled a cart, wins first post-war Derby – Arthur Smith picks the wrong one – Skinner for the books – The Panther an expensive failure – Buchan an unlucky loser – Odds-on Buchan finishes poor third in St Leger and Major Gerald Deane and Joe Childs nearly come to blows – Childs' last race in the Astor colours.

A famous theatrical impresario used to say that the play was the thing, and that audiences would queue up and sit on sugar boxes provided the entertainment was to their liking. That may have been true during the war, when even shows of no particular merit played to packed houses, but with the passing of the years theatre audiences and racegoers became more discriminating. In my opening chapter I have set the stage for the drama which was to be enacted in the next fifty years, and I have, if anything, understated the discomfort inseparable from a day at the races in those piping days of peace.

Post-war booms are short-lived, and racecourse companies, bookmakers and the army of spivs, who had never had it so good, found that the flood of easy money had dried up by the end of 1919. Fortunately for racing, there was a hard core of regulars still prepared to watch the show from sugar boxes. Excepting for a few courses, whose licences should have been withdrawn years ago, racecourse amenities have improved out of all knowledge in the past ten years, but a day's racing in this country still costs more than anywhere else in the world. There

B

is no getting away from the fact that the fare served up to the customers at many meetings does not represent value for money, an expression rarely employed fifty years ago. The rich were so rich and the poor so grateful for the crumbs which fell from the rich man's table that few questioned the sanctity of the *status quo.*

The land fit for heroes promised by Lloyd George seemed to be a long time materialising, but for six months following the Armistice the people of this country lived in a state of euphoria.

By the end of the summer, however, it began to dawn on the workers that the politicians had been guilty of a confidence trick of such proportions that compared with them the 'spot the lady' spivs were philanthropists: but there wasn't much they could do about it, though there was a brief railway strike, which made it even more difficult to get to and from our race-courses.

Racing always had been, and still was, carried on chiefly for the amusement of a few colossally rich men. We had been engaged for over four years in the most ghastly war in the history of mankind, but hereditary wealth was still intact, in addition to which vast sums of money had been accumulated by the war profiteers.

Eighty per cent of the horses in training were owned by men so wealthy that a little thing like value for money never entered their heads. They raced for one another's money and did not seem to think it strange that there was no prize money for winning the Derby and the Oaks.

Up to 1921, when the Derby was won by Humorist, the winning owner received £6,450, every penny of which was subscribed by the owners of the 335 entries. Had not Mr Joel been the breeder as well as the owner of Humorist he would have received only £5,950.

Long before my day, the Eclipse Stakes at Sandown had been worth £10,000, but this great prize had only cost the executive £1,000, the remaining £9,000 being subscribed by the owners. Sandown, however, has always been our most enterprising racecourse, and if the owners were content to sponsor a race for £9,000—it was no concern of theirs.

In these circumstances it was not altogether surprising that neither the Jockey Club nor the racecourse companies worried much about the comfort of those who wanted to attend the races. They gave us the impression that they could not care less whether we came or stayed away, and I think they considered themselves jolly decent for accepting our money and letting us in.

Until quite recently it was as difficult to get into the Private stand at Newmarket as it is alleged to be to get past St Peter, and vouchers had to be signed and countersigned by members of the Jockey Club. Today the Jockey Club welcomes all and sundry with open arms, and no past indiscretions will be raked up when you queue up for admittance to this one-time holy of holies. It is advisable, however, to remove the spent cartridges from your gun and the tell-tale stains from your knife. Such was the scene when the racing world went back to business as usual.

One figure stands out in my memory head and shoulders above all other racing men of his time, though he stood little more than an inch over five feet. The name Steve Donoghue was on the lips not only of all racegoers but of every housewife when she handed her bob (or perhaps it was only a tanner) to the milkman to put on 'what Steve rides in the three o'clock'. It was perfectly legitimate for the well-to-do to ring up their S.P. bookmakers and invest any sum they liked, but the less fortunate committed an offence every time they supported their fancy.

Bookies' runners were constantly harried by the police, but those who worked in the plush offices of the wealthy Starting Price bookmakers were respected members of the community.

Not since the days of Fred Archer had a jockey captured the public imagination to the extent that Steve Donoghue had done during the war years, and now that racing was returning to normal he was the most popular figure in the sporting world. I remember a newspaper carrying the banner 'Steve mobbed by the demobbed' after he had ridden a big winner, but this awful pun expressed no more than the truth.

Each succeeding generation makes its own idols, and the

acclaim given to Steve was on a par with that reserved for long-haired guitar players fifty years later.

He was always immaculate in suits from the most expensive tailors. His face was dominated by large brown eyes, irresistible when they smiled, as they did constantly. Young and old were bowled over by his charm, and he gave everyone he met the impression that he or she was the one person he had been longing to talk to.

I was first introduced to him at the age of thirteen, on a visit to the famous trainer Atty Persse at Stockbridge, and his smile was accompanied by a few words specially for me. His voice was husky, and his speech remained as ungrammatical as on the day he ran away from his home at Warrington, wearing clogs, at the age of twelve.

For six years from 1907 the great American jockey Danny Maher and the young Australian rider Frank Wootton had reigned supreme, Maher being champion jockey twice and Wootton four times. These men were before my time, though some years later I saw Wootton ride over hurdles, but there is no doubt that they were two of the finest riders of all time.

Wootton, however, became too heavy to ride on the flat soon after his twenty-first birthday, and Maher developed tuberculosis from which he died early in the war. By then Donoghue had been knocking at the door for several years, and in 1914 with the retirement of Maher and Wootton he topped the list for the first time with 129 winners.

In the limited amount of racing that took place during the war Steve's position as champion was never threatened, and he won the triple crown in 1915 on Pommern and in 1917 on Gay Crusader, whom he always maintained was the best horse he ever rode. These races were all run at Newmarket. When the war ended Steve's services were in tremendous demand for all the big races, but Sir Walter Gilbey managed to secure him to ride his colt Paper Money in the 1919 Derby, to the great excitement of the entire Gilbey family. Although I always called him uncle, Sir Walter was my father's first cousin, their respective fathers Walter and Alfred having founded the business which bears our name.

Sir Walter was a conspicuous figure in his immaculate tweed suits, with a mauve carnation in his buttonhole, and a bowler hat with an extra curly brim, which he had made specially for him. He was inclined to be self-opinionated, but he was a pretty good judge of horses of all kinds. He had very decided views on the make and shape of a horse and he liked to impress on people his knowledge of equine anatomy.

I remember remarking to him as Pasch was standing in the winning enclosure at Newmarket that I thought he was a very good Two Thousand Guineas winner, to which he replied, in a voice which could have been heard at the Bushes, 'I don't like him, his tail's set too low.' I have heard horses crabbed for a hundred different reasons, but never before or since for the position of their tails. A very kind man, he was devoted to his trainer Tom Cannon with whom he trained for well over forty years.

The Panther, who had won the Two Thousand Guineas, and was reported to have done a marvellous gallop, was all the rage for the 1919 Derby. As I have already said, everyone had money to burn that summer. Seldom can the bookmakers have reaped such a harvest. Having been backed down to the unrealistic price of 6/5 The Panther demonstrated that he was 100 per cent on the side of 'the enemy'. He did his best to get left at the post and succeeded in losing several lengths. He was never seen with a chance. The Panther's bad behaviour upset several of his opponents, notably Buchan, in the colours of Major Waldorf Astor.

Steve, on Paper Money, led till about two furlongs from home, when he was headed by Grand Parade and Buchan, the former winning by half a length, with Paper Money two lengths behind. Some people thought that Steve had made too much use of Paper Money, but he had ridden him in the same way that he was to ride four out of five Derby winners in the years to come. I think his tactics suited Paper Money, but I have always regarded Buchan as a most unlucky loser. In addition to being slowly away, he went at least three lengths further than the winner, who was beautifully ridden by Fred Templeman, still hale and hearty today I am glad to report.

Grand Parade was a chance ride for Templeman, as Arthur Smith, first jockey to Lord Glanely, chose to ride his stable companion Dominion, who started at 100/9; the winner started at 33/1. It was a huge benefit for the bookmakers, many of whom had not even written the winner's name in their books, though Frank Barling, trainer of both Grand Parade and Dominion, told me years later that he backed them both, and was delighted when Grand Parade won at the longer price.

Cardiff shipping magnate Bill Tatham, recently raised to the peerage as Lord Glanely, spent a goodly proportion of his vast fortune on yearlings, but the coal-black Grand Parade, whom he bought as a foal in Ireland, cost him only 470 guineas. Like his sire Orby he was not a particularly distinguished Derby winner, and his dam Geraldine was reported to have pulled a cart in Ireland though she was a grand-daughter of St Simon.

If ever a colt looked a certainty for the St Leger that colt was Buchan on whom Joe Childs was substituted for the luckless Brennan who had ridden him in the Derby. Backers had no hesitation in laying odds of 11/8 on him, which even the hard-headed professionals considered a generous price. But he was beaten six lengths and two lengths by Lord Derby's filly Keysoe, whose form was extremely moderate, and by Dominion, who had finished many lengths behind him in the Derby. The going was good and I never heard a satisfactory explanation for his failure.

Major Aston's notoriously hot-tempered racing manager, Major Gerald Deane, told Childs that either he had ridden the worst race in the history of the St Leger, or else he had pulled Buchan. Joe Childs had a bit of a temper himself, and he wasn't standing for this. So a slanging match ensued which would have ended in blows had they not been forcibly separated. Childs never again rode in the Astor colours, though he continued to ride for the other Manton owners. I think that the probable reason for Buchan's failure was that he did not stay a mile and three-quarters at racing pace: as we will see later, this view is not contradicted by the fact that he staggered first past the post in the following year's Gold Cup. Between Epsom and Doncaster he won the Eclipse stakes, and a month after his sensational defeat at Doncaster he took the Champion Stakes. I had only once been racing during the war years, and Buchan was the first really good horse I had seen. My memory of him is therefore clearer than that of several equally good horses who followed him.

3 Steve

Steve supreme—steals Derby mount from Jellis and it falls - Spion Kop wins Derby - Luckless Arthur Smith picks the wrong one again - Buchan disqualified after winning Gold Cup – The French hold up their heads again.

Although Steve Donoghue did not ride a classic winner in 1919 or 1920 he remained on the crest of the wave, finishing far ahead of his nearest rivals with 129 winners in 1919 and 143 in 1920. The now familiar cry of 'Come on, Steve!' echoed from one end of the country to the other and the crowd would rise to him as he rode into the winning enclosure, smiling his acknowledgement of the cheers. In those days my judgement was very immature, but from the moment Steve left the paddock to canter down to post you didn't need to be an expert to realise that you were watching an artist.

The Hon. George Lambton, who knew more about horses and the men who rode them than any man of his time, wrote that Steve could get more out of a horse with his little finger than any other jockey could with whip and spur, and that he could hold the hardest puller on a silken thread. Any trainer who knows his job can teach his apprentices to ride reasonably well, but 'hands' are a divine gift, and Steve had the hands of an angel.

As a young boy he was always on the move, so he received less tuition than does the average apprentice; but after a variety of jobs in France and Ireland he started riding in England in his early twenties, and it was apparent at once that he was not just a young man trying to make his way, but a fully fledged jockey. His first ride in the Derby was on Charles O'Malley, who finished third to Lemberg and Greenback in 1910.

In Steve's young days horses were part of the family and were loved for themselves as well as for the services they rendered. You made it your business to get to know their likes and dislikes, and, in return, they served you with unswerving loyalty, no matter if they were thoroughbreds, living in the luxury of a racing stable, or animals of mixed parentage, whose job it was to pull a cart.

Steve spent hours getting to know the horses in the stables that retained him, or for whom he rode work, but such was his intuition that before he reached the starting gate he had usually come to an understanding with a horse he was riding for the first time. If he had possessed the same understanding of his fellow men as he had of their horses he would not have had to wait from 1925 to 1937 before he rode another classic winner.

Steve's account of how he came to ride Abbots Trace in the 1920 Derby conflicts with that of Jellis, who as the stable jockey went to Epsom expecting to ride the horse for Mr Dewar, later Lord Dewar.

Steve had been engaged to ride Prince Galahad, but the colt went wrong and was scratched on the day before the Derby. Steve's version of what occurred is that Mr Jack Joel, for whom he often rode, told him that Mr Dewar was desperately keen that he should ride Abbots Trace, now that he had become available, and that it would be ludicrous for the champion jockey to watch the Derby from the stands.

Steve maintained that he first turned down the offer, but after a friendly interview between Mr Dewar, Jellis and himself, in which Mr Dewar promised Jellis the same present as Steve if Abbots Trace won, 'Jellis very sportingly smiled and agreed to the bargain'.

On the other hand Jellis told me that he first learned he was not to ride the colt when he went to change into Mr Dewar's colours and was told that Donoghue was riding him. 'I told him I hoped he would break his bloody neck,' he said, 'and, of course, I could have cut my tongue out when down he went, when leading, two out.'

This was my first Derby, and though I've only missed two in the intervening fifty years, I think it was the strangest. Brownie Carslake's mount Tetratema, who had inherited much of the speed of his sire The Tetrarch, generally agreed to be the fastest two-year-old that ever lived, had won the Two Thousand Guineas and was made a hot favourite. With the hindsight we now possess it was any odds against Tetratema getting the trip, but a lot of people, who should have known better, held the view that the moderate horses opposed to him would never get him off the bit, in which case his stamina would not be put to the test. In a somewhat substandard field Steve and most of the other jockeys had one idea in their heads—go like hell to beat the favourite. Steve admitted setting a mad gallop and riding a shocking race, but he was still in front with less than two furlongs to go when down he went and the field galloped over his prostrate body. By a miracle he was unhurt, and later in the day he rode a terrific race to win by a short head on a horse called Prince Herod, whose owner Jimmy White had £2,000 each way on him—quite a nice little bet when the pound was worth about six times what it is today.

No one, least of all Steve, could explain why Abbots Trace fell. He had galloped full out for one and a quarter miles; but horses that are exhausted slow down, they don't fall when still travelling at around forty miles an hour, and I think what probably happened was that he crossed his legs when he saw Sarchedon swerve towards him, though they did not touch.

On the other hand, he may have skidded on one of the numerous bare patches which disfigured the Derby course in those days, when the track received no attention from one year's end to another. A heatwave was in progress and the going was as hard as a rock, which made Steve's escape all the more miraculous.

The race was won by Spion Kop in the Pretty Polly colours of Major Giles Loder, a serving officer in the Scots Guards. He owed his success largely to the fact that the great French-based American jockey Frank O'Neill had other ideas than beating Tetratema, who, in point of fact, was a spent force at Tattenham Corner.

For the second year running poor Arthur Smith picked the wrong one. He was now first jockey to the Fairhaven Lodge trainer, Peter Purcell Gilpin, who had won the Derby with Spion Kop's sire Spearmint, and in the morning papers Smith was down to ride Spion Kop. But he changed his mind at the last moment and decided to ride the ill-tempered Sarchedon, who he thought had gone the better in their final gallop. Sarchedon started at 9/1 and Spion Kop at 100/6, so for the second year running the Derby had been won by a stable's second string.

Smith received some consolation when he won the 1920 St Leger on Caligula, who, like Tetratema, was by The Tetrarch, but was much more stoutly bred on his dam's side.

Caligula was trained by an up-and-coming trainer, still in his mid-twenties, named Harvey Leader, who today could still pass for fifty. Known to everyone in the racing world as 'Jack', Harvey Leader is one of the finest trainers and best-loved characters in the racing world. I was fortunate that he took me under his wing when I was very young, and he not only taught me the rudiments of the racing business, which was to become my profession, but set me an example of how to win and how to lose without being a bore to one's friends. I did not make Jack's acquaintance till several years after Caligula's victory, but I have been with him in triumph and disaster and I know that Kipling must have had a man like Jack Leader in mind when he wrote 'IF'.

With his usual modesty, Jack described Caligula as an easy horse to train, but the obstacles he had to overcome before he hoisted Smith into the saddle at Doncaster were of the sort which would make any normal man old before his time. Caligula was going better with every gallop, but the same could not be said of his owner Lord Wilton, whose financial affairs were in a terrible tangle. A court order forbade his running his horses, which were to be sold, a reserve of 6,000 guineas being placed on Caligula. Unless a buyer could be found who was prepared to pay this price, the colt could not run, and Jack searched far and wide for such a saviour, but in vain. Then, a few days before the race, Jack, now in despair, heard that a rich Hindu called Mr Goculdas might be interested.

A cable was sent to Bombay, and the reply was to the effect that Jack had found himself a new owner. Years later, when I was a stipendiary steward with the Royal Western India Turf Club, I met Mr Goculdas. He was a charming old gentleman, and though he had lost all his money, he retained his enthusiasm for racing. Spion Kop was unplaced behind Caligula, and he never won another race after the Derby. He and Grand Parade were probably two of the least distinguished Derby winners of my time, though Spion Kop became the sire of the 1928 Derby winner, Felstead.

Few Derbys can have required less winning than Spion Kop's, as he was the only genuine stayer in the field in a race run at a mad gallop. Orpheus, who finished third, did not get a yard over ten furlongs, but he was a top-class colt up to that distance. Buchan was the only really high-class one-and-a-half mile colt to run in the first two post-war Derbys, though he may have been even better over one and a quarter miles.

I have not forgotten, nor am I likely to forget, that Buchan won the 1920 Gold Cup (two and a half miles) but was disqualified, the race being awarded to Tangiers. Buchan, at odds on, was no use to an impecunious bank clerk such as myself, so I had supported Sir William Nelson's colt. It was not considered the right thing to do in those days to lodge an objection at Royal Ascot, and Buchan's disqualification was received in shocked silence. He was, however, desperately tired at the end of a race over double his best distance, and he was rolling from side to side. I have no doubt that the stewards today would have acted on their own initiative and relegated him to second place, but under the absurd rules in force in those days he was placed last.

No praise could be too high for Buchan, who kept plodding on, though reeling with fatigue, and he must have been possessed of an iron constitution because a few weeks later he won the Eclipse Stakes for the second year running.

Spion Kop, ridden by Steve, started a hot favourite for the Grand Prix de Paris, but was unplaced; a thrilling race was won by his stable companion Comrade, superbly ridden by Frank Bullock. Comrade had no classic engagements, but his victory in this race and in the Prix de l'Arc de Triomphe stamped him as the best colt of his generation. It is interesting to note that Spion Kop's Derby was worth £6,450, but that Comrade earned £13,235 by his victory in the Grand Prix and £6,000 for winning the Prix de l'Arc de Triomphe. The latter was a brand-new race, and though it carried considerable prestige, many years were to pass before it superseded the Grand Prix as Europe's greatest race. Galloper Light, trained by Jack Watson of Newmarket and ridden by George Hulme, had won the Grand Prix in 1919, and Lemonora, ridden by Joe Childs and trained by Alec Taylor, won it in 1922. He was the last English-trained horse to do so.

In the First World War France was one huge battlefield. Chantilly was in the hands of the Germans and a number of the leading studs ceased to exist. It was therefore not surprising that our horses were superior to the French in 1919 and remained so till a grand little chestnut colt called Ksar, ridden by George Stern, pulverised the English representatives in the 1922 Prix de l'Arc de Triomphe, and won it again the following year in the hands of Frank Bullock.

The French had, with justification, considered themselves the senior partner in the Entente Cordiale, but when the war was ended the franc was devalued to fifty to the pound, and their most valuable races were won by horses from England.

Ksar, a son of Bruleur, was therefore hailed as a hero, and I have seldom heard a horse given such an ovation as he received at Longchamp when accounting for a high-class field, including Square Measure, Pomme de Terre and Blue Dun, all from England. Despite his name, Pomme de Terre was 100 per cent English bred. He was owned by Lord Zetland and trained by his son, Lord George Dundas. Ridden by Robbins, he had won the previous year's Prix du President de la Republique, as the Grand Prix de St Cloud was then known.

Judged by any standards Ksar was a smashing good colt, and following his victory at Longchamp my French friends told me: 'We can hold up our heads once again.' Ksar was the sire of Tourbillon, who was worth his weight in gold both as a racehorse and as a sire to M. Marcel Boussac.

4 Humorist, the brave

Steve rides the race of his life on a dying horse to win the 1921 Derby – His tribute to Humorist – Lord Derby releases him but says 'never again' – Captain Cuttle wins first Derby for which there is prize money—bookmakers think he is lame and pay dearly for their mistake – Lord Woolavington gives Steve generous present and retainer for next season.

In 1921 Steve Donoghue fulfilled his dearest wish—to win an Epsom Derby. But the machinations which led up to his association with the immortal Humorist sowed the first seeds of the disapproval from owners which was to have such a disastrous effect on his career.

In the previous year he had ridden Humorist for Mr Jack Joel and had fallen in love with him. It was therefore a surprise to his friends, whom he had told that Humorist might be a Derby colt, when he accepted a retainer to ride for Lord Derby in 1921, as it was almost certain that the latter would have a runner in the race which bore his name.

Steve was able to ride Humorist in the Two Thousand Guineas, in which Lord Derby had no runner, and he finished third, after looking all over a winner. Some people thought that he had been caught napping, while others declared that Humorist was a rogue. Steve knew that neither view explained his defeat, but he could not put his finger on the reason for the colt's stopping as if he had been shot.

For the next three weeks Steve rode him nearly every day,

and Humorist thrived on his work for the first time in his life. Horse and jockey became devoted to one another, and it never seemed to enter Steve's head that he might be called upon to honour his contract with Lord Derby. But Lord Derby had a colt called Glorioso engaged, and decided to run him.

Steve was flabbergasted when George Lambton told him he would be required to ride Glorioso. 'But he's got no chance,' Steve protested, to which Lambton replied that retainers were like marriage lines—for better or worse.

Steve begged and pleaded, and Lord Derby, great sportsman that he was, finally agreed to release him, though he made it quite clear that he was doing so solely on account of his respect for Mr Jack Joel, an owner and breeder on the very best lines. Racing was Mr Joel's sole recreation and he had founded the Childwick Bury stud twenty-five years earlier. He was one of the best judges of a pedigree in the country and his exceptional intelligence, allied to the skill and experience of his trainer, Charles Morton, were productive of a long series of triumphs.

Samuel Johnson wrote: 'As a man advances in life he gets that which is better than admiration—judgement to estimate things at their own value.' Looking back over the years, I am undecided as to when my estimates became solely of my own making and were not tinged with the views of my elders. I believe that Steve Donoghue's handling of Humorist in the 1921 Derby constituted one of the finest pieces of jockeyship in my lifetime, though I am not certain whether I should have been so convinced had not his skill that day been lauded to the skies by those with far more knowledge of racing than I had at that time. When we became friends, years later, Steve told me that this was the best race he ever rode, and the one which gave him most pleasure. There is no shadow of doubt that had anyone else in the world ridden Humorist, Lord Astor's Craig an Eran would have won.

As Major Waldorf Astor, Lord Astor had seen his Buchan most unluckily defeated two years earlier, and now only a superhuman effort by the greatest living jockey prevented the victory of his Craig an Eran, a son of Sunstar, with whom Mr Joel had won the race ten years earlier. Jack Brennan rode both

Buchan and Craig an Eran, but he certainly could not be blamed for the latter's defeat: he was just unlucky in running up against one of the greatest jockeys and the bravest horse that ever lived.

Steve described the last moments of that historic race in the following words: 'Leighton, the leader, was beaten in the dip, but I did not take up the running as that would have been asking too much of my little friend, so I tucked him in on the rails behind Alan Breck. When the latter faltered I slipped between him and the rails, and as I did so I saw Craig an Eran gaining on me. Every yard counted now and as I knew my little fellow was doing all he could I would have sooner cut off my right arm than hit him with the whip. So with Craig an Eran creeping up on me I sat still, and gave him all the help I could with my hands, and we passed the post a winner by a neck.'

Humorist did not run at Ascot. Charles Morton had noticed a fleck of blood inside his nostril when he arrived at the royal meeting, so he was sent home to Wantage. A few days later Sir A. J. Munnings went down to paint his portrait. He had worked on him in the morning, but when he went into the box after luncheon he found the little horse dead on the floor in a pool of blood. A post-mortem revealed that Humorist had a tubercular lung condition and there is no doubt that from time to time he must have been in great pain. His sudden collapse at the end of the Two Thousand Guineas was no longer a mystery.

Steve had ridden him with all the tenderness for which he was famous, and Humorist had responded like the great-hearted little warrior he was. His death was not only a tragic loss to Mr Joel but to British bloodstock, as it was as certain as anything can be in racing that a horse of such breeding, quality, ability and courage must have become a successful stallion in the ordinary course of events.

Steve's reputation as a jockey stood higher than ever following his victory in the Derby, though as far as the future was concerned it might have been better had he stood by his contract and ridden Glorioso. Lord Derby and his trainer George Lambton considered Steve to be the greatest jockey in the world and they also had a great affection for him, but they decided there and then that they must look elsewhere for a stable jockey. Their choice was Ted Gardner, a capable rider, who would not consider himself entitled to pick and choose his mount when under contract. Had Steve not ridden Humorist in the Derby he might have won the race for Lord Derby on Sansovino and Hyperion, and ridden any number of other big winners in the black jacket and white cap.

But in 1922 the boot was on the other foot. Steve was engaged to ride Captain Cuttle for Lord Woolavington in the Derby only a few days before the race, and this time it was Vic Smyth who was 'jocked off' to enable Steve to ride the horse of his choice.

Captain Cuttle, a massive, heavy-topped chestnut son of Hurry On, was not an easy horse to train. He disappointed in the Guineas, after which he was found to be suffering from a digestive disorder. Fred Darling rode him himself in most of his work and he looked the hell of a horse when stripped in the paddock at Epsom. He had been the medium of a gamble, but when Steve mounted him he was found to be lame and it was discovered he had spread a plate. He therefore had to be re-shod, and when he finally cantered to post, long after the others, he seemed to be a bit stiff, and rumours spread around the course that he was lame.

The bookmakers knocked him out to 10/1 and took a caning for their foolhardiness. Steve had Captain Cuttle in the leading bunch from flagfall and he was clear at Tattenham Corner. From that point the race was a procession, Captain Cuttle winning by four lengths from Tamar, a full brother to Buchan in the colours of Lord Astor, who therefore had the mortification of seeing a horse of his finish second in the Derby in three years out of four.

Captain Cuttle was undoubtedly one of the best Derby winners between the wars. He went on to Ascot and won the St James's Palace Stakes, but could not be trained for the St Leger. His trouble was that his legs were not up to supporting his great body. Thirty-one years later Pinza, who weighed even more than Captain Cuttle, was similarly handicapped and broke down before the St Leger.

C

This was the first Derby for which the Epsom authority donated any prize money, and winning owner Lord Woolavington is reputed to have given the £3,000 prize money, plus another £2,000, to Steve. This I can well believe. Born James Buchanan, millionaire Lord Woolavington was seventy-three years old and raced originally as Mr Kincaid. He had raced on the best lines for twenty years before Captain Cuttle, whom he bred himself, made him 'the happiest man in the world', so he told his friend and business rival Sir Walter Gilbey.

5 Lord Derby's Derby

Steve up to his tricks again—refuses to ride for Lord Woolavington, and completes Derby hat-trick on Papyrus— then sacked by Fred Darling – The luck of Ben Irish – Gardner sacked by Lord Derby – Lambton engages Tommy Weston – Lambton's magnanimity – Tranquil wins St Leger trained by Charlie Morton – Sansovino's Derby, wettest ever – Stanley House back to its former glory – The Aga Khan wins with second string.

So delighted was Lord Woolavington at Steve's riding of Captain Cuttle that he gave him a fat retainer for the following season. Steve therefore started in 1923 with the job coveted by all jockeys—first jockey to the great Beckhampton trainer, Fred Darling. A dynamic figure, quick-tempered and a martinet, the master of Beckhampton has never had and never will have a superior at the art of timing a horse's preparation so that he reaches the pinnacle of physical fitness on the day of a great race; but one did not need to be a very astute judge of character to realise that he would stand no damn nonsense from anyone, and this included owners as well as jockeys.

If any owner did not agree with his decision he was welcome to send his horses elsewhere, and if a jockey did not carry out his instructions he could look for another job. His employees were scared stiff of him, but they respected him and carried out their jobs to the best of their ability. His horses' coats shone so brightly that some evil-minded people suggested that this effect was produced by something stronger than grooming. Such an idea, however, was never entertained by the Jockey Club.

'Steve won't be able to try any of his tricks on Fred Darling,' was the unanimous opinion of the racing profession, but Donoghue, to his ultimate cost, had already demonstrated that he was no respecter of persons. He had only one idea in his head—to ride a third consecutive Derby winner, and when he found the Beckhampton three-year-olds were below standard he began to look elsewhere for his Derby mount.

Lord Woolavington, however, also had horses in training with Gilpin at Newmarket, and decided to run both Town Guard and Knockando. The latter had been beaten a head by Ellangowan in the Two Thousand Guineas, but Steve did not fancy either, and was determined to ride Papyrus, trained at Newmarket by Basil Jarvis.

When told he would be required to ride one of Lord Woolavington's pair he affected pained surprise and replied that he thought his retainer was only for horses trained by Fred Darling. This was complete nonsense and only goes to show to what lengths Steve would go to get his own way where the Derby was concerned. Lord Woolavington's present to Steve for winning on Captain Cuttle was reputed to be the largest ever given to a jockey, whilst his retaining fee for the 1923 season was also an extremely generous one: but here was Steve once again trying to wriggle out of his commitments.

He had won the Criterion Stakes on Papyrus, who beat the 4/1-on chance Town Guard the previous autumn. And when he won the Chester Vase on him the following spring, Steve was determined that by hook or by crook he would ride Papyrus at Epsom. This victory revealed that Papyrus was not only a very handy horse, but that he was certain to get the Derby distance. As he was by the St Leger winner Tracery out of Miss Matty by Marcovil, sire of Hurry On, out of Simonside by St Simon, Papyrus had an ideal Derby pedigree.

Mr Ben Irish, a local farmer, and a close friend of Basil Jarvis, asked the latter to buy him a yearling, which he did for 260 guineas. The colt, Periosteum, won the Gold Cup, ridden by Frank Bullock. Mr Irish decided to play up some of his winnings and bought Papyrus, who was bred at the Worksop

Manor Stud, for 3,500 guineas. Steve eventually got his way, as he always did, though this time at the expense of the patronage of one of the Turf's richest and most generous owners.

By this time, Steve was a national hero, and the crowd gave him a great cheer as he cantered to the post on Papyrus for the 1923 Derby. He rode with the father and mother of a black eye, and some wags put it about that it had been administered by Lord Woolavington: it was in fact the result of a stone thrown up when he was riding in the first race.

From Tattenham Corner the Derby was to all intents and purposes a two-horse race. Steve sent his mount into the lead before reaching Tattenham Corner, as he usually did, but early in the straight he was headed by Pharos, and Lord Derby's colt appeared to be going the better of the two. Inside the last furlong, however, Papyrus's stamina was the deciding factor as Steve was sure it would be, and he regained the lead and won by a length. Gardner was blamed for coming too soon on Pharos, but the latter was a free-running horse and his jockey had no alternative than to make his effort when he did. The unlucky horse was Mr Goculdas' Parth, who lost many lengths at the start and appeared to be completely out of the race. But he finished like a train and galloped past sixteen horses in the straight to finish third. Parth was subsequently sold to Mr A. K. Macomber, for whom he won the Prix de l'Arc de Triomphe. Although he ran well in a number of good-class races, Papyrus's solitary victory after the Derby was at York, where he was awarded a race on an objection. In the St Leger he again finished in front of Parth, but both were beaten by Lord Derby's filly Tranquil.

Tranquil had won the One Thousand Guineas, and started an even-money chance for the Oaks, but she could only finish fourth after a rough passage, the race being won by Brownhilda, trained by Dick Dawson and ridden by Vic Smyth.

This certainly was not Gardner's lucky week, and at the end of it he got the sack, his job being given to Tommy Weston. Lambton's choice of new jockey created considerable surprise as Weston's bodily weight was less than seven stone, and he would therefore have to put up two stone deadweight in the classics. Lambton, however, argued that Frank Wootton was also very young and weighed little more than Weston when he won the St Leger for Lord Derby on Swynford, a big horse who needed a lot of driving. Twenty-year-old Weston had been reared in a hard school. The North Country trainer Mc-Cormack had spotted him riding a trace horse shunting railway trucks and between them they brought off some very lucrative coups for Drake, a North Country bookmaker. In addition to his classic horses, Lambton trained a number of handicappers and with Weston as his stable jockey he would have no worries about overweight no matter how low they were in the handicap. Weston's first ride for Lord Derby was on Silurian in the Gold Cup, and he clearly demonstrated that Lambton had not over-rated his ability. Riding a terrific finish for a boy of his size, Weston was only beaten a short head by the favourite Happy Man, a seven-year-old ridden by Vic Smyth.

Tranquil was ridden by Carslake in the Coronation Stakes at Ascot, but she had to give lumps of weight away all round and could only finish fourth. The favourite, the Aga Khan's Teresina, was ridden by the stable jockey Hulme, while Paola, carrying the Aga's second colours, was ridden by Vic Smyth. Smyth could do no wrong at this time, and here he was fortun-ate in that Hulme picked the wrong one. Paola, conceding seven pounds, beat her comfortably.

Anyone who knew anything about racing must have seen that the two fillies had run strictly on their merits, but accusations of sharp practice were levelled at Dawson, Hulme, and even the Aga himself. The stewards were, of course, perfectly satisfied, but the Aga Khan, who had only recently come into racing, was very upset.

Tranquil was a big filly and as she did not appear able to stride out on the firm going on Newmarket Heath, Lambton advised Lord Derby to send her to be trained for the St Leger by that wonderful old horsemaster Charles Morton at Wantage. This action revealed the stature of Lambton as a man as well as a trainer. He thought the world of Tranquil, a daughter of his old favourite Swynford, yet he was big enough to realise that another man had better prospects of producing her fit to run for her life in the greatest race of her career in September.

For magnanimity on the part of a trainer, this has only once been equalled. Marcel Boussac sent several high-class animals to be trained by Lambton in the thirties, among them being Corrida. Lambton knew she was a potentially great filly, but she seemed unhappy at Newmarket, and try as he might, Lambton could not arouse her from her lethargy. He therefore advised M. Boussac to take her back to Chantilly and see how she responded to Jack Watts' training in her native environment. Back home again, Corrida proved herself the best of her sex over a period of three seasons.

Tranquil thrived during her stay at Wantage and she beat Papyrus fairly and squarely in the St Leger. Lord Derby was delighted at her success, his second St Leger victory with a filly in the space of five years. In winning this great race only three months after his appointment as first jockey to the Stanley House stable, Weston had abundantly justified Lambton's faith in him.

No Earl of Derby had won the Derby since the twelfth Earl won the race in 1787 with Sir Peter Teazle. How many horses carried the black jacket and white cap in our greatest race between that date and 1924 I have never been told, but it must have been a formidable number.

The Stanley House stable was back to its former glory, and the performance of Archaic in finishing a creditable second to Spion Kop in 1920, together with Pharos' fine effort against Papyrus in 1923, indicated that victory for the seventeenth earl would not be delayed much longer.

Sansovino, like Tranquil, was by Swynford, her dam being Gondolette, whom Lord Derby had bought when she was ten years old from Colonel Hall Walker (later Lord Wavertree). Although she had previously changed hands for as little as 75 guineas and 360 guineas, Gondolette was probably the best buy Lord Derby ever made as she bred him six winners. Her daughter, Serenissima, bred eight winners of forty races, including the Gold Cup winner Bosworth, Tranquil and Selene, dam of Hyperion. She also bred Sickle and Pharamond, brilliantly successful sires in the U.S.A.

I do not believe that there has ever been a stud comparable to Stanley House during the lifetime of the seventeenth earl. He neither bred nor raced on the scale of the Aga Khan or M. Boussac, but for a period of over fifty years it was a rarity for a great race to be won by a horse which had not Stanley House blood close up in its pedigree.

Like Swynford, Sansovino was a big colt, but he did not take so long to mature as did his sire, and he won both his races as a two-year-old, though he did not beat much. He was not entered for the Two Thousand Guineas, and in any case he would not have been forward enough to run in it: but he was saddled for the now defunct Newmarket Stakes (a mile and a quarter) and right well he ran, finishing third, beaten a neck and a head by Hurstwood and Bright Knight. This was a good performance as Bright Knight had run Diophon to a short head in the Guineas, and had I been the judge the verdict would have gone the other way although I had backed Diophon. The race brought Sansovino on a ton and in his final gallop for the Derby he made hacks of Pharos and Tranquil, both of whom he met on considerably worse than weight-for-age terms. Lambton's only fear was firm going, and there wasn't much fear of that in 1924. By the time the Derby was run the course was barely fit for racing, the track resembling a ploughed field. While most of the trainers were bewailing their luck, Lambton was rubbing his hands with glee, knowing that Sansovino, with his big feet, would revel in the conditions.

Weston was actually pushing his big lazy mount on his way up the hill, but Sansovino fairly took hold of his bit at the mile post and the race was all over at Tattenham Corner. In the straight, Sansovino was the only horse able to raise a gallop in the mud, and he won by six lengths from Lord Astor's St Germans, who was also by Swynford. This was the sixth postwar Derby, in four of which Lord Astor's representative had finished second.

A hundred and thirty-seven years is a long time to wait, and Lord Derby made no secret of the fact that Sansovino's victory gave him the greatest thrill of his life. Minoru's victory was before my time, but those who had been present told me that the reception accorded to Lord Derby as he led in Sansovino was comparable with that which greeted King Edward VII when he led in Minoru fifteen years earlier.

What a day it was. The rain teemed down without ceasing on a course on which several inches of rain had fallen over the previous weekend. With the exception of Troytown's National in 1920 it was the wettest day on which I have ever been racing. Buses sank up to their axles and the course was in such an appalling state that the start of racing on the following day was delayed for over an hour. No announcement was made, and the crowd was in an ugly mood. Eventually Lord Lonsdale, in top hat and morning coat, and smoking a huge cigar, cantered past the stand on a skewbald hack. Reassured at the spectacle of the 'Yellow Earl', who was presumably doing his best to get things moving, the crowd's boos turned to cheers. It was finally decided that racing was possible except on the five-furlong course, and the two races over the minimum distance were abandoned.

The Coronation Cup at this 1924 Derby meeting was won by Lord Coventry's remarkable filly Verdict, who was not in the stud book. Trained by Willie Waugh at Kingsclere, and brilliantly ridden by Michael Beary, she had won the previous year's Cambridgeshire by a neck from the great French horse Epinard (also a three-year-old), who was conceding her no less than eighteen pounds. Epinard, who had cantered away with the Stewards' Cup under 8 stone 6 lb, must have been a horse and a half. The Rowley Mile course was not railed off as it is today, and a strange jockey could well get lost on its wide expanse. Epinard's American jockey Haynes wandered from one side of the course to the other and, even so, Epinard was only beaten a matter of inches by a super game filly on whom Michael Beary rode the race of his life. Ridden by a Brownie Carslake, Epinard would have won the Cambridgeshire on the bit, and forty-seven years later I still regard Epinard's performance as one of the best I have seen in any handicap over any distance—perhaps only surpassed by Sayani who won the same race 23 years later, carrying 9 stone 4 lb.

Epinard possibly did not stay one and a half miles, but had

he been as good over that distance as he was over nine furlongs, he would presumably have won the Coronation Cup with 10 stone 7 lb on his back! Parth had given Verdict three pounds and beaten her by a short head in the Jubilee at Kempton, but on the same terms as Epsom, Verdict, ridden this time by Steve, turned the tables, winning by half a length. At stud, Verdict produced Quashed, who was even better than her dam. In the colours of Lord Stanley, to whom she was leased, Quashed won the Oaks and the Gold Cup at Ascot in which she beat the famous American horse Omaha by a short head. Not a bad performance for a half-bred.

6 Back from the wilderness

Manna kicks Fred Darling and wins 1925 Guineas and Derby – Steve makes it four Derbys out of five—his last classic win for twelve years – Brown Jack – Steve and Frank Bullock injured in Grand Prix pile-up – Steve comes in from the cold to win 1937 One Thousand Guineas and Oaks on Exhibitionnist in the year of his retirement – Apprentice Charlie Elliott ties with Steve for the championship.

Except for the fact that both men were superbly good at their respective jobs no two men could have had less in common than Fred Darling and Steve Donoghue. Steve's easy-going charm infuriated Fred almost as much as did his unpunctuality and unbusinesslike approach to life when he was not on a horse's back.

Steve's refusal to abide by his contract to Lord Woolavington over the 1924 Derby was no direct concern of Fred Darling's, but he realised that what Steve had done to Lord Derby and Lord Woolavington might be done to him. He therefore made a vow that in no circumstances would Steve ride again as first jockey to Beckhampton.

If one of his owners chose to make a private arrangement with Steve that was his affair, and Darling made no objection in 1925 when Mr H. E. Morris engaged the man who had ridden three of the previous four Derby winners to ride his colt Manna.

Mr Morris, a Shanghai bullion broker, had instructed Fred

Darling to buy him the best yearling at the Doncaster Sales, and Darling, a great judge of horses of all kinds, paid 6,300 guineas for a bay son of Phalaris, from the famous Confey Stud in Ireland. This was the equivalent of 30,000 guineas today, and was a hefty sum, but the colt, whose dam Waffles never raced but was inbred to St Simon, was a bargain.

When subsequently mated with Sansovino this tiny mare, about the same size as Stroller, bred Sandwich, winner of the St Leger. Mr Morris called his expensive purchase Manna, and following his colt's victories in the Two Thousand Guineas and Derby he was always known as 'Manna' Morris.

Manna was a beautiful little colt, and a very good one indeed, but he was fortunate in that his contemporary Picaroon suffered from a mysterious ailment which caused his death as a four-year-old, and also in that Solario became caught up in the tapes at the start for the Derby and lost many lengths.

As round as a ball, Manna was so beautifully made that he looked smaller than he actually was. With the exception of Fairway, who was light of frame, the best of Phalaris' stock were beautifully proportioned, muscular and low to the ground, and Manna was typical of them.

He was, however, a little devil, both in his stable and on the gallops. One of his claims to fame is that he is the only horse who ever kicked Fred Darling. He didn't do it twice, but he remained the most exuberant horse in his yard. Steve, of course, had no difficulty in handling him, and told his trainer that Manna's antics were solely the result of his high spirits.

He had not ridden him as a two-year-old when Manna had looked a smasher to me when winning the Richmond Stakes at Goodwood. I thought he was sure to win the Imperial Produce Stakes at Kempton, but he was no match for Picaroon, trained by Alec Taylor. Frank Bullock, who was associated with some great horses, told me that Picaroon was the best two-year-old he had ever ridden, and during one of his rare spells of freedom from illness as a three-year-old he beat Pharos in a match for the Champion Stakes. He could not run in any of the classics, but had he been blessed with normal health he might have been a Triple Crown winner.

The going at Beckhampton had been so wet that Fred Darling feared that Manna was not fit enough to win the Two Thousand Guineas, and he started at 100/8, but he made every yard of the running to win by two lengths.

Phalaris had had stamina limitations, and it was thought at that time that his stock might not stay much more than a mile. Manna was therefore opposed in the Derby market, despite the fact that he would again be ridden by Steve who had no doubts concerning his stamina. He described Manna's action to me as so perfect that galloping seemed to require no effort from him.

Looking back over the years, it nearly always seemed to rain on Derby day, and though the weather was an improvement on that of the previous year, it was extremely unpleasant, and the going was soft. This caused Manna to drift, much as Captain Cuttle had done, and he started at 9/1. In the race, however, he was never out of the first three, and he was clear at Tattenham Corner. In the straight he drew further and further ahead to win by eight lengths. Despite being hopelessly left, Solario finished fourth.

Steve told me that he had asked Mr Morris for £5,000 if he won, but the latter had promised him £20,000. He eventually gave him £1,000 and Steve went on to say how much he appreciated the pillars of the Turf, whose word was as good as their bond. What a pity it was that as the result of his own disregard of contracts Steve no longer rode for these gentlemen.

With the breakdown of Manna in the race for the St Leger, Steve's career as a classic jockey was virtually at an end. He had antagonised most of the leading owners by his disregard for contracts, and no longer would any of them retain him, knowing that if he took a fancy to a horse in another stable he would consider it his right to ride it in the Derby.

After nine years as the undisputed champion jockey an apprentice attached to Jack Jarvis' stable called Charlie Elliott tied with him for the championship in 1923, and in the following year won it outright. From that point Steve became just another jockey, and not a particularly successful one at that, although he did win the Queen Alexandra Stakes at Ascot six years running on Brown Jack, perhaps the most remarkable gelding in the history of the Turf. An absurd rule forbids geldings participating in the Gold Cup, though they are allowed to run in the Goodwood Cup, so Brown Jack's name does not appear on the role of honour with such great stayers as the White Knight, Bayardo, Prince Palatine and Alycidon. When in 1934 Brown Jack, at the age of ten, won our longest race for the sixth time the crowd went wild, and these two wonderful old gentlemen were responsible for a display of emotion such as I have never seen before or since on a racecourse.

A few weeks after he had won the Derby on Manna, Steve was injured in a terrible pile-up in the Grand Prix de Paris in which Frank Bullock was also involved. Amongst other injuries, Steve sustained a fracture of the shoulder, and as a result of this he was never again quite as effective in a close finish. The injury prevented his getting as low in the saddle as he had previously done. In all other respects he remained a great jockey, though after he had reached the age of fifty he would sometimes seem wearier than his mount as he returned to the paddock. In this chapter I intend to skip a few years to describe Steve's later career.

He had always loved the bright lights and the company of attractive women. For many years his name was associated with that of a lady of title, and when that romance ended others took its place. He loved pink champagne (who doesn't?), and enjoyed few things more than to sit at a *chemin-de-fer* table in a casino, with a pile of chips in front of him, his current girl friend at his elbow and a bottle of what he called 'The Rosie' in an ice bucket within reach.

Although they came from very different backgrounds Steve and Aly Khan had many characteristics in common, not the least being the charm which turneth away wrath.

Steve's ability to charm irate owners, trainers and sometimes fellow jockeys into sitting down and accepting his hospitality was matched by Aly's ability to pacify outraged husbands who had vowed to kill him. Lovable, infuriating, feckless and apparently oblivious of his own shortcomings, Steve Donoghue was easily the most fascinating character among the jockeys of the past fifty years, and I have known them all.

Jockeyship is a skilled profession, but it requires no more skill than that of a highly competent workman. Steve Donoghue, Sir Gordon Richards and Lester Piggott have brought a new dimension to jockeyship, but we must retain a sense of proportion in assessing their skill. If they were geniuses what word can we use to describe Michelangelo, Rembrandt, Velasquez or Cézanne? Until some etymologist invents a new word I refuse to describe a man as a genius on account of the fact that he can induce a horse to cover the distance between two given points in a shorter space of time than his rivals.

Steve had passed his heyday when we got to know each other well, but we had many friends in common, were often asked to the same parties and stayed at the same hotels for race meetings. Although his earnings had dropped considerably, his style of living was as high as ever, with a luxurious flat in Albany.

Over dinner at the Adelphi Hotel, Liverpool, in the autumn of 1936 Steve told me that next day he was to ride a very nice two-year-old filly called Exhibitionnist, belonging to Sir Victor Sassoon and trained by Joe Lawson, and he advised me to have a bit on her, which I did. She won in nice style but hadn't beaten very much, and I was surprised when Steve said, 'I think she may be a classic filly next year.' Steve hadn't ridden a classic winner for eleven years and as he was due to retire at the end of 1937 I thought that his optimism was the result of wishful thinking.

It was evident that the official handicapper did not rate Exhibitionnist as highly as Steve did: he gave her only 7 stone 7 lb in the Free Handicap, twenty-one pounds less than the top weight.

She had wintered well, but Lawson had not hurried this big filly and Steve told me she was still backward when I met him at the Craven Meeting. He added, however, 'I think she'll run well in the Free Handicap, and after it we shall know whether she's a classic filly.'

That Free Handicap was without precedent, and I am sure that the finish of this race will never again be fought out by two lightly weighted candidates, both by the same sire (Solario), who will go on to win the Derby and Oaks respectively. As I watched Mid-day Sun, ridden by Kenny Robertson and carrying only 7 stone 1 lb, win by a neck from Exhibitionnist (ridden by Cliff Richards as Steve could not do the weight) who was giving him six pounds, I reflected that this race had certainly shed no light on the classics. But when I met Steve that evening he was bubbling over with delight. 'The race will have brought her on a ton,' he told me, 'and if it was re-run she'd win a minute. I *think* she'll win the One Thousand but she's certain to win the Oaks, as there's no doubt she'll stay a mile and a half.'

Gainsborough Lass was a screaming hot favourite at 11/10 for the 1937 One Thousand Guineas, and I got 10/1 without any difficulty about Exhibitionnist, despite the fact that Mid-day Sun had finished third in the Two Thousand Guineas two days earlier. Steve had her well placed throughout and, galloping smoothly, she ran on up the hill to win comfortably by half a length from Spray, with the favourite a head away third.

Steve had ridden a beautiful race on her; his services had not been in great demand for the past ten years, he was well into his fifties and he was not quite the finisher he had been, but he was still a magnificent horseman. Riding Exhibitionnist so tenderly he insured that she would benefit from the race, and when Mid-day Sun, ridden by Michael Beary, won the Lingfield Derby Trial Stakes she looked something to bet on in the Oaks.

But three days before the race she came into season, and Lawson announced that it was no more than a fifty-fifty chance that she would be fit to run. She would be taken to Epsom, and Steve would ride her a canter on the morning of the race, after which a decision would be made.

I was on the course at 7.30 a.m. to do a story for the *Evening Standard* and as I reached the paddock I saw Steve approaching with Bobby Jones, who also rode for the Manton stable. At a distance of fifty yards Steve's smile told me all I wanted to know: yes, she could not have gone better, and was fighting fit.

My brother Geoffrey and I were under contract to broadcast most of the big races that year, and on the Wednesday we had described Mid-day Sun's victory over the 100/1 chance Sandsprite in the Derby, with Michael Beary in the saddle. I had not

1 Steve Donoghue's greatest feat: winning the 1921 Derby on Mr. J. B. Jael's *Humorist*. 'The bravest horse I ever rode'

2 Joe Childs on *Coronach*, winner of the 1926 Derby. 'The bastard ran away with me'

3 Two irascible characters, Joe Childs and Fred Darling

4 Charlie Elliott wins the 1927 Derby on Mr. Frank Curzon's *Call Boy*

backed the winner, but I was able to generate some enthusiasm into my commentary, as his victory made Exhibitionnist appear a bigger certainty than ever for the Oaks.

The 1937 fillies' race was a piece of cake, and a more appetising piece of cake I've never tasted. Steve rode her in much the same way he'd ridden Captain Cuttle and Manna in the Derby all those years ago, and there was really only one in it all the way up the straight.

After twelve years in the wilderness the little man had come back to end his career on a triumphant note. He had never before won the One Thousand Guineas and his only previous victory in the Oaks had been in a wartime event at Newmarket, when his mount My Dear was awarded the race on an objection.

Steve had never been one to hide his feelings behind a poker face, and he was obviously very moved as he rode Exhibitionnist through the cheering crowd to the winning enclosure, where her owner, Sir Victor Sassoon, was waiting in his wheel-chair. Steve was smiling, as he always was when he had ridden a winner, but there were tears in his eyes, and he was not ashamed of them.

Steve had his faults, but he was a lovable character and I am proud to have been his friend. His disregard of contracts was infuriating to his employers, but though he might leave an owner stranded he would never 'shop' him. Once he was on a horse's back he was 100 per cent on the side of his owner.

He was not a compulsive gambler, but everyone knew he betted. Even when he was at the top of the tree he would not only listen to, but also act on, so-called 'information'. On a number of occasions he backed a horse in a race in which he was riding, and then won it himself. He rode his share of non-triers, unfancied horses, if you prefer it, but always with the connivance of the owner and trainer. Just because a jockey gives a horse an easy race it does not follow that it would have won had he given it a hard one.

His delinquencies, for which he paid a high price, were motivated by his desire to ride winners, which, after all, is what a jockey's career is all about.

Every jockey of my acquaintance, with the exception of Bill Rickaby, has at some time or other angled for a mount which

D

rightfully belonged to someone else, but no jockey other than Steve has considered he could have his cake and eat it. Either a jockey is retained by a stable or he rides as a freelance. Mounted on a horse, Steve Donoghue was an artist; on his flat feet, like so many of us, he was a bit of a mug.

7   Old Joe and Brownie

Coronach and Solario run away with Joe Childs to win Derby and Coronation Cup in 1926 – Solario one of the greatest—wins 1927 Gold Cup on three legs – Coronach becomes a roarer – Colorado proves himself a champion – Carslake wins 1924 St Leger on Salmon Trout—and faces ruin – His version of the story – Fellow jockeys and Alec Taylor vote for Frank Bullock as the best all-round jockey. – Cricket with the jockeys.

'The bastard ran away with me!' This exclamation of disgust was accompanied by a crash, as a saddle, complete with irons, struck the weighing-room wall. This outburst of temper did not emanate from the lips and hands of a 'chalk' jockey, who had been unable to control his mount, but from those of a celebrated rider who a few minutes earlier had realised the ambition of every jockey from the day he first joins a racing stable by winning the Derby.

The jockey was Joe Childs, the horse which had incurred his wrath was Coronach, and the year was 1926. With his lean, deeply lined face and piercing eyes, which glared from under beetle brows, Joe was a formidable figure, and on the first occasion I was deputed by my editor to interview him I was so scared that I forgot what it was I had to ask him. No wonder the apprentices were frightened to death of him, but those who knew him far better than I did declared that he was a very kind man, something one would never have suspected.

His constant companion was the professional backer Canny

Watt, while he was also on very friendly terms with his fellow jockey Fred Lane; but he did not much care for the society of most other men and if any man can be said to have kept his own counsel it was old Joe. I have no idea how old he was, but he looked a middle-aged man when I first saw him ride in 1919, and very much the same when I last saw him shortly before he died. Like most of us he had softened with retirement, and he gave me a warm handshake and a friendly smile, something he had never done in the old days. It was quite impossible to believe that he had ever been young and guilty of the pranks to which all boys are prone. Life to him was an immensely serious business, and he was about as flexible as a concrete lamp-post.

He was, however, a great jockey, though he would have been an even greater one had he been endowed with a little flexibility. The word compromise did not figure in his vocabulary, and like Frank Sinatra he insisted on doing it 'my way'. The fact that fairly late in life he had won his first Epsom Derby gave him no pleasure, as he had not won it 'his' way but in a manner dictated by Coronach.

I have no hesitation in saying that Joe Childs was the greatest rider of a waiting race in my time, but I do not place him among the dozen greatest jockeys, as he insisted on riding all horses alike. He was a strong man, and only the hardest puller could overpower him. I must have seen him ride in many hundreds of races, but Sir Cosmo, in a race over the Old Mile at Ascot, was the only other horse apart from Coronach I can recall that got the better of Joe and made all the running.

I have heard it said that he was no flier at the gate, but this was of his own volition. The last thing he wanted was to find himself in front early in a race, even in a five-furlong event over a fast course like Epsom. Coronach was the hell of a horse on Derby Day, and he must also have been blessed with abnormal intelligence, as having overpowered Joe in the first couple of furlongs, he dropped his bit and dictated the pace at which the remainder of the race should be run. He ran an identical race when winning the St Leger over an extra two and a half furlongs.

Brilliant as he was, I hesitate to say that Coronach was the best of his generation, as in his four encounters with Colorado, Lord Derby's little colt won three times, his only defeat by Coronach being in the Derby, in which Colorado was left with far too much to do.

Not even the greatest trainers are infallible, and the Hon. George Lambton erred in instructing Weston to ride a waiting race. Colorado had slammed Coronach in the Two Thousand Guineas, and as a four-year-old he beat him just as easily in the Princess of Wales' Stakes at Newmarket and in the Eclipse Stakes.

By this time, however, Coronach was a roarer; his wind had always been slightly suspect, and after his collapse at Newmarket it was astonishing, and completely out of character, that Fred Darling should have allowed Lord Woolavington to run him again against Colorado a fortnight later. No two colts could have been more dissimilar than were Coronach and Colorado. The former, a typical son of Hurry On, was a big powerful light chestnut, with a flaxen mane and tail. Such markings sometimes denote a soft spot, but there was no lack of resolution about the way Coronach went about his business till his wind infirmity asserted itself.

Colorado was a big little horse, as although he stood only 15.1 hands he was deep through the heart, and combined tremendous power with superb quality. We all have a picture in our minds of the horse we should most like to own and Colorado, a typical son of Phalaris, was my *beau idéal*.

His dam Canyon won the One Thousand Guineas, and his pedigree was a tribute to the judgement of his owner-breeder and his trainer who worked in perfect unison. Lord Derby and British bloodstock suffered a cruel blow when Colorado died in 1929, as had he lived I think he might have proved himself as great a sire as another big little horse who carried the famous black jacket and white cap, called Hyperion. In only two seasons at stud Colorado sired Felicitation, winner of the Gold Cup, Loaningdale, winner of the Eclipse Stakes, Colorado Kid, winner of the Jubilee, the Royal Hunt Cup and the Doncaster Cup, Coroado, winner of the Wokingham Stakes and July Cup, and Figaro, winner of the Stewards' Cup.

Michael Beary had ridden Solario when he was virtually left at the post in the 1925 Derby, but Joe Childs rode him in the Ascot Derby in which Manna was penalised. I do not think Manna was quite the colt at Ascot that he had been when winning at Epsom, but Solario demonstrated what a close thing he would have made of it in the Derby by trouncing Steve's mount.

Their meeting in the 1925 St Leger was eagerly awaited, but Manna broke down in the course of the race, and Solario, again ridden by Joe Childs, won much as he pleased. By this time Solario was a really great horse, but his trainer Reg Day told us after the St Leger that he would be an even better one with another year over his head—and how right he was!

I have been fortunate in seeing about 90 per cent of the most memorable races of the past fifty years, and the Coronation Cup of 1926 was certainly one of them. Making his first appearance of the season in a field of five, Solario was opposed by a very good colt in Zambo, and they were almost inseparable in the betting, Solario starting at 2/1, and Zambo, in the colours of the Aga Khan, at 9/4; but Solario beat his market rival out of sight. Solario did not run away with Joe Childs from the start as Coronach had done in the previous day's Derby, but he spreadeagled his field approaching Tattenham Corner, and drew further and further away all the way up the straight to win by the unprecedented margin of fifteen lengths, despite the fact that Joe was sitting up in the saddle endeavouring to restrain him.

On his return to Newmarket, Solario developed leg trouble and Reg Day had the sort of fortnight which can make trainers old before their time (though I am glad to say that forty-five years later that great trainer is still hale and hearty). If ever a horse looked a certainty for the Gold Cup, that horse was Solario, but within a week of the race he was still hopping lame. The injury responded to treatment, but he hadn't done a gallop since his victory at Epsom, and he moved feelingly to the post for our greatest long-distance race. Joe could be severe on a horse, but he could also be tender, and not even his great rival Steve Donoghue ever nursed his mount more effectively, with the result that although he was short of about three gallops, and finished virtually on three legs, Solario proved too good for the opposition.

Steve Donoghue, Joe Childs and Brownie Carslake were known as the triumvirate and were racing's counterpart to golf's Vardon, Braid and Taylor, but whereas even the twenty-four handicapper of today, struggling round to break a hundred, can relate anecdotes concerning the prowess of these masters of the 'gutty' ball, memories of the exploits of three of the greatest jockeys ever to appear in public at one and the same time are beginning to fade. In conversation with four racing enthusiasts, all of them well over thirty, at a recent meeting, I discovered that the sum total of their knowledge of Carslake was that he was ruined financially as a result of winning the St Leger on the Aga Khan's Salmon Trout in 1924. I am raking up this old scandal for no other reason than to give Carslake's version of the story as he told it to me when we were both dining with Gordon Richards in Paris on the eve of the Grand Prix de Paris fourteen years later. He told me that he did not think that Salmon Trout had any chance of staying the St Leger distance, so he instructed his friend, bookmaker Moe Tarsh, to lay it on his behalf to lose him a very large sum of money indeed, though he did not specify the exact sum.

My reaction to this was to ask him why, therefore, did he ride Salmon Trout in the only way possible to enable a doubtful stayer to get the trip. Entering the long Doncaster straight last, he rode one of the most perfectly timed waiting races that even this wonderful judge of pace had ever ridden. His reply was in the nature of a question. 'D'you think I'm a bloody fool or a bloody crook, or both? D'you think I should be such a fool as to stop a horse of the Aga's in a classic? I was first jockey for him at the time and I was getting the biggest retainer ever paid to a jockey. I believed Salmon Trout wouldn't get the trip, no matter how he was ridden, but I was determined to give him the best ride possible.'

That was Brownie's version, but though I begged him to allow me to publish it he declined, pointing out that it was an admission that he had betted, which was, in itself, a warning-off offence. The version which 99 per cent of racing men believed at the time was that the stewards had got wind of Carslake's and Moe Tarsh's market transactions, and had sent for Carslake and told him that every action of his throughout the race would be scrutinised, and if the stewards were not satisfied that he had done his best to win he would be warned off.

Morals aside, Carslake's story to me is plausible in that no leading jockey, unless he was in the hands of the bookmakers, would pull a horse belonging to the richest man in the world by whom he was employed. Like so many fabulously rich men, the Aga Khan was extremely careful over trifling sums, and it is said of him that in the year Bahram won the Triple Crown he would take time to consider whether to give his caddy two bob or half a crown. But he could be very generous to a jockey who had won him a great race, and Rae Johnstone told me that the Aga gave him the stake after he had won the Grand Prix on My Love, the first horse to complete the Epsom Derby–Grand Prix double since Spearmint forty-two years earlier.

The belief that Carslake had originally intended to stop Salmon Trout from winning but had changed his mind was supported by the market, as in the transactions up to the off he was as firm as a rock. Had the ring believed that the Aga Khan's colt was 'dead meat' every bookmaker on Town Moor would have been screaming his head off in his endeavour to lay him.

Personally I am content to believe what Brownie told me, though I agree that it is almost inconceivable how a jockey of his experience could have made such a blunder concerning a colt's stamina. Admittedly, Salmon Trout was by The Tetrarch, whose son Tetratema had been beaten in the Derby of 1920, with Brownie in the saddle, before he reached Tattenham Corner; but Salmon Trout was far more stoutly bred on his dam's side than was Tetratema, and The Tetrarch had already sired two St Leger winners in Caligula and Polemarch.

Whichever version you accept, Brownie emerges as a 'fly mug', and as I can vouch for the fact that he was nothing of the sort I can only assume that he was already in dire financial trouble and seized on the 1924 St Leger, as a drowning man will clutch at a straw, to straighten out his affairs.

Jockeys are notorious for being the world's worst tipsters, and if Brownie had dissipated what must have been a considerable fortune by gambling, one can be sure that his own judgement was at fault. While happy-go-lucky Steve would take a tip from a raw novice like myself, Brownie was very self-opinionated, and never (so far as I can recall) sought the advice of anyone except that of a trainer whose horse he was riding for the first time.

Saturnine and sardonic were two adjectives invariably employed by those who had endeavoured to interview him, usually without success. With his black hair, brushed straight back from a high forehead, eyes of the same hue, an aquiline nose and dark skin, hence his nickname (his real name was Bernard), he was a handsome man of about the same height as Lester Piggott. He was very vain about his appearance and was always immaculate.

Sardonic he certainly was; without even opening his mouth, his expression left you in no doubt that in his eyes you were something the cat had brought in which would have been better left outside.

Although in the late thirties I probably knew Brownie better than did any of my colleagues I did not know him well, and that occasion in Paris was the only one on which he talked about himself to me. He was much older than I was, and middle-aged jockeys do not open their hearts to aspiring journalists, with only one foot in Fleet Street and the other still in the Strand. By this time he was a teetotaller, and could be relied upon to retain his geniality throughout an evening. When I first met him in the mid-twenties he would become very cantankerous after a few drinks. He was in no sense of the word an alcoholic, but not having had a square meal for days on end a couple of drinks had a disastrous effect on him.

I have described him as of the same height as Lester Piggott, but he was bigger-boned, and the fact that he rode far less made 'wasting' all the harder. Diets had not been worked out by experts in those days, and Brownie would often exist for forty-eight hours on nothing more substantial than dry toast and an occasional cup of weak tea.

He and Lester Piggott have been described as the most powerful finishers of all time. I do not question the assertion that they were two of the most effective, but the word powerful suggests that they were men of muscle, built on the lines of all-in wrestlers, whereas they were as thin as rails. By superhuman efforts they kept alive that spark of energy which galvanises all great jockeys into action at the crucial moment, but it is sheer nonsense to suggest that Brownie or Lester owed their success to physical strength.

I have heard it said, and have even written myself, that a certain jockey had lifted his mount past the post, but this is, of course, an optical illusion. What has happened is that he has retained a fraction of the horse's energy so that when he has called on him for a supreme effort in the last few strides the horse's response has appeared to emanate from his rider, rather than from himself.

If a horse has no more to give it would make no difference if his jockey has the strength of a weight-lifter, and what has been mistaken for power is in reality a combination of timing and rhythm, plus, of course, physical energy.

If a jockey loses his rhythm he loses the race, unless he has ten pounds in hand, in which case he has no cause to move anyway, and I once caused considerable merriment by describing a jockey as going faster than his mount. The race was at New-market, and a horse ridden by one of the less competent French jockeys was very tired as he met the rising ground in the final furlong. Not so his jockey, who pushed, scrubbed and kicked in inverse ratio to his mount's flagging strides. I need hardly add that the horse slowed down to little more than walking pace, and was well beaten.

Mention of Newmarket brings me back to Brownie Carslake, who had no equal over any portion of either course at head-quarters. In those days there were a number of winning posts, but Brownie knew to an inch the exact position of all of them. I can recall no more inspiring sight than that of Brownie, with his mount perfectly balanced, after the lead had changed hands several times, waiting to pounce. He had been riding for many years before I went racing regularly and he may have lost a race he should have won on Newmarket Heath, but I can vouch for the fact that never in my time did he come a fraction too soon or a fraction too late. He did not always win, but when he was beaten by a narrow margin I invariably got the impression that no other jockey would have got so close.

An Australian, he had ridden for many years on the Continent before he settled in this country, when he decided to adopt the English style by letting down his leathers several holes, and riding with a long rein.

He was reputed to dislike sharp courses and Epsom in particular, but the fact that he never won the Derby was due to his never having ridden the best horse, and not the result of any lack of courage on his part.

Very late in his career I saw him ride a lovely race to win the Oaks on Lord Durham's Light Brocade. Luck plays a big part in racing, no matter how good a jockey may be, and Steve would never have ridden a Derby winner had he had Brownie's mounts. Brownie and I became friends as the result of our common love of cricket. A very sound right-handed bat, he was also a highly competent slow left-hand bowler. I do not think he was up to county standards, but he would have proved an asset to most club teams.

In the thirties, the Press and the Jockeys played each other three times a year—at Lord Glanely's ground at Exning, at the Sussex county ground at Hove, where that great little sportsman Harry Preston was our host, and at Lord's. The standard of the cricket was not high, and goodness knows why anyone paid to watch us.

Lord Glanely's and Harry Preston's hospitality was of the highest standard and the side which batted second was at a big disadvantage. The result of the Lord's match, where we had to pay for our own drinks, was therefore more reliable. This match was played on the Monday of the St Leger meeting and as the cricket season was over they gave us a pitch in the middle of the ground.

When Steve came in my brother Geoffrey, bowling from the Nursery End, bowled him a slow long hop to enable him to get off the mark. Steve swung at it with all his might and hit it full in the centre of the bat. Up and up it soared, a truly colossal hit for so small a man, but after what seemed several minutes I realised that if I remained absolutely still it would drop into my hands, fielding on the boundary under Father Time. This it did, and I managed to hang on to it, at which a voice from the crowd shouted: 'Now you've got your own back for some of his stiff 'uns.'

At luncheon, Brownie, who was captaining the jockeys, said: 'We've just seen two miracles. Steve's nearly hit a six at Lord's and Quinny caught it.'

As a jockey I rank Brownie superior to Joe Childs as he was the more flexible, though he was as left-handed as Joe was right-handed. It probably seems strange to present-day racing enthusiasts that neither of these two great riders ever pulled his whip through in the course of a race. Horses, however, did not hang with them, and if they began to do so they were promptly straightened out. I can only assume that being tall men they did this largely with their legs, a physical impossibility for a jockey riding as short as our leading riders do in the seventies.

I have described Steve, Joe and Brownie as the triumvirate, but I would have included Frank Bullock, and made it a quartet, had he not retired as long ago as 1925, the same year that another splendid rider in Vic Smyth hung up his boots.

For two of the six years prior to Bullock's retirement I was living in Paris, and it was there that I saw Frank ride some of his greatest races. The French considered him superior to both Donoghue and Childs, and he rode in France every Sunday throughout the season. For some reason Carslake seldom rode in France. It is possible that he did not relish competing with the French jockeys who were, at that time, somewhat wild and undisciplined. A more likely reason, however, is that he did not relish two Channel crossings in the space of twenty-four hours on an empty stomach.

Frank was a magnificent rider, more flexible than either Childs or Carslake, and though he may not have been Steve's equal as a horseman, he was more versatile. Steve could, of course, ride a waiting race, but he was somewhat loath to do so, and was far happier when bowling along, not necessarily in front, but within striking distance of the leaders. Frank, unlike Joe, did not insist on doing things his way, and rode each horse in the manner which he thought would suit it best. I have seen him make all the running in one race, and come from last to first in the straight to win the next. I remember dining with a party of jockeys at Liverpool in the year of Frank's retirement, and a vote was taken as to who was the best all-round jockey in the world. Frank Bullock received a unanimous vote.

He rode with great success for the Manton stable, and in particular for Lord Astor, following Buchan's defeat in the St Leger, when ridden by Joe Childs. Alec Taylor, who employed more great jockeys in his long career than did any of his contemporaries, described Frank Bullock as a very great jockey indeed. Frank was one of the most honourable men ever to hold a jockey's licence. After he had lodged an objection to 'Snowy' Whalley's mount Western Wave, who had hampered his mount Plymouth Rock in the closing stages of the 1920 Stewards' Cup, Frank considered he was in duty bound to tell the stewards that it was his mount that had first deviated from a straight line. His objection was overruled: had he said nothing he would almost certainly have been awarded the race. Whalley was one of a large number of competent senior jockeys riding at the time—not an artist, but strong and very determined.

Frank Bullock, who was no relation of Billy Bullock (who won the Derby and Oaks in 1908 on Signorinetta, and received a cup of tea and a small cigar for his pains), won the One Thousand Guineas and Oaks on Lord Astor's Saucy Sue in 1925. A super-brilliant filly but very headstrong, she hung so badly at Epsom that not even Bullock's superb skill could keep her straight. It was of no consequence, however, as the daughter of Swynford beat Miss Gadabout, in the same colours, by eight lengths, with Riding Light, ridden by Steve, the same distance away third. Strange to relate, these two successes on Saucy Sue were Frank's only classic victories, though everyone, bar the judge, thought he had won the Two Thousand Guineas on Lord Astor's Bright Knight.

8 Michael and Freddy

Michael Beary, man about town, humorist and 'mickey-taker'. – Redeems his overcoat and wins 1937 Derby on Mid-day Sun – Freddy Fox, racing's forgotten man, makes a sensational come-back and wins Derby on Cameronian – Freddy beats Gordon by one for 1930 Championship – 1931 a vintage year – Gordon rides for Lord Glanely – Bahram wins 1935 Triple Crown – Accident on eve of St Leger ends Freddy Fox's career.

The twenties have often been described as the golden age of jockeyship, and with good reason. I have already referred to the superb race Michael Beary rode to win the 1923 Cambridge-shire on Lord Coventry's Verdict. Had this mercurial little Irishman learned to let sleeping dogs lie and refrained from taking the mickey out of people who held the ace, king, queen and knave of trumps his life would have been a great deal easier, but then, of course, he would not have been Michael Beary. In no circumstances would he have died a rich man, as he was the only man I ever met with less idea of the value of money than Steve Donoghue.

Michael had a positive genius for rubbing the right people—or the wrong people, according to which way you looked at it—up the wrong way. He did this deliberately. There was nothing naive about Michael, but his impish sense of fun could only be appeased by sallies, which inevitably came back like boomer-angs.

Had I not known him well I should have thought he was

bent on self-destruction. At an hour when most jockeys were tucked up in bed, or having a night-cap at the Craven Club at Newmarket, Michael, resplendent in white tie and tails, would be driving up to some stage door to escort the girl of the moment to supper at a night club. His stories in the weighing room the next day of how he had met such-and-such an owner, whom he referred to by his Christian name, did not endear him to his fellow jockeys; they suspected that Michael had been doing a little propaganda on his own behalf at their expense while burning the midnight oil.

Michael and Jack Leach had the entrée to a society to which most of their colleagues could not aspire, but Jack never boasted about his social triumphs. Most of us are snobs of one kind or another, and I include inverted snobs, but Michael was a bit of a name-dropper and such men are seldom popular.

He was, however, a close friend of mine, and I always enjoyed his company. He had no reason to try to take the mickey out of a man several years his junior, who was no rival to him, but who might be useful in putting over some propaganda on his behalf. Unlike many jockeys, he had a wonderful sense of humour and was the only one in my experience who delighted in telling stories against himself.

One I particularly remember concerned his bankruptcy, and was told in a broad Irish brogue. Having related in some detail the indignities to which he had been subjected, he went on to say: 'But the wickedest thing they did to me was to take away m' ould overcoat. Would you believe it that men could be so heartless as to take away a man's overcoat? Things were bad, but I said to meself the luck will change if only I can get back m' ould overcoat.

'So I told the man in charge he could have everything else I owned if he'd give me back m' ould overcoat. This melted his black heart, and he gave it me back, and that afternoon I won three races at Hurst Park and six weeks later I won the Derby.'

How could one help liking a man like that—though I might have found it possible if I had been a brother jockey or a trainer from whom he was for ever trying to take the mickey. His prime act of mickey-taking, or self-destruction—the same in his case—was to turn up at the royal meeting at Ascot on the Wednesday, immaculate in top hat and morning coat, having been stood down the previous day for the remainder of the meeting for some infringement or other.

He was escorted from the course soon after his arrival, as he knew he would be, but he had achieved his object—he had infuriated the stewards. One of the best men to hounds in England, or his native Ireland, he was a superb horseman and loved horses. To Michael, Steve Donoghue was the greatest jockey that ever lived, and I well remember meeting him at a dinner party in Cheshire after he had won the 1931 Chester Cup on Brown Jack a chance ride for Michael as Steve was injured.

'What a horse and what a jockey' were his first words to me, and he went on to say that no man in the world could have 'made' Brown Jack except Steve. A mile in circumference, Chester is our sharpest course, but Michael said that Brown Jack was so responsive to the lightest touch of the rein that it would have been just as easy to ride him round a sixpence.

Once we drove through a winter's night from Paris to Normandy, where we spent the day visiting the Aga Khan's studs. Michael was the Aga's stable jockey at the time. Michael had never ridden Mumtaz Mahal, the fastest filly that ever lived, then nearly white, and, as usual in January, heavily in foal, but he was delighted when another pregnant mare, whose name I cannot recall, trotted over and rubbed her nose against his arm. He had ridden her to win several races and there were tears in his eyes as he fondled her, cooing 'You remember me, old girl, you remember me.'

Michael's only Derby victory was on Mid-day Sun in 1937, but had not Solario become entangled in the tapes, and been virtually left at the post, it is quite conceivable he would have beaten Manna in 1925, in which case it is on the cards that he would also have won the St Leger and Gold Cup on Sir John Rutherford's colt. He picked Ruston Pasha in preference to Blenheim in 1930, of which I shall have more to say in a later chapter.

Michael would also have won the 1929 Derby on Trigo had

5 Mr. Curzon, a dying man, summons his last reserves of energy to lead in *Call Boy*

6 Tommy Weston, on Lord Derby's *Fairway*, who lost his tail to the souvenir hunters on the way to post for the 1928 Derby

7 Charlie Elliott, Freddy Fox and Tommy Weston (1930). Three great classic jockeys

7a Lord Derby's *Hyperion*, winner of 1933 Derby and St. Leger, a great racehorse and an even greater sire

he not been claimed by the Aga Khan to ride his colt Le Voleur. He did, however, win the St Leger on Trigo, who beat Lord Derby's Bosworth by a short head after the most exciting finish for that race in my experience. Both Beary and Tommy Weston got every ounce out of their mounts and Michael told me that Trigo was the gamest horse he had ever ridden. He must also have been a very tough one, as a week later, carrying 9 stone 12 lb and again ridden by Michael, he won the Irish St Leger by a short head from Visellus, to whom he was conceding 12 lb. In those days the Irish St Leger was a conditions race, with penalties and allowances.

In 1949 Michael won the St Leger for Noel Murless' stable on Ridge Wood. He was now a veteran and life was not treating him too well, so it was a welcome change of luck for him when his friend Gordon Richards chose to ride stable companion Krakatoa, whose best distance was one and a quarter miles. This was one of the poorest St Leger fields of all time, and the Aga Khan's Dust Devil, second to Ridge Wood, was a maiden.

Although Michael Beary rode for the Aga Khan for a number of years, he rode only one classic winner for him—Udaipur in the 1932 Oaks. In that year Michael had the mortification of finishing second in the Two Thousand Guineas, Derby and St Leger on the Aga Khan's Dastur; in the St Leger he was beaten a neck by his stable companion Firdaussi, who was ridden by Freddy Fox. This was a truly remarkable race as horses carrying the Aga Khan's colours filled four of the first five places. Dastur was certainly one of the unluckiest horses of my time, but I am not altogether sure that he was 100 per cent genuine. In any case, he had neither the ability nor the courage of his half-brother Bahram.

Michael and Freddy were not exactly bosom friends, and to have been beaten in the final classic by Freddy, as the result of picking the wrong one, must have been very hard to bear.

The first thing which struck one on meeting Freddy Fox was that he resembled the animal of that name. There was nothing sly about his expression, but with his reddish hair, fresh complexion and slightly startled eyes he had a distinct look of the Brer Fox of our childhood days. The impression was only a

E

momentary one as the startled look would invariably give way
to a beaming smile. He was four years younger than Steve, and
like him was a most friendly person. He positively exuded good-
will, and required no encouragement to embark on his latest
story. It was seldom very funny, and often one had heard it
before, but he derived such pleasure from telling it that one
could not hurt his feelings by telling him so.

Apprenticed to Fred Pratt, as far back as 1910 he finished
second in the St Leger on Mr James de Rothschild's Bronzino,
beaten a head by the mighty Swynford with the Derby winner
Lemberg one and a half lengths away third. At this time he was
a highly promising young lightweight jockey and neither Frank
Wootton on the winner, nor Freddy Fox on the second, weighed
more than a few pounds over seven stone.

When racing got back to normal, after World War I, nothing
would go right for Freddy, and at one time it seemed as if he
might drop out altogether. Fortunately for him, however, he
had a good friend in Captain Gooch, a fine trainer of stayers,
and an extremely patient man to boot. It so happened that at
the time Freddy's prospects were at their lowest, and he was
getting very little riding, Dick Gooch had his stayers very fit,
and, just as important, in a number of handicaps with weights
which he regarded as eminently satisfactory.

Freddy was an excellent judge of pace, and was very little
heavier than he had been when coming so near to winning the
St Leger in his youth. It only remains for me to say that up
came the winners, one after another at nice prices, and Freddy
Fox was back in business. But if Captain Dick Gooch had not
had those stayers on the right mark at the right time, who
knows?

From then on the forgotten man's telephone never stopped
ringing, and one day it was Fred Darling, master of Beckhampton, on the line. Things had not been running all that
smoothly for him, and Joe Childs, the stable jockey, had been
very put out when Gordon Richards, who had been engaged to
ride the lightweights, was put up once or twice on horses on
which old Joe could have done the weight. The truth of the
matter was that Fred and Joe were not one another's cup of tea,

but when a jockey has won a Derby and a St Leger for a stable, as Joe had done on Coronach, all differences are forgotten for the time being, and owner, trainer and jockey become a mutual admiration society.

In point of fact, the inflexible and somewhat touchy Joe maddened Fred Darling as much as the charming and reckless Steve had done in the early twenties. Even at this time Fred had set his heart on having Gordon Richards as stable jockey. He had a high opinion of him on account of his skill as a jockey and his integrity. It would also be very handy to have a man as stable jockey who could ride at around 7 stone 8 lb. Fred Darling will always be remembered for his classic winners, but he invariably had a horse or two in his yard which he hoped would win a nice handicap, and with such horses he could be very patient.

A young man of Gordon's weight would be an all-purpose rider and Fred knew that although he had been champion jockey for several years he was still willing to obey riding orders, and learn what it takes to win big races.

Not even a Fred Darling can change his jockey without consulting the owners who pay his retaining fee, and while negotiations were in progress Gordon, not realising that the Beckhampton job was about to fall into his lap, signed up to ride for Lord Glanely, for whose trainer Tommy Hogg Gordon had ridden from his earliest days with Marty Hartigan. Freddy Fox, although much older than Gordon, was almost the same weight.

That telephone call from Fred Darling was an offer to Freddy to ride as first jockey for Beckhampton. Needless to say, the offer was accepted. Despite the split with Fred Darling, Joe Childs remained on friendly terms with the master of Beckhampton, and when the latter decided to run two in the Two Thousand Guineas in 1931 Childs was given the ride on Cameronian, the less fancied of the two. Fox rode Lord Ellesmere's Lemnarchus, who started second favourite. Cameronian had been regarded as the stable's Derby hope at the end of the previous season, but he had disappointed in the Craven Stakes, and was thought to be still backward.

That race, however, must have brought him on at least a

stone, as he gave Joe a lovely ride, to win by two lengths from
M. Boussac's Goyescas, who lost several lengths at the start but
could never have beaten Cameronian.

It is always irritating for a jockey to pick a wrong one in an
important race, but it happens with unfailing regularity, and
cheerful Freddy was not the man to allow an occupational
hazard to get him down. On the strength of his polished display
at Newmarket, Cameronian started a good favourite in the
Derby, and, ridden with the utmost confidence by Freddy, Mr
John Dewar's colt beat the Manton-trained Orpen by three-
quarters of a length. The latter was well ridden by Bobby Jones
to get as close as he did. He had finished third in the Two
Thousand Guineas and went on to finish second to Sandwich
in the St Leger.

Sandwich had not had a clear run at Epsom, where he
finished third, but the luck certainly changed at Doncaster.
Cameronian started at 6/5 on for the St Leger, but he was never
in the race with a chance and his extraordinary behaviour has
never been satisfactorily explained. Normally, he was as quiet
as a lady's hack, but on this occasion he behaved like a mad
horse, both at the start and in the course of the race. Before the
tapes went up he administered a savage kick to the luckless
Orpen, and when he returned home was found to be running a
temperature, which persisted for several months. If ever a horse
gave one the impression that he had been got at that horse was
Cameronian, but Fred Darling and the stewards were apparently satisfied that his strange behaviour, and inability to run
within two stone of his true form, was due to natural causes.
With Cameronian to all intents and purposes out of the race,
and Orpen slightly *hors de combat* as the result of Cameronian's
attentions, Sandwich may not have had a great deal to do, but
he did it in the style of a very good horse. Lord Rosebery was
the last man to make excuses for the defeat of one of his horses,
but he regarded Sandwich's defeat in the Derby as the result of
sheer bad luck, a view which was shared by his jockey Harry
Wragg.

I have always regarded the 1931 three-year-olds as a vintage
crop, as until Cameronian's inexplicable fall from grace at

Doncaster they had run most consistently, reproducing their form with one another to an ounce.

In the previous year, 1930, Freddy Fox became champion jockey for the only time in his career, with 129 winners, beating Gordon Richards by one. I shall never forget that final day at Manchester, which began with Freddy leading by one, having begun the final week of the season at Warwick with a lead of six. Gordon won the first race by ten lengths: all square. Then Gordon went one up by winning the Manchester November Handicap on Lord Glanely's Glorious Devon. Freddy levelled the score by winning the fourth race. Gordon had no ride in the last two races, but Freddy rode the favourite Landsong in a field of twenty-two for the fifth race to win by a head, with a short head separating second and third, to become champion jockey.

Gordon told me that he couldn't bring himself to watch that race, and while it was run he was enjoying (if that is the right word) a cup of tea. There was dead silence for what seemed an eternity, and then a roar went up, and Gordon knew that the 1930 championship was one championship he was not going to win.

There has never been such a finish to a season's racing in my professional career, though Steve Donoghue and Charlie Elliott had dead-heated in 1923. In 1963 Scobie Breasley had only one to spare over Lester Piggott, but the lead did not change hands in the final week of the season.

Gordon, as was typical of him, was the first to congratulate Freddy and I quote his words to me that afternoon at Manchester. 'If ever a man deserved his triumph it's Freddy. He's a grand fella and as popular with the public as he is with us in the weighing room, and that's saying something. I've not forgotten what a friend he was to me when I was a kid, and though no one likes finishing second, if I had to be beaten I'm glad it's dear old Freddy who's done it.'

The two Freds, Darling and Fox, had appeared to be working in complete harmony, but maybe Freddy had tried out one of his not-so-funny stories on the guv'nor once too often. Anyhow, at the end of the 1931 season, a triumphant one for Beck-

hampton, Fred Darling offered Gordon the job of first jockey to
Beckhampton.

Gordon had been riding with great success as first jockey to
Lord Glanely, but I think that it was out of loyalty to his old
friend Tommy Hogg, rather than because of any great affection
for his Lordship, that Gordon rode for the Exning stable for as
long as he did.

Although 'Guts and Gaiters', as Lord Glanely was known on
the racecourse, would often squander money at the yearling
sales on animals of no great distinction, against the advice of
his trainer, he was always striving to get something for nothing,
or at any rate as cheaply as possible. Twice he had delayed
renewing Gordon's contract until November, when he knew
that the other big stables would have made their plans for the
following season. He then offered him £1,000 less than his
previous retaining fee.

Twice bitten, three times shy, and Gordon informed Lord
Glanely that only if he would make up his retainer to what it
had been previously would he sign on for another year. But his
Lordship still shilly-shallied, and Gordon, his patience at an
end, signed as first jockey to Beckhampton, a post he held for
the remainder of Fred Darling's career as a trainer. When
Darling retired Gordon continued to ride as stable jockey to
Noel Murless, and was riding a horse trained by him when he
met with the accident at Sandown in 1954 which put an end to
his career as a jockey.

Freddy Fox was getting any amount of riding as a free-lance,
but shortly after leaving Beckhampton he entered into some
form of agreement with the Aga Khan, whose horses had left
Dick Dawson, and were now trained by Frank Butters at
Newmarket. Numerically, this was the most powerful stable in
the country, and in nearly every big race the stable had more
than one representative. For more reasons than one the jockey
situation was in something of a tangle. The Aga Khan had
wanted Gordon, but he was employed by his chief rival. Such
was the Aga's admiration for the champion (he regained the
title in 1931 and retained it till 1953, except in 1941 when he
broke his leg) that he gave him a second retainer even though

it was most unlikely he would be available for big races.

Frank Butters disliked all jockeys on principle, and would not trust one further than he could see him. He and Michael Beary were at daggers drawn for years, but their association was amicable by comparison with that between Butters and Charlie Smirke in the years to come. So suspicious was Butters of all jockeys, except Gordon and Doug Smith, that even in the final gallop before a big race he would put up his 'work' riders rather than the jockeys who were to ride the horses in the forthcoming event. He had, however, a real affection for Gordon and he agreed with the Aga that 'Gordon when we can get him is better than no Gordon at all'. The Aga therefore made an arrangement with Freddy Fox and Dick Perryman to ride his horses when the champion wasn't available, though I never knew the exact terms of the agreement.

Freddy's greatest season was in 1935 when he won two classics, but, sad to relate, it was also his last. He and Dick Perryman had both ridden Bahram to victory as a two-year-old, but by this time Perryman had succeeded Weston as first jockey to Lord Derby, so Freddy was engaged to ride Bahram in all his races as a three-year-old.

A slight mishap prevented Bahram running at the Craven meeting, but he was fully recovered by Guineas day, though he had missed a couple of gallops, and Butters feared he might not be fully wound up. The Beckhampton three-year-olds were below par and for once in a way Fred Darling had no runner in the race. Gordon Richards therefore rode the Aga Khan's Theft. Running into the Dip, Theft appeared to be going the better of the two, but Bahram's giant stride enabled him to pull away up the hill to win in storming fashion.

A Derby with no runner from Beckhampton was a rarity, but Darling would never saddle a horse for a race unless he thought he would prove a real contender. Gordon therefore was available to ride for the Aga Khan, and chose Hairan in preference to Theft, who was most unlikely to get the trip, and was ridden by Harry Wragg. Had not Freddy been engaged to ride Bahram in all his races, Gordon would have won both the Guineas and Derby that year, and would not have had to wait a further eighteen years before realising his most cherished ambition on Pinza.

The St Leger appeared to be a mere formality for Bahram, and Freddy was all set to complete the Triple Crown, when disaster struck. Riding a horse belonging to Herbert Blagrave in a selling race on the opening day of the Doncaster meeting his mount came down and Freddy sustained grievous injuries. The sympathy of the entire racing world went out to this grand little sportsman as he lay in a Doncaster hospital while Smirke rode Bahram to complete the Triple Crown.

Bahram, like many great horses, was lazy, and would do no more, off his own bat, than was absolutely necessary. In his unbeaten career he had never won a race by more than two lengths, but as this was to be his last race it was decided to let the public see what he was capable of. Smirke, therefore, set him alight halfway up the straight and he raced away to win by five lengths.

No matter how good a horse may prove himself to be he will always have his detractors, and some people wrote Bahram off as being the best in a bad year. This was to some extent true in that he never met a horse except those of his own generation. But in race after race, over distances varying from five furlongs to one mile six furlongs 132 yards, he proved himself overwhelmingly superior to his contemporaries, and I for one regard Bahram as one of the great horses of all time.

During the few short years after his retirement, before he met his death in a motor accident, Freddy, who was affectionately known as the Mayor of Wantage and was a J.P., remained the cheerful, kindly little man he had always been. Never a word of complaint passed his lips regarding the accident which robbed him of the Triple Crown and prematurely ended a career in which he had achieved high distinction, and in the course of which he had set a wonderful example to those who were to follow him.

9 Charlie Elliott

The rise to fame of Charlie Elliott – An incredible horse called Golden Myth – Elliott wins 1923 Guineas for Lord Rosebery on Ellangowan – Mumtaz Mahal, the wonder filly, fails to stay – Charlie Elliott wins 1927 Derby on Call Boy for dying owner – Frank Curzon's courage – Charlie Elliott wins two more Derbys – Pharis, the horse with horns, wins sensational race for 1938 Grand Prix.

In the preceding chapters I have dealt almost exclusively with the careers of those who were established in their professions when the First World War ended, but within a period of five years a crop of young men had forced their way to the front, and their names had become household words.

First of these was Charlie Elliott, the son of a Newmarket stableman. He began by being articled to an obscure Epsom trainer who treated him with such cruelty that he ran away to become something of an embarrassment to his family. An extra mouth to feed means scantier rations all round when the bread-winner earns thirty shillings a week.

An apprentice who has run away from one master has difficulty in finding another trainer willing to engage him, but Jack Jarvis was impressed by the boy's enthusiasm, and, after a short period of probation, had his indentures transferred to him. It proved a wise decision.

Jack Jarvis, who was knighted shortly before his death, told me that young Charlie Elliott was a 'natural' in that he automatically did the right thing. 'I don't think he knew what he was doing half the time,' Sir John told me, 'but as it was the right thing I never enquired what went on in his young head. He was learning all the time and by the age of nineteen he was the equal of any jockey in the world.'

In an incredibly short space of time Charlie was riding winners and before he had celebrated his eighteenth birthday Jack Jarvis decided he was competent to become the stable jockey. It was, however, one thing for Jack to form this opinion but quite another to convince his owners, of whom the fifth Earl of Rosebery was the doyen, that a boy with three years of his apprenticeship still to serve was capable of holding his own with Donoghue, Carslake, Childs and Bullock in the classics.

Lord Rosebery had won the Derby with Ladas, Sir Vista and Cicero, and for a number of years had employed Danny Maher, considered by many to be the greatest jockey of all time. Jack, however, had remarkable powers of persuasion, and after giving the matter considerable thought Lord Rosebery and his fellow owners decided to give the boy the chance their trainer considered he deserved.

It was a tremendous responsibility for such a young boy, for although he had ridden a considerable number of winners, there is a world of difference between winning a handicap on a horse whose patient trainer had decided was carrying a convenient weight, and taking on Steve, Joe, Brownie and Frank on level terms. Tommy Weston had justified George Lambton's confidence in him by riding a succession of big winners for Stanley House, but he was several years older than Charlie Elliott when the latter became stable jockey to the Park Lodge stable.

Apprentices were allowed a 5 lb allowance, which they lost after riding fifty winners. Elliott's services were in just as much demand after he had lost the right to claim—a sure sign that trainers, other than his master, had a high opinion of young Charlie. Many boys who have shone when they have had a few pounds in hand, as is often the case when they are claiming an allowance, have disappeared from the scene when they have lost it, but Jack Jarvis' telephone continued to ring with requests from trainers who wanted Elliott to ride their horses.

He was not placed in a classic race in 1922, his first season in his new and responsible job, but so far from being overawed, when he went out to ride in a great race the excitement of knowing that history was about to be made seemed to inspire him. He was not conceited, but the thought that he might not be able to hold his own with the greatest riders in the world never entered his head. He had supreme confidence in his own ability; he knew he was a good rider, and was determined to become an even better one. The young man who thinks he knows it all is insufferable, but an aspiring jockey who is not full of self-confidence hasn't a hope in hell of making the grade.

To every boy who entered a racing stable between 1914 and 1926 Steve Donoghue was a hero. Michael Beary, when apprenticed to Atty Persse at Stockbridge, thought the sun shone out of his eyes, and long after Steve had become just another jockey Michael still thought that there was no one like him. Michael and Gordon, at Chattis Hill and Foxhill respectively, had the opportunity of studying the great little man at close range, but Charlie Elliott could only worship him from afar. All the same one had only to watch Charlie canter to the post, with his perfect seat and riding with a long rein, to realise that he had modelled himself on his childhood hero.

In his very first year in his new job Charlie and a horse called Golden Myth accomplished one of the most extraordinary performances in the history of racing. So moderate was Golden Myth's form as a three-year-old that he was set to carry only 7 stone 6 lb in the Queen's Prize in the spring of his four-year-old career. The famous hurdler Trespasser, who was no world beater on the flat, had to give him 20 lb. Golden Myth won all right, as Jack Jarvis had thought he would, but he beat Trespasser by only three-quarters of a length, though it was apparent he had a bit in hand. Even so, it seemed that Jarvis was aiming rather high in saddling him for the Gold Vase, as the Queen's Vase was then known.

In between these two races Golden Myth had been beaten eight lengths by Chivalrous, to whom he was conceding 2 lb, in the King Coal Stakes at Manchester over two miles. It seemed therefore that he was no more than just a fair handicapper. The Gold Vase was run only four days after the Manchester race, but despite this short rest and a couple of long journeys Golden Myth looked better than ever when he arrived at Ascot, and he proceeded to win the important two-mile event from another four-year-old, Vilna, to whom he was conceding 19 lb. Trespasser, who met him on 16 lb better terms than at Kempton, was fifth, but it is interesting to note that a three-year-old called Selene was fourth. In the years to come she was to immortalise herself as the dam of Hyperion and Sickle.

'But you ain't heard nothing yet,' as Al Jolson used to say. Two days later Golden Myth won the 1922 Gold Cup by three-quarters of a length from a very good stayer in Flamboyant, with Yutoi, who had won the previous year's Cesarewitch under a 10 lb penalty, fourth.

His most extraordinary achievement of all was yet to come. Having won two races over two miles, and one over two and a half miles in which he beat the best stayers in the country, Golden Myth's next objective was the Eclipse Stakes.

Buchan, a ten-furlong horse, had struggled on to finish first in the Gold Cup, only to suffer disqualification, but Jarvis was asking an out-and-out stayer, who seemed to get better the further he went, to take on the leading ten-furlong horses over their best distance. I was convinced they would run away from him, and I have never been more surprised in my life than when Golden Myth produced the speed to beat the even-money favourite Tamar by a head. Had it not been for Captain Cuttle, Tamar would have won the 1922 Derby by three lengths.

Charlie did not have to wait long for his first classic winner, as in 1923 he rode a magnificent race to win the Two Thousand Guineas on Lord Rosebery's Ellangowan, a son of the 1910 Derby winner Lemberg. What astounded those who had been racing ten times as long as I had was Elliott's maturity, a quality which one associates with long experience. The infant prodigy may excel one day, and be made to look rather foolish by a senior jockey the next, but Charlie Elliott could already ride any kind of race on any kind of horse against any kind of jockey.

It was as if he had done it all before in a previous incarnation.

When riding his first classic winner he was up against the American George Archibald, riding Lord Woolavington's Knockando. Archibald, the father of the successful steeplechase jockey George Archibald, was a very strong finisher, but Charlie Elliott, on Ellangowan, rode like a man inspired to win by a head. The pundits compared him to Frank Wootton, who was champion jockey at the age of seventeen with 165 winners in 1909, and no one was in any doubt that a new star had been born.

Triumph followed triumph and Charlie tied with Steve Donoghue for the 1923 Jockeys' Championship with eighty-nine winners, Steve having been undisputed champion for nine years. The following year Charlie was champion on his own with 109 winners. But there was already another young man breathing down his neck. A shock of black hair had earned him the nickname of Moppy, and he was to be champion jockey on no fewer than twenty-six occasions.

In the year following his success on Ellangowan in the Two Thousand Guineas Charlie Elliott won the One Thousand Guineas on Lord Rosebery's filly Plack, the most sensational race for this event in my time.

Mumtaz Mahal was the fastest filly anyone had ever seen, and some impartial judges thought that over five furlongs she was even faster than her sire The Tetrarch, who was before my time. I did not see Mumtaz Mahal make her début at New-market, but in the Queen Mary Stakes at Ascot she was so quickly into her stride that most people thought it had been a false start (of which there were plenty in those days); but not a bit of it, and the starter, Captain Allison, told me that she had not got a flier, but had gained a lead of half a dozen lengths in the first furlong by her incredible initial speed.

There was obviously a doubt as to whether she would stay the Rowley Mile, but backers fell over one another to support her, and she started a screaming hot favourite. At the Bushes she was eight lengths clear, but when she met the rising ground her stride became shorter and shorter. It must have been agony for George Hulme trying to drag the winning post towards him. All credit to him that he sat as still as a mouse in an endeavour to conserve her failing energy, but it was to no avail: Plack swept by her in the final fifty yards to win by half a length with Straitlace the same distance away third.

Plack, a big chestnut daughter of Hurry On, used to gallop with her tail going round like a windmill, but it was only a mannerism as she was as game as they come. In the Oaks Sir Edward Hulton's Straitlace, ridden by Frank O'Neill turned the tables on her. This lovely filly of medium size was the only offspring of Son-in-Law to win a classic.

The first of Charlie Elliott's three Derbys was on Call Boy in 1927. Like most of the best sons of Hurry On he was a chestnut, but he was not typical of his breed, being cast in a smaller mould. He was much more compact than such as Captain Cuttle and Coronach and I fell in love with him when I first saw him as a two-year-old. He was bred by his owner, Mr Frank Curzon, who had bought his dam Comedienne for only 130 guineas, and was trained by Jack Watts, whose father rode four Derby winners, including the Prince of Wales' Persimmon, and whose son and grandson are both particularly successful trainers.

After a highly promising two-year-old career Call Boy looked a picture when I first saw him the following year at Newmarket. I thought he was sure to win the Two Thousand Guineas, but in a terrific finish he was beaten a whisker by Mr C. W. Whitburn's Adam's Apple, trained by Harry Cottrill and extremely well ridden by Jack Leach. Jack was a very good friend of mine and I was delighted to see him win a classic though I could have wished he had done so in a race in which I was less financially involved.

One did not have to be a pedigree expert to realise that the extra half-mile at Epsom would be all in favour of Call Boy, and so it proved to be, Mr Curzon's colt winning by two lengths from the second favourite Hot Night, in the colours of Sir Victor Sassoon.

Call Boy had been easy to back in the ante-post market, for the sad reason that it was known that Mr Curzon had not long to live. If he died before the race Call Boy would automatically be debarred from running, and ante-post backers would lose their money. This rule has long since been changed.

As Call Boy passed the post Mr Curzon summoned his last reserves of strength and walked on to the course to lead in his winner. He stumbled, and his friends had to support him, but he made it. Less than a month later he was dead. People said 'What a tragedy', but I disagree. We all have to go some time, and what better time than when we have just realised our most cherished ambition? The tragedy would have been if he had died the day before the Derby.

Call Boy appeared to possess all the requisite qualities to make a successful stallion, and was sold for £60,000 to Sir Harry Mallaby-Deeley, a brother of Mr Curzon who had changed his name when he went on the stage as a young man. Sir Harry received no return for his big outlay as Call Boy proved to be virtually sterile. Not so Lord Derby's little colt Sickle, who injured himself in the course of the race. After being sold to America he was a brilliant success at stud, his descendants including the famous Native Dancer. Charlie rode two more Derby winners—on Bois Roussel in 1938, and on Nimbus in 1949. Bois Roussel was bred in France by M. Leon Volterra and was out of that remarkable mare Plucky Liege, by Spearmint out of Concertina by St Simon; she was twenty-three years old when she foaled Bois Roussel. She had been bought in 1915 by that colourful character Jefferson Davis Cohn who was Horatio Bottomley's son-in-law, and when Cohn went broke in 1934 Leon Volterra, who had also had his ups and downs, bought all his racing interests, including Plucky Liege, for the proverbial song, the market being somewhat depressed at the time.

Mr Cohn knew far more about racing and breeding than did M. Volterra, and it must have been a cruel blow to him when he had to dispose of his stock at a time when years of careful planning were beginning to bear fruit. Prior to Bois Roussel Plucky Liege had had twelve foals, the most celebrated being Sir Galahad III and Bull Dog, both by Teddy, and Admiral Drake by Craig An Eran. Sir Galahad III won the Two Thousand Guineas and the Lincoln, and was the sire of Galatea II, winner of our One Thousand Guineas and Oaks. Exported to America, he was four times leading stallion in the U.S.A., where Bull Dog was also a very successful sire. Admiral Drake, ridden by Steve, won the Grand Prix, and was the sire of Phil Drake, winner of our Derby and the Grand Prix in 1955.

Bois Roussel started his career by winning the Prix Juigne for three-year-olds that had never run, a race which corresponds to our Wood Ditton Stakes except that it is about ten times as valuable. The merit of success in such a race is hard to evaluate as one can only guess at the strength of the opposition, but Mr Peter Beatty took a great fancy to Bois Roussel who was a most attractive colt. Short in the leg he was beautifully put together, and already had the appearance of a potential classic winner.

Every horse Leon Volterra owned was for sale—at a price—and Aly Khan, acting on Beatty's behalf, had to go to £8,000 for Bois Roussel, which was about twice the sum the buyer had in mind. All's well that ends well, and after he had won the Derby he appeared to be a very cheap horse indeed.

When he first arrived at Beckhampton Bois Roussel did not impress either Fred Darling or Gordon Richards. Pasch had won the Two Thousand Guineas in great style and both trainer and jockey had a very high opinion of him. Mr Beatty had bought Bois Roussel with the Derby in view, but in his work on the Beckhampton downs in the first couple of weeks after he had arrived from France it did not seem that he would prove much of a danger to Pasch at Epsom. About ten days before the Derby, however, Bois Roussel, having become acclimatised, started to thrive and was altogether a different colt from the one who had moved so sluggishly earlier on. But when a jockey has won the Guineas on a potential stayer (Pasch was by Blandford) a rival must prove himself a world-beater to make him want to swop mounts. The two colts were not tried against one another, but with every gallop Bois Roussel pleased Fred Darling a little bit more, and I think that by this time he had a suspicion that Pasch, who was a very free runner, might not get the trip. So he decided to have £1,000 to win on each of his two runners. As Bois Roussel started at 20/1 and Pasch at 9/4 he could be forgiven if he did not appear unduly depressed when the 'neglected' beat the 'selected'.

He was, however, geneuinely sorry that Gordon, whom he described as having done all the work, should have been on the loser, and told him so as soon as the jockeys had weighed in. Charlie Elliott was based in France, where he was first jockey to M. Boussac, but immediately it was known that the latter would have no runner in the 1938 Derby Mr Beatty engaged him. Although he had been riding in France for nearly ten years Charlie's services were in as much demand for the big races in this country as they had been when he was riding for Jack Jarvis.

Pasch and Scottish Union, ridden by Carslake, were battling it out, quite early in the straight, and when Pasch cracked it looked a million to one on Brownie winning a first Derby for Mr Jimmy Rank, Noel Cannon and himself. Bois Roussel had been idling along at the rear of the field and neither he nor his jockey seemed very interested. Charlie had ridden him in only one work-out and had not been very impressed with the Prix Juigne form. As the field approached Tattenham Corner with Bois Roussel at least a dozen lengths behind the leaders Charlie gave his mount a back-hander, and it worked like magic.

With two furlongs to go, he was still six lengths behind Scottish Union, but he was now in full spate, and he swept by Mr Rank's colt as if the latter were standing still, to win by four lengths. Pasch did not get one and a half miles, but Scottish Union subsequently won the St Leger, and for Bois Roussel to have trounced him in the way he did Mr Peter Beatty's colt must have been a pretty good Derby winner. Unfortunately he only ran once again—in the Grand Prix de Paris.

The Longchamp course is often referred to as Epsom in reverse, but it has always seemed to me that luck plays an even bigger part on the French course than it does over our Derby track with its longer straight. At Epsom, despite being in the last two all the way to Tattenham Corner, Bois Roussel had a perfectly clear run, but at Longchamp Gordon Richards found himself in a terrible tangle and was knocked from pillar to post as he endeavoured to extricate himself.

In no circumstances would Bois Roussel have beaten the

F

Italian colt Nearco, who had already proved himself the hell of a horse and was to turn out an even greater stallion, but with a clear run Bois Roussel would have undoubtedly have beaten Canot for second place.

Charlie Elliott's first two Derbys required no exceptional skill on his part, but he rode a terrific race to win the 1949 Derby on Nimbus, who beat Amour Drake by a head with Swallow Tail a head away third—the closest finish for our greatest race in my fifty years' experience of Epsom.

Nimbus, a son of Nearco, had beaten Abernant by a short head in the Two Thousand Guineas, but I was a little doubtful whether he would stay the Derby distance as his dam, Kong, was a sprinter. Charlie Elliott, however, had no doubt that he would do so, and as the colt's trainer George Colling was confined to his bed with a serious illness he and the head lad were responsible for the preparation of Nimbus. By this time unimportant races had little interest for Charlie, but when he had been engaged to ride a horse in a classic he would not spare himself, no matter where racing was due to take place, in order to ride him every day even if the animal were to do only a canter.

He would spend hours getting to know his prospective mount so that on the big day there was a complete understanding between them. Charlie was always the boss, but there was no problem about doing it 'your' way or 'my' way. 'We were allies,' Charlie told me, 'and we did it our way.' He had no opportunity to get to know Bois Roussel, but Call Boy and Nimbus were like members of his family, and what he didn't know about them wasn't worth knowing.

Charlie's faith in Nimbus' stamina was apparent when he set out to make all the running. He succeeded in doing so, though it is possible that Swallow Tail may have headed him for a few strides a furlong from home. Nimbus fought back, but he hung to the right, and I thought he interfered with Swallow Tail. This left a gap between Nimbus and the rails, and Johnstone, on the fast-finishing Amour Drake, switched to the left and was through it, or perhaps I should say nearly through it, in a flash. I thought he had got up, but the photograph revealed Nimbus as the winner. Had not Amour Drake split Nimbus and Swallow

Tail I think Doug Smith would have had grounds for an objection—which would have been the first in the Derby since the stewards, on their own account, objected to Craganour in 1913 and awarded the race to the 100/1 chance Aboyeur.

Charlie won every big race there was to win in France, many of them several times, in the orange jacket and grey cap of M. Marcel Boussac, and he considers Pharis II to be the best horse he ever rode. Like Bois Roussel, Pharis ran only three times. I saw him win his three races, and he was indeed a remarkable horse. In the first place he had horns of about half an inch protruding from his forehead, which M. Boussac believed were a relic from some prehistoric animal ancestor of the horse family. A coal black, he was not outstandingly tall, but he had an exceptionally deep body which fairly exuded power. His sire, Pharos, was one of the most powerful horses I had ever seen, but Pharis, who closely resembled him, was just that bit heavier. He had tremendous shoulders, and above them a thick neck, which made one wonder whether he was entirely clear winded, and it was no surprise when Charlie Elliott confided in me after he had won his first race that the colt was already a slight 'whistler'.

Such a heavily built colt was not suited to the Longchamp gradients, and at the bottom of the hill in a small field for the Prix Lupin, his first race, he was last by several lengths. But when he reached the level ground he flew past his rivals to win as he pleased. In the straight in the French Derby at Chantilly he stumbled, and Charlie told me that there were traces of grass on his muzzle when he pulled up; but Pharis was so superior to his rivals that he was able to pick himself up and go on to win.

In the Grand Prix he met with as much interference as Bois Roussel had done the previous year, largely because of his inability to act on the steep descent. Charlie, knowing his dislike for galloping downhill, would have been better advised to have taken him to the outside instead of keeping to the rails, where he had to contend with beaten horses slowing down in front of him. The result was that with only a furlong to go Pharis' chance appeared hopeless.

I shall never forget the closing stages of that race. One often hears of a horse leaving the opposition standing, but Pharis made them appear to be going backwards.

In the late summer of 1939 M. Boussac sent him over to Steve Donoghue's place to complete his preparation for the St Leger, but before that race was run Hitler had marched into Poland. We too had a great horse that year in Lord Rosebery's Blue Peter, winner of the Two Thousand Guineas, Derby and Eclipse Stakes with E. Smith in the saddle. Jack Jarvis had no doubt that this chestnut son of Fairway was by far the best horse he had ever trained. The meeting between him and Pharis at Doncaster was eagerly awaited, but even if Hitler had waited another month (or Chamberlain had done another Munich) these two great horses would not have met. Soon after his arrival at Blewbury, Pharis went so badly in a gallop that it was evident that he had no chance in the St Leger. Steve Donoghue and Elliott informed M. Boussac of this and he ordered him to be returned to France. I never heard exactly what ailed him, but I suspect that this great horse, whose wind had always been suspect, had become a 'roarer'.

After the fall of France the Germans stole Pharis, but when he was recaptured in 1945 it was evident that he had been well treated. So fat was he that he had to be put on a slimming diet.

When I saw him at Fresnay le Buffard in 1946 he was still overweight, though he was ridden out every morning and served forty mares a year. I was warned that he might bite me when I entered his box, and to obviate this possibility the stud groom gave him a stick which he clenched between his teeth with obvious enjoyment.

Until I saw Sea Bird win the Prix de l'Arc de Triomphe by five lengths from the French Derby and Grand Prix winner Reliance in 1965 I had considered Pharis' Grand Prix to be the most spectacular performance I had ever seen on a racecourse. Charlie Elliott regards Tourbillon and the latter's sons Caracalla and Djebel as the next-best colts to Pharis. The best mare he ever rode was undoubtedly Corrida. Charlie's association with M. Boussac began in 1929. His great friend Charlie Smirke had been warned off the previous year, while Charlie had lost his job as first jockey to Jack Jarvis and was riding for the latter's brother Basil.

It was common knowledge that the two Charlies had been betting in large sums and Charlie Elliott thought that the stewards were gunning for him. Normally a super-confident young man, he was on tenterhooks and expected to be hauled up after every race. Whether or not his fears were justified I would not like to say, but the stewards were determined to stamp out betting among the jockeys and I think he was well advised to jump at the offer made to him by M. Boussac, who already had a powerful string of horses and whose ambition it was to become the most successful owner in the world.

10 Harry Wragg brings back sanity

Harry Wragg does it his way and wins 1928 Derby on Felstead – Charlie Elliott and Gordon Richards cut each other's throats – Fairway mobbed, loses his tail and his backers' money – None-the-worse wins 1928 Eclipse Stakes and St Leger – First classic success for royal colours for nineteen years – Trouble behind the scenes at Stanley House – Butters takes over from Lambton, who stays on as manager – Half-bred Quashed beats American champion Omaha in 1936 Gold Cup – Harry Wragg wins another Derby, this time for the Aga Khan.

After Steve Donoghue had won the Derby three years running and four times in five years people began to talk about his magic wand and the more gullible believed that he possessed some supernatural power which could turn a slow horse into a fast one.

A newspaper, trading on this belief, announced that it had prevailed upon Steve to confide the secret of his success to its readers. I hope Steve got well paid for it, for the promise that he would divulge his innermost secrets certainly sold a lot of copies. The article was quite a long one, but the only part of it written by Steve was his signature at the end of it, and it is quite on the cards that he didn't even write that.

What it all boiled down to was that if a jockey was to have any chance of winning the Derby he must be in the first three at the top of the hill, with nearly a mile still to go. Admittedly, Steve had ridden his Derby winners in this way, and he may have told his ghost writer that this was the secret of his success, but Steve knew as well as you and I know today that though it is one way to win the Derby it is by no means the only way. This contention of Steve's and his ghost writer's received support a few weeks after the article appeared when Joe Childs made all the running on Coronach. Headlines of the size usually reserved for the outbreak of a war announced that even Joe Childs, the greatest exponent of waiting tactics, had taken Steve's tip, though everyone who knew the first thing about racing knew that the old boy had been run away with.

But there was one young man who was convinced that Steve, through his ghost writer, was talking a whole load of nonsense, and he was determined to prove it at the earliest opportunity. His name was Harry Wragg, the year was 1928, and the horse he was to ride in the Derby was called Felstead.

The favourite was Lord Derby's Fairway, an own brother to Pharos but dissimilar to him in every respect. While Pharos was powerfully built, Fairway was made like a greyhound. He had not run in the Two Thousand Guineas, owing to a slight mishap, but he demonstrated that he had fully recovered by winning the Newmarket Stakes over a mile and a quarter in great style. The first classic had been won by the tough, courageous little Flamingo, ridden with his usual skill by Charlie Elliott, who scored by a head from the big grey colt Royal Minstrel. The latter had a somewhat high action, unsuitable for Epsom, in addition to which, being by Tetratema, he was unlikely to stay a mile and a half. Flamingo, each way, looked a gilt-edged investment: in fact, Fairway, who as a two-year-old had won the Coventry Stakes, the July Stakes and the Champagne Stakes, appeared to be the only danger.

On the book Fairway was entitled to be favourite, but when he reached the starting gate it was apparent that his chance had gone. What the police were up to when they should have been shepherding the runners across the course to the start I have never been told, but they allowed the crowd to get out of control. There must have been a number of souvenir hunters amongst those who mobbed the favourite, as by the time Captain Allison called the roll Fairway had lost almost every hair from his tail. He was trembling with fright, and having shown speed for only three furlongs he disappeared from the race.

Realising that Fairway was no longer at the races, Charlie Elliott, on Flamingo, and Gordon Richards, on Sunny Trace, each thought he had only the other to beat, and if either of these two great jockeys ever rode a worse race I was not present to see it.

They were at it hammer and tongs from the mile post, after which point neither horse was on the bit for a single stride. With two furlongs to go Sunny Trace had had it, and those of us who had had a great deal more on Flamingo than our bank managers would have approved of, our eyes fixed on the leading pair, began to shout 'Come on Charlie!'.

But what's that going like a bomb a couple of lengths behind him in green? And no sooner had we realised that it was Felstead, in the colours of Sir Hugo Cunliffe-Owen, than he swept past the stone-cold Flamingo to win by one and a half lengths.

As a two-year-old Felstead had been unplaced in all his four races, and though he had won a maiden race at Newbury and the Davis Stakes at Hurst Park his form did not give him much chance of beating colts of the quality of Fairway or Flamingo. While giving Felstead's trainer Captain Ossie Bell full credit for the improvement he had brought about in him I believe that if Fairway had not been subjected to mobbing and tail pulling and if Charlie Elliott had ridden with his customary judgement Felstead would have finished third. Gordon Richards rode with no more discretion than Elliott had done, but in no circumstances would Sunny Trace have stayed the distance. Chief praise, however, must go to Harry Wragg: he had proved conclusively that the Derby, like any other race, could be won by waiting, thus reintroducing sanity into the race.

Fairway was a sorry sight when he arrived home at Newmarket, almost tailless and a bundle of nerves, but it was not long before he recovered his composure, although his tail took several months to regain its luxuriant growth. As he was soon working even better than before he went to Epsom it was decided to let him take his chance in the Eclipse Stakes.

Punters, however, believed that a highly strung colt who had undergone such diabolical treatment as Fairway had had to contend with on the way to the post for the Derby would remember his nightmare experience when he left the paddock and might decline to participate. But the preliminaries at Sandown are mercifully short and when Fairway reached the starting gate he was cool, collected and rarin' to go.

Book Law was made a hot favourite, but Lord Astor's filly was only a shadow of what she had been as a three-year-old, when following a short head defeat in the Oaks by Lord Durham's Beam, trained for him by his brother George Lambton, she won two races at Goodwood before trouncing the colts in the St Leger. Lord Astor owned some magnificent fillies in the twenties and thirties, all bred by him at Clivedon, but I regard Book Law as the best of them—even though Pogrom, Saucy Sue, Short Story and Pennycomequick won the Oaks, in which Book Law was so narrowly defeated.

I rate Fairway's performance in the 1928 Eclipse Stakes as one of the most remarkable I have seen on a racecourse. Excuses had been made for Book Law, when with odds of 5/2 betted on her she could only finish third to Apelle and Silverstead in the Coronation Cup, but there was no excuse for her at Sandown. From the moment the field entered the straight there was only one in it, and Fairway drew further and further away to win by eight lengths from Royal Minstrel, with Book Law half a length away third.

With Book Law obviously over the hill, the opposition in what was in those days our most valuable race may not have been very strong, but Fairway won like a world-beater, which he undoubtedly was as a three-year-old. He and Solario were certainly the two best horses to have been beaten in the Derby in my time. Had the police been carrying out their job as efficiently as they perform it today Fairway must have won the Derby by several lengths, unless, or course, Weston had joined Charlie Elliott and Gordon Richards and played into the hands of Harry Wragg.

Fairway started a hot favourite for the St Leger, and demonstrated that he was just as good over a mile and three-quarters as he was over ten furlongs, beating the French-trained Palais Royal very comfortably. The result, however, demonstrated that the handicapper had made a *faux pas* in giving Palais Royal only 7 stone 13 lb in the Cambridgeshire. He started at 5/1 and made virtually all the running to win comfortably and land a substantial gamble for his Belgian owner Jacques Wittouck, a most genial man and a fine sportsman.

Stanley House had received some consolation for the Fairway catastrophe in the 1928 Derby, when, two days later, Lord Derby's Toboggan ran away with the Oaks. King George V's Scuttle had won the One Thousand Guineas (for which she started a hot favourite) by a length from Jurisdiction, with Toboggan no fewer than six lengths away third, but not before she had given heart failure to all loyal subjects present that day at Newmarket. She had never been the most tractable of fillies when faced with several strands of rope, but on this all-important occasion she was on her worst behaviour. Joe Childs displayed remarkable patience for a man not renowned for that virtue, and Captain Allison should have been knighted for his services to the crown.

After what seemed an age their patience was rewarded: Scuttle was facing the right way for long enough for the starter to press the lever and they were away. In the race the royal filly did nothing wrong, settling down as good as gold, and lengthening her stride immediately Joe gave her the office.

The royal colours had been through a very thin time in the years preceding Scuttle's victory, the previous classic in which they had been carried to victory being the Derby of 1909, won by King Edwards VII's Minoru. Scuttle was trained by William Jarvis, elder brother of Basil and Jack and father of Ryan, a highly successful trainer today.

Scuttle and Joe Childs were given an ovation and it was hoped she would follow up this success by winning the Oaks. Toboggan was no danger to her on the book, but an awful lot can happen between Guineas week and Derby week, and Toboggan, like so many of Hurry On's offspring, improved out of all knowledge in the course of that vital month. Furthermore, bred as she was, the extra half-mile was all in her favour.

Scuttle started at even money, but it was evident a long way from home that Toboggan had taken her measure, and Lord Derby's filly galloped right away from her to win by four lengths. Toboggan was one of the best Oaks winners between the wars, and in the Coronation Stakes of a mile at Ascot she confirmed her superiority over Scuttle. With odds of 7/2 betted on her she finished third of four in the St George Stakes at Liverpool, but this shock defeat was redeemed when she won the Jockey Club Stakes from a good class field.

The Stanley House stable was on the crest of the wave in the twenties and thirties, but all was not going smoothly behind the scenes. George Lambton was deposed as trainer by Frank Butters, but remained in the capacity of manager. When Butters got the sack at the end of only a couple of seasons Lambton again took over the role of trainer, but at the end of 1933 (Hyperion's year) he was kicked out once more and College Leader moved into Stanley House.

Leader was a very genial, mild-mannered man, but he made one stipulation: he wasn't going to take over Tommy Weston, who had been Lambton's right-hand man since the latter engaged him as first jockey for Stanley House in 1921. In the course of those ten years Stanley House had won the Derby twice (Sansovino in 1924 and Hyperion in 1933), the Two Thousand Guineas (Colorado in 1926), the One Thousand Guineas (Fair Isle in 1930), the Oaks twice (Beam in 1927 and Toboggan in 1928), and the St Leger three times (Tranquil in 1923, Fairway in 1928 and Hyperion in 1933).

Weston had ridden all these winners, but Leader doubted whether he could establish a harmonious relationship with a man so steeped in the Lambton tradition, who would regard him as an intruder. 'Weston would have gone to the ends of the earth at a nod from George Lambton, but God help the man who took over his job,' Leader told me.

'Coll' Leader had employed Dick Perryman for a number of years, and they had been very successful with horses that were some way removed from classic standard. A very level-headed, hard-working young man, Perryman had been apprenticed to Coll's brother Fred, for whom Joe Childs rode whenever he was not claimed by one of the stables that retained him, and young Dick modelled his style on that of the great exponent of waiting tactics.

He realised, however, that no two horses are alike, and while he copied the old maestro's tactics on horses who were prepared to drop their bits, he suited his style to the horse he was riding.

Tommy Weston had been brought up in a rough, tough school in the North, and though under Lambton's guidance his technique improved, his riding lacked polish. No jockey, however, rode a more vigorous finish and his records showed that though inelegant he was most effective. He was in fact a far better jockey than he appeared to be from the stands.

Dick Perryman, like Childs, was reputed to be a bit slow out of the gate, but like him he preferred to settle his mount down, give it time to find its stride, and get it properly balanced. He was an excellent judge of pace and though some may have been more subtle and others more brilliant Dick Perryman had always been in great demand by betting stables, a sure sign that he was not in the habit of losing races he should have won. His only classic victory for Lord Derby was on Tide-way in the 1936 One Thousand Guineas, but he would undoubtedly have ridden several more had not a motor accident during the war years cut short his career as a jockey.

His greatest triumph for the Derby family was on Quashed in the 1936 Gold Cup. A daughter of the 'half-bred' Verdict, who has figured in an earlier chapter as the winner of the Cambridgeshire and the Coronation Cup, Quashed had been leased to Lord Derby's son Lord Stanley for her racing career. As the stable second string, ridden by Henri Jellis, she had got up in the last stride to win the Oaks. Freddy Fox had won the Derby two days earlier on Bahram, and looked all set to complete the double on Mrs G. B. Miller's Ankaret, but Quashed, running on with great courage, got her nose in front on the line. Incidentally, Mrs Miller became the first lady to win an Epsom Derby when her Mid-day Sun, ridden by Michael Beary, won the big one two years later.

Omaha had been sent over from America to be trained by

Captain Boyd Rochfort, without an equal as a trainer of stayers, for the Gold Cup. He was reputed to be one of the best stayers ever to run in the U.S.A., and he was thought sure to achieve his objective. And so he would have done had not Quashed, like her dam, been one of the bravest fillies that ever looked through a bridle. What a race it was, with Omaha holding a fractional advantage till Quashed poked her nose in front right on the line just as she had done when winning the Oaks the previous year.

Both Perryman on the winner and Rufus Beasley on the loser rode like heroes, getting every ounce out of their mounts with the minimum use of the whip. Rufus dropped his in the concluding stages of this memorable race, but the American horse had given all he had to give and I don't think it affected the result.

I never knew what led up to the final split between Lord Derby and George Lambton, but the parting must have been a painful experience for both men, as not only had their association brought unprecedented success to Stanley House, but away from the racecourse they had been close friends for many years.

After Fairway's Eclipse Stakes, Carslake complained to the stewards that Weston had interfered with his mount The Wheedler, who was unplaced in the colours of the Duke of Portland. In other words, Carslake accused Weston of foul riding. Weston admitted having bumped The Wheedler, but said that it was because the horse in front of him had stopped. The stewards were satisfied that Weston was not guilty of any intentional malpractice, but they considered his method of riding had been very rough, and severely cautioned him as to his future riding.

After Lord Derby's Caerleon, an own brother to Colorado, won the Eclipse Stakes of 1931 by half a length from Goyescas, with Sandwich, who was to win the St Leger that autumn, and the previous year's St Leger winner, Singapore, both unplaced, he was booed by the crowd as he entered the winning enclosure. The stewards held an enquiry into the discrepancy between his performance in this race compared with that in the Duke of Cambridge Handicap a fortnight earlier in which he had finished unplaced, as he had done in his two previous races.

George Lambton stated that his horses had been coughing badly in June, that Caerleon was a peculiar tempered horse who could not be relied on, that he had great difficulty in training him, but that the horse had made great improvement since his previous race. This final observation was apparent not only to the stewards but to every racegoer who owned a form book.

The stewards, in view of the fact that they considered that this had been a false-run race, were satisfied with Mr Lambton's explanation. Lord Derby was very upset that the crowd, with whom he was so popular, should have demonstrated against one of his horses, and that the stewards should have thought it necessary to enquire into its running. It was rumoured at the time that Lambton would be relieved of his duties by Lord Derby immediately the latter could find a suitable man to take his place. But this was idle speculation, and when the dust settled Lord Derby and his trainer appeared to be once again on good terms. When the break came two years later it created a big surprise, especially in view of the fact that Lambton that year had saddled Hyperion to win the Derby and the St Leger.

Most jockeys live their lives by a series of reflex actions, directed by their subconscious minds. Thinking is a chore which can be left to those with nothing better to do, but as the mind, like every other part of our bodies, ceases to function if it is never exercised, jockeys have fewer interests outside their profession than any other men of my acquaintance.

War, famine and pestilence only happen to other people. The idea that they might happen here need not be taken seriously, thank goodness, as they might stop racing next week. If there has to be an earthquake let it happen on a Sunday, unless, of course, they happen to be riding in France that day.

A colleague with interests outside racing is regarded as 'not one of us'. Jockeys make a great deal of money, but though most of them spring from humble origins they evince little interest in the fate of the have-nots. They will pull up one of the floorboards to find a tenner for old so-and-so, who's down on his luck, but that's as far as it goes. A marvellous man is one who carries large sums of ready money in his pocket which he drops to his jockey when he wins a race, and a proper so-and-so is one who pays by cheque. A bastard is a jockey who gets the ride on a horse you have set your heart on, and a smart guy is yourself when you pinch a ride which rightfully belongs to another.

A national catastrophe is when the telephone breaks down when you are ringing up a trainer to ask for the ride on a horse which your best friend rode last time out, when it wasn't having a pop.

The above is a very long way from Harry Wragg, Felstead and the other horses which Harry's carefully laid plans landed in the winning enclosure. Harry has a first-class mind, which he used unsparingly from the days of his apprenticeship with old Bob Colling, and is still using today as a highly successful Newmarket trainer. I have said that Joe Childs was the greatest rider of a waiting race, but Harry Wragg was the finer jockey. Although he was nicknamed the Head Waiter, he could ride any sort of race on any sort of horse.

From his earliest days he was always thinking things out for himself, and was therefore something of a heretic in the eyes of his contemporaries, who called him, somewhat contemptuously, 'Brains'. Brains, like birthmarks, were best concealed. Unlike Charlie Elliott and Gordon Richards, he did not immediately hit the high spots, and I recall that when he was riding for Mr Solly Joel, who trained with Walter Earl, he was sometimes criticised by owner and trainer. Both men liked to bet, so somebody had to carry the can.

Some years later Harry teamed up again with Earl at Stanley House, where they enjoyed great success, winning the Derby with Watling Street, the Two Thousand Guineas with Garden Path, the One Thousand Guineas and St Leger with Herringbone and the One Thousand Guineas with Sun Stream. All these were wartime events.

Two years after his success on Felstead, Harry Wragg won the Derby on the Aga Khan's Blenheim. The luckless Michael Beary was on stable companion Rustom Pasha, who started second favourite at 9/2, while Blenheim was an 18/1 chance. Diolite, who had won the Two Thousand Guineas ridden by Freddy Fox, was favourite. Rustom Pasha had won the Nonsuch Stakes at Epsom, which corresponded to the Blue Riband

Stakes, and had acted so well on the course when winning by four lengths that the Aga Khan believed he would win him his first Derby.

Rustom Pasha was the product of extremes, being by Son-in-Law out of the flying mare Cos. Such a pedigree can confound the most profound students of the stud book when they try to assess the animal's potential stamina.

Rustom Pasha led into the straight, but failed to get the trip. Iliad, a son of Swynford, looked the likely winner for Mr Somerville Tattersall when he got the better of Diolite. Harry Wragg, riding almost the identical race he had ridden on Felstead, brought Blenheim along with a devastating run to win by a length. Dick Dawson therefore saddled the Derby winner two years running, having won in 1929 with Trigo. This was a remarkable feat in itself, rendered all the more noteworthy by the fact that both the horses were by Blandford, whom he owned in partnership with his brother.

A delighted Aga Khan led in his Derby winner. He is alleged to have cooed 'good old Rustom' as he entered the winning enclosure, but to have corrected this to 'good old Blenheim' when he noticed that the jockey was Harry Wragg, wearing a green cap, and not Michael Beary in a brown one. I must add that the Aga hotly denied this story. Blenheim fell lame in the course of his preparation for the Eclipse Stakes, but Rustom Pasha won that race ridden by Harry Wragg and actually finished third in the St Leger, over a distance half a mile in excess of his best. In the Derby, however, Michael Beary had made a lot of use of him, while at Doncaster Harry Wragg rode one of his most patient races. Back to his best distance Rustom Pasha, again ridden by Harry Wragg, won the Champion Stakes.

11 Beckhampton: Gordon and Fred

Gordon Richards – Early years at Foxhill – Steve, his boy-hood hero, takes him in hand – An apt pupil – The fabulous Jimmy White – Gordon's first winner needed a longer distance! – Marty Hartigan, 'a great guv'nor', moves to Ogbourne – Jimmy White tries to buy Gordon for £3,000, but he's not for sale – Champion jockey for first time in 1925—but a serious illness threatens to end his career – Champion again in 1927 – Wins Oaks on Rose of England and St Leger on Singapore – On the mat – Words with Old Joe – The war years and a great royal double – Big Game and Tudor Minstrel fail to stay – The Derby at last – Arise Sir Gordon.

In a book of mine published in 1937 I described what for me was the most beautiful scene in the world: Gordon Richards, leading by two lengths with a hundred yards to go and his whip still swinging, when you have had twice your limit on him and four times as much as you can afford to lose.

If ever a jockey was the answer to a punter's prayer it was the little man, who was born at Oakengates in the Shropshire coal-fields, and might have spent the rest of his life in them had not his boyish imagination been fired by the deeds of Steve Donoghue. Being the smallest in a family of eight, none of whom was very big, he had answered an advertisement for stable boys inserted in a newspaper by Mr Martin Hartigan of Foxhill. He was told to come to Foxhill for a month's trial, and that's how it all began.

G

Looking back over the years and the thousands of races in which I watched Gordon through my raceglasses I think the sentence 'with his whip still swinging' sums up not only his method but his whole way of life.

Well before the day he had his first ride in public on a horse called Clockwork, who was fourth in a big field at Lingfield, Gordon was determined to become a famous jockey, and it was this single-mindedness which was to stand him in such good stead throughout his career. All apprentices bet amongst themselves, and today they may have friends with access to a betting shop, but unlike some of the men I have already written about in this book, betting was no temptation to Gordon. His parents were Primitive Methodists and Gordon went to chapel three times every Sunday, but I don't think it was his strict upbringing that kept him off betting so much as the realisation that it might stand between him and the top of the tallest tree. Gordon set his sights very high and he never lowered them.

The image of Gordon 'still swinging his whip' symbolises for me the character of a man who took no chances, but would still go for the narrowest opening if he considered it expedient. 'Winning cleverly', however, made no appeal to Gordon, who realised that it was most unlikely to deceive the handicapper, and that in a classic or important weight-for-age or condition race it is sheer lunacy.

Occasionally a disgruntled opponent would complain that Gordon's swinging whip served a dual purpose, acting not only as an incentive to his own mount but as a deterrent to those in his vicinity. The stewards, however, were satisfied that Gordon's tactics infringed no rules, and only once was he up before them for rough riding. The race was the Cesarewitch of 1927, and Gordon on St Reynard and his great friend Johnny Dines on Eagle's Pride had a battle royal over the last fifty yards. The horses were almost touching one another and with whips flying Gordon caught Johnny a mighty crack, to which Johnny retaliated by hitting St Reynard, though I don't think he hit Gordon. Watching broadside on it was impossible to see exactly what happened, but I formed the impression that Johnny was more sinned against than sinning, and that if the short head had gone in St Reynard's favour he would have been disqualified. The stewards took no action, but the protagonists carried on their feud at the start of the following race, and a steward who overheard them had them both on the mat. Both jockeys protested that they were unaware that anything untoward occurred, but Gordon was severely reprimanded.

I am not suggesting that Gordon rode every horse out to the bitter end, but though I think I can safely say that I saw him ride more of his 4,870 winners than any man alive today I never once saw him caught napping. No jockey wants to give a horse a harder race than is necessary, but Gordon held the view that it took no more out of a horse to be kept going till the winning post was safely behind him than to be eased in the last hundred yards and run the risk that something will come from out of the blue and pip him on the post. Lester Piggott is the only jockey in my experience who can look round several times without unbalancing his mount, but even he cannot be quite sure that there is no possible danger, especially when the runners are spread across the width of the course.

Gordon's swinging whip was a part of a machine which produced the maximum momentum through perfect rhythm. In his early days he was thought to be too free with his whip, but only by those who did not realise that it was being propelled back and forth with the regularity of a piston and was not making contact with the horse's quarters or flanks. Unorthodox he certainly was, though he had modelled himself on his boyhood hero Steve Donoghue, who was essentially a stylist. Steve was riding as first jockey for that colourful character Jimmy White, who owned Foxhill at the time when Gordon was articled to White's trainer Martin Hartigan.

I have already described Steve's charm, and Gordon, who had expected that a champion jockey would take the view that apprentices should be seen and not heard, was entranced by his friendliness. Steve, who liked the company of young people, took a lot of trouble in teaching Gordon the rudiments of riding. Gordon was an apt pupil and watched everything Steve did.

Although Steve's and Gordon's styles were so dissimilar at the

end of a race, in all other respects it was apparent that they had
been master and pupil. They had the identical seat and both
rode with a long rein, though Gordon's reins seemed to get
longer as the winning post approached. Steve had the God-
given ability to extract every ounce from his mount with the
minimum movement, but Gordon realised that this was something Steve could not pass on to him, and in the closing stages
of the race he would throw everything he had in the direction
of his mount's ears.

Gordon copied Steve's tactics to the extent that he liked to be
among the leaders, and if he had a fault it was that he occasionally made too much use of his mount, though I can only recall
two instances when he came too soon and he might have won
with a little more patience instead of finishing second. Gordon
won innumerable races through his ability to induce a horse to
drop his bit and lob along, having taken up the position which
he considered the most advantageous. Sometimes it would be
in front, if no other jockey wanted to make the running, but his
exact position was dictated by the pace at which the race was
run.

How he contrived to induce a free-running horse to amble
along, taking nothing out of itself, I do not pretend to know, and
it is possible that he never knew himself. About three furlongs
from home Gordon would appear to be uneasy, and three or
four others would seem to be going better than he was. This,
however, was a bit of kidding on Gordon's part and it usually
succeeded in inducing some jockey to make his effort before he
had intended, while lulling others into a sense of false security.
Gordon's mounts used to enter into the spirit of this ruse and
would take no notice until they were picked up and reminded
that there was a job still to be done. In a few strides they would
be galvanised into action, and a few seconds later the number
hoisted into the frame would denote that Gordon Richards had
ridden yet another winner.

It was a bad sign if Gordon, two furlongs out, was seen to be
sitting motionless, as it meant that he knew his mount was
dying under him and was nursing it to conserve what little
energy it had left.

Noel Murless, one of Gordon's most ardent admirers for whom he rode as first jockey after the retirement of Fred Darling, told me that the greatest race Gordon ever rode was in the Two Thousand Guineas of 1949. His mount Abernant, trained by Murless, had terrific speed, but he did not stay a mile and Gordon sat and suffered, holding him together in an endeavour to keep him going up that last furlong to the winning post. Although unspectacular from the crowd's point of view it was jockeyship at its best, and it deserved to succeed. But Nimbus, very strongly ridden by Charlie Elliott, caught him in the last stride to win by a short head.

Most of the great rainers for whom Gordon rode are no longer with us, but Noel Murless is our number one trainer, a position he has held for many years. He has employed some of the greatest jockeys in the world, but when I asked him last summer who he considered was the greatest jockey of his time he answered, without a moment's hesitation, 'Gordon Richards', adding, 'and off the racecourse one of the greatest men'.

There can never have been an establishment like Foxhill in the early twenties, and the whole set-up was more like something from a spectacular musical show than a training stable. The musical-comedy actress Ivy Tresmond acted as hostess, and Mr White's guests were mostly from the theatrical and sporting worlds. Few of them knew anything about horses except that they ate with one end and kicked with the other, but this did not stop their host taking his house-party round the stables on Saturday evenings. Every horse had been groomed till its coat shone, and the stable lads and apprentices were dressed in spotless white jackets.

The horses were paraded before the guests on Sunday mornings and in the afternoon there was a football match between the Foxhill apprentices and those from one of the neighbouring stables. This was followed by a Donkey Derby in which the actresses and the apprentices were in opposition. There was also boxing, the feature being a bout between Jimmy Wilde, the greatest flyweight of all time, against some man about four stone heavier than he was; Wilde always won.

Gordon has often told me that with his strict upbringing he

should have been shocked at such extravagant and (at least by the standards of those days) permissive behaviour, but his reactions took the form of a resolve—to make as much money as Mr White or any of his guests and, unlike them, to keep it. That was exactly what he did.

I do not think that Gordon was ever in Steve's class as a horseman, and all through his career he marvelled at the way even the most excitable horse would behave itself immediately Steve got on his back (even though, as I shall explain later, there was one horse who resisted all Steve's endeavours to make him co-operate). I once asked Gordon how much of his success was due to having Steve as his mentor. 'You've got me beat there,' he answered, 'but it was a marvellous bit of luck for a kid who didn't know the first thing about riding to have Steve take an interest in me.' He went on to say: 'If it hadn't been for the guv'nor' (Marty Hartigan) 'I'd still be doing my two, as no matter how hard you work or who your teacher is it's the trainer who gives a boy the chance to show what he's made of.'

No jockey has ever pulled his whip through from one hand to the other as fast as Gordon, while continuing to ride for his life, except possibly for Geoff Lewis, who modelled his style on Gordon's and has become almost as expert at it in the past few years. I suspect that this is one of the reasons why Geoff is now first jockey to the Warren Place stable. No man can succeed by slavishly copying the methods of another, and having realised that Steve's finishing methods were not for him Gordon adopted a style peculiar to himself in which he would pivot so far in the direction of his whip hand that he sometimes gave the impression of riding back to front.

Although we have been friends for well over forty years, neither of us can remember when first we met. I did not see him ride his first winner at Leicester on a horse called Gay Lord. There were no horse boxes in those days, and Gordon had to walk Gay Lord five miles to Shrivenham station from Foxhill, and the best part of three miles from Leicester station to the course. The horses of today do not seem to stand up to the amount of racing they had in my young days and I think the answer may be that like many human beings they do not walk as much as they used to. I imagine that any stable lad or apprentice who reads this will say: 'Perish the thought that I should have to walk eight miles with a horse before he runs, and another eight miles on the way home.'

Marty Hartigan was not at Leicester on that momentous occasion, and the job of hoisting Gordon into the saddle was left to Laing Ward, the travelling head lad. Laing told Gordon that he thought Gay Lord would be a good thing if the race were a bit longer. In the course of the race Gordon refused to give up the outside to anyone, but though Gay Lord went about eight lengths further than any other horse he won easily. As a jubilant Gordon was unsaddling his first winner Laing asked him why he had gone so wide. 'You said he wanted a longer distance—so I gave it him,' was the reply.

Having broken the ice Gordon was soon back in the winning enclosure, riding in a highly professional style to win an apprentice event at Lewes by a neck on a horse called Spiral Spin that belonged to Mr White. Later in the day he rode a horse called John Charles, who also won by a neck. I don't suppose anyone had 'mixed doubles Gordon Richards' mounts' on that far-off day, but in the years to come this became a most popular form of wagering, and I have often wondered how many million times the bet was struck in the course of his career.

Marty Hartigan was a highly professional trainer, and all the ballyhoo associated with training for Jimmy White was not really his cup of tea. Marty and his brother Paddy were devoted to one another and it was a great grief to Marty when Paddy met his death in an accident. Marty resigned as private trainer to Mr White and moved into his brother's stables at Ogbourne, where he set up as a public trainer, taking Gordon and his other apprentices with him. Mr White and Hartigan parted on good terms and Mr White sent several horses to be trained at Ogbourne. He also offered Hartigan £3,000 for Gordon's indentures, quite a lot of money at that time, but Hartigan wouldn't take it; which shows what a high opinion he had of him even in those early days.

After those two winners at Lewes more winners came rolling in. Marty Hartigan had a number of horses where he wanted them in the handicap, and so had his close friend Tommy Hogg, who trained at Russley. Gordon, who could ride at a little over six stone (he had weighed 4 stone 10 lb when he went to Foxhill), lost the apprentice allowance in 1923, but he was riding with such success that he still got all the mounts he wanted. Both Hartigan and Hogg liked to have a few quid on one they thought had a few pounds in hand, as did their owners, and the two stables must have won a small fortune during the time in which Gordon was claiming the 5 lb.

I was living in France when Gordon rode his first winners but very early in his career I saw him ride a very strong finish to win a race at Kempton on a horse called Squarson, trained by Tommy Hogg. I think Gordon had ridden about a dozen winners by this time, but some of the pundits still wouldn't stand for him at any price. 'Has anyone ever heard of a jockey being any good who doesn't look where he's going and finishes with a loose rein?' they asked, and concluded: 'He'll never be heard of again when he loses the five.' However, Brownie Carslake was far more circumspect, and when he was asked what he thought of the infant prodigy, he answered: 'If I did one of half a dozen things this kid does I should fall off, but they seem to work with him. They can laugh at him, but I seem to remember they laughed at Tod Sloan.'

The laugh was a short one, and at the end of his apprenticeship Gordon had ridden 114 winners. Gordon Richards, the little boy with the shock of black hair from Oakengates, had certainly arrived, and he was being tipped as the next champion jockey. The tip was a good one, but I don't suppose even his most ardent admirers at that time thought that he would head the list on twenty-six occasions and become the most successful British jockey of all time.

In 1925, his first season as a fully fledged jockey, Gordon rode as first string for Captain Hogg. Marty Hartigan did not have enough horses to employ a jockey on his own and Gordon therefore accepted a second retainer from his old master. He ended up that season as champion jockey with 118 winners, an extraordinary feat as he could ride at 6 stone 12 lb. Many leading jockeys from Fred Archer to Lester Piggott have had their weight problems, and would have given anything to have been ten pounds lighter, but jockeys can also be too light, and in 1925 Gordon had often to put up to two stone or more deadweight. This is an even bigger disadvantage when a jockey is as short in the leg as Gordon was, and confines his contact with his mount to the reins. Two stone of unyielding lead between you and your horse makes him seem a very long way away indeed.

The disadvantage of being very light is largely offset by the advantage of having the whole scale of weights in a handicap at his disposal: a Carslake or a Piggott normally has only half a dozen to choose from, at the top of the handicap. This partly explains why throughout his career Gordon seldom rode in fewer than five races in an afternoon, though in the last years of his career he declined to do less than 8 stone 2 lb. When a man has been champion jockey more than twenty times he cannot be expected to jeopardise his health in order to ride the winner of a handicap, and in any case he got all the riding he could possibly cope with at 8 stone 2 lb. What wouldn't Charlie Smirke have given to have been that weight?

When a young man, or a young horse for that matter, makes the headlines there are always those who belittle his success with such remarks as 'What did he beat?' or 'The best of a bad lot', which means precisely the same thing. No one, however, who has read the earlier chapters of this book can question the strength of the opposition to Gordon Richards. All the men I have mentioned were still in their prime (though Frank Bullock and Vic Smyth retired at the end of 1925, not because they were over the hill but because their doctors had advised them not to continue their battle against increasing weight).

Gordon did not ride many big winners in his first season as champion jockey, the most important being the great Metropolitan and the Ebor handicaps. The Lincoln meeting of 1926 was the coldest I have ever experienced. The draughty old Carholme stands offered few amenities at the best of times, and when the wind, laden with sleet, blew straight into them from the North Sea one felt stark naked. I had draped myself with every garment I could lay hands on, and I pitied the jockeys, clad only in silks and the lightest of breeches.

Gordon had only just recovered from the removal of his appendix, and caught pleurisy. Although he was feeling very unwell he soon returned to the saddle, but had only ridden five winners when Marty Hartigan sent him off to be examined by his brother John, who was a doctor. The X-ray revealed that he had T.B.

Six months in a sanatorium, followed by three months in a bungalow on the Ogbourne Downs, and he was pronounced cured. Although he had been champion jockey in 1925 he was still something of a stranger to the stay-at-home punters, but he had already endeared himself to the racing profession, of which I had become a member in 1925. (Previously I had gone racing whenever possible, and sometimes when I should have been doing something else infinitely less entertaining and would have got into hot water had I been found out.)

Gordon, though a very friendly person, never sought popularity, but once he accepted you as a friend you were one for life. No one whose eyes looked so straight into yours could be capable of deceit; owners and trainers had complete faith in him, and his honesty of purpose became a legend while he was still a young man.

I believe that the Turf is as straight in the seventies as it was when Gordon retired in 1954, which is a tribute to the example that he set and shows that the Gordon Richards tradition lives on. He was knighted not because he had ridden more winners than any man had ever ridden before, but for his services to racing.

A lot of dirty linen was washed in public in the years preceding his rise to fame, and indeed for several years afterwards. Stories circulated concerning the villainy of men whose names were household words; most of these were without foundation, but there was a grain of truth in some of them, which was sufficient to make the public wonder whether they were getting a run for their money.

When he was struck down, with a disease which in those days often proved fatal, our sympathy went out to the young man who was doing such a great job for racing, quite apart from riding winners. Soon after his triumphant return to the saddle in 1927 the slogan 'When in doubt back Gordon' was born, and when he retired twenty-seven years later those whose job it was to give winners, as well as those who just tried to back them, felt lost.

The 1927 season was only a few weeks old when his services were in demand by the big battalions. Alec Taylor, Fred Darling and P. P. Gilpin all employed him, and he rode the Manton-trained Duke of Buckingham to win the Ascot Stakes. Lord Glanely was so impressed by Gordon's riding that he sent several of his horses to be trained by Tommy Hogg at Russley so that he could be sure Gordon would ride them. At the end of 1927 he was champion with 164 winners. What a comeback! To cap it all, when he went for his check-up his lungs were found to be as sound as a couple of bells.

From then on the jockeys' championship became Gordon's property, except in 1930, when Freddy Fox beat him by one, as I've already described, and in 1941, when he broke his leg and Harry Wragg became champion with seventy-one winners, a highly creditable total in wartime, when racing was greatly restricted. Gordon had been champion jockey four times before his mounts began playing an important part in the classics. In 1930, however, he was destined to atone for previous failures by winning the Oaks on Rose of England and the St Leger on Singapore, both owned by Lord Glanely and trained by Tommy Hogg who by this time had moved to Newmarket. At the Doncaster sales in 1928 Lord Glanely had paid 12,500 guineas for a lovely colt by Gainsborough out of Tetrabazzia, the equivalent of about 50,000 guineas today, as well as 3,100 guineas for a filly by Teddy out of Perce Neige. He called the colt Singapore and the filly Rose of England. Hogg decided to give both plenty of time to mature, and neither ran as a two-year-old. Rose of England ran with great promise in the One Thousand Guineas to finish fifth, and Singapore showed equal promise to finish sixth in the Greenham Stakes. Her next race was in the Oaks, which she won in great style to give Gordon his first classic victory.

Singapore was the more backward of the two, but he went on improving all the summer, though his only success was at

Sandown. At Goodwood, however, where he was unluckily beaten in a 'muddling' sort of race, he gave Gordon the right sort of 'feel', and from that moment his objective was the St Leger. He did extra well in the final month, and his connections thought he was sure to win, which he did by one and a half lengths from the Beckhampton-trained Parenthesis, ridden by Freddy Fox, with Rustom Pasha three-quarters of a length away third.

In the following year Singapore was beaten a short head by Trimdon in the Gold Cup. The latter hung towards Singapore, and as he did so Gordon and Joe Childs got their whips entangled and Joe dropped his. This upset the old gentleman, and he made some very uncomplimentary remarks about young jockeys who rode with a loose rein and didn't know where the hell they were going. No one of my acquaintance is more capable of holding his own in a battle of words than Gordon, especially when, as in this case, he knows he's in the right. I didn't hear what passed between them, but a jockey friend of mine, who did, told me that it was most enlightening. I had backed Trimdon and as the seconds ticked away and the 'all right' was announced I breathed a sigh of relief, as I fully expected that Gordon would lodge an objection and be awarded the race.

On the previous day, however, Grand Salute, owned by Lord Glanely, trained by Tommy Hogg and ridden by Gordon, had won the Royal Hunt Cup very easily, landing a gamble for owner and trainer, neither of whom was afraid to put his money down when he thought there was a few pounds in hand. After the race, owner, trainer and jockey were up before the stewards, who asked for an explanation as to why Grand Salute's form at Ascot was so superior to previous form. The stewards pointed out that the market suggested that this improvement had been expected by owner and trainer. The explanation was accepted, but the stewards made it abundantly clear that they hoped Lord Glanely's horses would run more consistently in future.

When Gordon announced that he wanted to object to Trimdon, Lord Glanely, who believed in calling a spade a spade, answered, 'Not bloody likely, I saw enough of those buggers yesterday to last me a lifetime.' This answer revealed a misconception: neither owner nor trainer would ever be called on to give evidence in an objection lodged by their jockey.

In the Doncaster Cup that autumn Singapore put up one of the best performances I have seen in a Cup race. He was carrying 9 stone 12 lb and was opposed by two crackerjacks in Brown Jack and Noble Star. Gordon had approximately 35 lb of lead between him and Singapore, but the St Leger winner of the previous year would have won with another 10 lb on his back. The race was run at a very fast pace, but Singapore sprinted away up the straight to beat Brown Jack by four lengths, and as Steve said to me that evening: 'It takes a pretty good horse to do that.'

In due course Lord Glanely mated Singapore with Rose of England, and their offspring was called Chulmleigh. He took even longer to come to hand than had his sire, but I formed a tremendous liking for him when I saw him finish second at York. He was ridden by Harry Wragg, who for once had appeared to overdo his famous waiting tactics.

A lot of water had flowed under the bridges since Gordon had ridden Chulmleigh's sire and dam to victory in the same year, and with Gordon installed as first jockey to Fred Darling Lord Glanely had changed his jockey after every defeat. 'Mike' Vergette, who was apprenticed to Tommy Hogg, was a very strong boy. He had ridden several winners for Lord Glanely, and it was announced he would ride Chulmleigh in the St Leger. The latter, therefore, remained at long odds, but having a high opinion of Vergette I backed Chulmleigh at 28/1. In the week before the race Fred Darling announced he would not have a runner so Gordon was without a ride. On reading this at the breakfast table Lord Glanely could not get quickly enough to the telephone, and Gordon was of course pleased to let bygones be bygones.

I was writing for the *Daily Sketch* at the time, and when I ran into Gordon on the course on the morning of the race he said, 'I see you've gone for my horse; surely his form isn't good enough to win a St Leger?' I explained that I didn't think the three-year-olds were a very good lot that year (1937), and that

I thought he would have won at York in a few more strides. I also reminded him of what tremendous improvement Singapore had made in the month before the St Leger. He scratched his head and answered: 'Now I come to think of it you may be right.' When Gordon was announced as Chulmleigh's jockey his price came down to 18/1, but editors are satisfied with a winner at that price—as well they might be. I had only recently joined the paper and I needed a good-priced winner to consolidate my position.

Chulmleigh, a very big, strong horse, needed a lot of driving, and although Gordon could ride any sort of horse I always thought he was seen at his very best on a big powerful animal who needed all the help he could give him. In a terrific finish, Lord Derby's Fair Copy ridden by Perryman led till well inside the last 100 yards, where Gordon drove the game Chulmleigh into a narrow lead. Derby winner Mid-day Sun finished faster than either of them, but through no fault of his jockey, Beary, he had made his effort too late and Chulmleigh won by half a length from Fair Copy with Mid-day Sun three-quarters of a length away third. Michael Beary described Mid-day Sun as the unluckiest loser he'd ever ridden, but when you have napped a horse and stand to win more money over him than you've ever won before you only have eyes for one.

I think that with the exception of Pinza's Derby, Chulmleigh's Leger gave Gordon as much pleasure as any winner he ever rode. He invariably developed a real affection for a horse which had carried him to victory in a big race, and Rose of England and Singapore, who gave him his first two successes in the classics, had a special place in his heart; what therefore could be more fitting than he should win the St Leger on their son?

Gordon's luck in the Derby was atrocious, no matter whether the race was run at Epsom or at Newmarket, as it was in the war years. In the spring of 1941 he broke his ankle when a filly lashed out at him at the gate before a race at Salisbury, and this stopped him riding for the remainder of the season. He is sure he would have picked Owen Tudor for the Derby, though Fred Darling saddled four in the race and Owen Tudor had let the

stable down when ridden by Gordon in the Two Thousand
Guineas. Ridden by Billy Nevett, he won the Derby very easily.
In the previous year Gordon had chosen to ride Tant Mieux,
who had failed to stay, the race being won by Pont L'Eveque
running in Fred Darling's own colours and ridden by Sam
Wragg. I was on sick leave with a broken jaw and smashed
teeth when the 1940 Derby was run. I should like to be able to
say that I had sustained this injury while displaying great
courage in the face of the enemy, but truth to tell it was a singu-
larly unglamorous accident, the result of a brother officer who
had consumed too much gin and French failing to notice a
stationary lorry in the blackout. The July course was ill-
equipped to accommodate a Derby Day crowd, even when we
were at war, and after he had saddled his runners Fred Darling
hailed me to ask if I would take him to watch the race from the
press stand.

While the horses were cantering to the post he told me that
Newmarket Derbys weren't like the real thing and he couldn't
get worked up about them. As the horses disappeared our conversation turned to my accident, and Fred said how sorry he
was for me that after my jaw had healed I should have to be
fitted with a plate. The off was signalled, but Fred went on
talking about the inconvenience he suffered now that few of
his teeth were his own, and how he no longer enjoyed his
meals.

The horses came into view and we focused our attention on
the race, but Fred showed not the slightest emotion when Pont
L'Eveque, carrying his colours, drew right away to win very
easily. As he left me to greet his winner he said: 'Thanks for the
view of the race and I hope your false teeth are better than
mine.'

Harry Wragg rode all the Beckhampton horses while Gordon
was incapacitated, and after he had won the Oaks on Commo-
tion poor old Gordon must have been quite relieved to hear
that Owen Tudor, who never ran twice alike, was unplaced in
the 1941 St Leger. That race was won by Sun Castle, owned by
Lord Portal, trained by Captain Boyd Rochfort and ridden by
the French jockey George Bridgland.

Big Game and Sun Chariot were unbeaten as two-year-olds, but Sun Chariot had developed into a holy terror, and if she had not been due to carry the royal colours in the classics Fred Darling might have turned her out of training and sent her back to the National Stud.

Gordon could do nothing right at the beginning of the 1942 season, and after being beaten on Sun Chariot at Salisbury he began to worry. He was always highly strung and lived on his nerves, in contrast with most jockeys who are so confident in their own ability that they give the impression that they have no nerves at all. Gordon's vivid imagination was not an asset to him, and on one occasion he was not far short of a nervous breakdown. But he conquered his nerves and few people knew of the mental anguish he was suffering.

Harry Wragg had been brilliantly successful when substituting for Gordon and on the first occasion Gordon rode Sun Chariot she was beaten. It was, however, her only defeat, as Gordon and Fred Darling (ably assisted by Warren, the boy who did her) were able to make her see reason, and though she remained temperamental she proved herself the best filly Fred had ever trained and Gordon had ever ridden.

One day when the King and Queen came down to Beckhampton to see her and Big Game each do a gallop (they never worked together) she went down on her knees and roared like a bull. Neither Fred nor Gordon had ever seen a filly do this—though colts, when their minds are far from racing and are centred on a life in which business is combined with exquisite enjoyment, will sometimes behave in this way. On the racecourse, however, she behaved herself reasonably well except in the Oaks. Big Game won the Two Thousand and Sun Chariot the One Thousand Guineas in tremendous style and started hot favourites for the Derby and Oaks respectively. Although he was rather a free runner Big Game was a paragon of virtue, but in a gallop before the Derby he gave Gordon a nasty suspicion that he might not be as good over a mile and a half as he was over a mile. His pedigree certainly raised doubts concerning his stamina, as although his sire Bahram had won the Triple Crown, he was out of a Friar Marcus mare, while Big Game's

8 The Aga Khan leads in Triple Crown winner *Bahram* (Freddy Fox) after winning 1935 Derby. Frank Butler in is rear

9 *My Love* (Rae Johnstone) after his victory in the 1948 Derby

10 M. Marcel Boussac leads in *Galcador* after his victory in the 1950 Derby

11 Charlie Elliott (left) on *Nimbus*, beats Gordon Richards on *Abernant* by a short head in a terrific finish for the 1949 Two Thousand Guineas

dam Myrobella had been one of the fastest fillies every trained at Beckhampton, but had failed to stay the mile of the One Thousand Guineas. There was therefore a weakness on both sides of his pedigree.

Notwithstanding this Big Game started at odds on for the Derby, though Gordon's confidence in his ability to get the trip decreased as the day drew near. I decided to oppose him, but chose Lord Rosebery's Hyperides, as Watling Street had been easily beaten in the Guineas and I was not sure he was completely genuine.

Big Game dissipated whatever slight chance he may have had of getting the trip by running too freely, and after Hyperides had looked all over a winner, with only 100 yards to go, Harry Wragg brought Watling Street with a beautifully timed run to win by a neck.

Gordon had no doubt of Sun Chariot's stamina but she gave her jockey and everyone else heart failure by her atrocious behaviour at the start of the Oaks, and when the gate went up she darted off the course to the left. Gordon managed to bring her back again, but by this time her chance appeared hopeless as she was 100 yards behind the last horse. It was not until the field had gone a mile that she got within hail of her opponents, but by this time she was thoroughly enjoying herself, and galloped straight by them to win by a length.

There is an old saying that horses can give away weight but they can't give away distance, but whenever I hear that said I always answer: 'What about Sun Chariot?' In the St Leger she treated Watling Street and Hyperides as if they were a couple of selling platers. By this time she was far more tractable and behaved herself like a perfect lady.

King George VI won four of the five classics, but though it was a joy to see the royal colours carried to victory in our greatest races, Fred Darling had voiced the opinion of all of us when he told me the previous year that wartime races were not like the real thing. Our joy was therefore tempered with sadness that Sun Chariot's victories in the Oaks and St Leger had not taken place at Epsom and Doncaster.

When writing about Sir Gordon Richards one can only touch

H

the fringe of his great career, and mention a few of the greatest horses with which he was associated.

Year after year I wrote in my Derby article: 'Gordon Richards has never won the Derby because he has never been lucky enough to ride the best horse.' It might be thought that this was apparent to everyone, without this constant repetition from me, but it is quite extraordinary how much nonsense is talked every day of the week by racing enthusiasts. Amongst them I do not include racing professionals though even they can talk a good deal of rot—especially when some horse they thought unbeatable has achieved the impossible. In the same way that some foolish people thought that Steve was endowed with supernatural powers after he had won four Epsom Derbys out of five, they thought that there was a jinx on Gordon after he had ridden twenty-five consecutive losers in our most famous race. Several times he picked the wrong one and on other occasions he would have ridden the winner had he disregarded contracts in the way that Steve had done in the twenties; but most of his mounts simply weren't good enough over one and a half miles, though Pasch and Tudor Minstrel had proved themselves unbeatable over a mile.

One of his Derby rides Gordon fancied most strongly was Manitoba in 1933, as like me he had not been very impressed with Hyperion's victory in the Chester Vase. How wrong we were, as Hyperion was one of the easiest and certainly one of the best of the Derby winners between the wars and he won the St Leger almost as easily. Gordon got a little bit of his own back in the following year's Gold Cup in which he rode the Aga Khan's Felicitation, who had won the Churchill Stakes two days earlier ridden by Freddy Fox. Felicitation was the nearest approach to perpetual motion I have ever known a horse to be. Gordon set a very strong gallop on him and one felt that no horse could keep this up for two and a half miles but Felicitation was galloping as strongly at the finish as he was when passing the stands first time round, and Hyperion could never get a blow in at him.

At the end of 1946 Gordon described the unbeaten Tudor Minstrel as the best two-year-old he had ever ridden, and after

he had won the Two Thousand Guineas by eight lengths he was
in no doubt that he was the best miler. But as Derby Day approached I realised Gordon had something on his mind, and
one day he said to me: 'I hope I'll be able to settle him down,
but he's a very free runner, and in none of his races so far has he
seen another horse.'

When a horse has won the Guineas as Tudor Minstrel had
won it it is hard to visualise any of those who finished behind
him turning the tables, no matter what the distance might be,
but though I'd backed Tudor Minstrel at odds against before
the Guineas (he started at 7 to 4 on) I wasn't happy. Free runners do win the Derby from time to time, and I have told how
Coronach took charge of Joe Childs and won by five lengths.
But in order to make all the running in the Derby a horse must
be an out-and-out stayer, and I was sure that Tudor Minstrel
was nothing of the sort. He had proved himself the best horse by
a long way over distances varying from five furlongs to a mile,
and if he had been endowed with stamina to match his speed
he would have been all the greatest horses that ever lived rolled
into one. Although his dam, Sansonnet, was by Sansovino the
bottom line of his pedigree was all speed.

After pulling Gordon's arms out, and racing with his head on
one side and his mouth wide open, he was stone cold by the
time he reached the straight. The race was won easily by the
French colt Pearl Diver, ridden by Bridgland, but never before
or subsequently did Pearl Diver run within a stone of his Derby
form. Mr William Hill had bought the French horse Chanteur
as a stallion, but before being sent to stud, where he became the
sire of Pinza, he won the principal race at Hurst Park on succes-
sive days, ridden by the Frenchman Roger Brethes who had
never ridden at Hurst Park before. Roger requested me to point
out the landmarks and pitfalls, and after his two victories he
thanked me and advised me to save my Tudor Minstrel bet on
Pearl Diver, which I did at 40/1 and therefore won on the race.

But at last, at very long last, came Pinza. Trained by Norman
Bertie, who had been head lad to Fred Darling who bred him,
Pinza had been sold as a yearling to Sir Victor Sassoon for only
1,500 guineas. Pinza was one of the biggest and most power-

fully built two-year-olds of his year. He was very impressive when cantering away with the Tattersall's Sale Stakes over seven furlongs at Doncaster, but was surprisingly beaten by the Aga Khan's Neema in the Royal Lodge Stakes over a mile at Ascot. In a small field the race was won at a muddling pace which did not suit Pinza, but if Neema had not gone wrong early in her three-year-old career she might have proved herself the best filly of her generation.

Pinza won the Dewhurst Stakes as impressively as he had won at Doncaster. Horses seldom raise a laugh on the way to the post but when Pinza, ridden as usual by Gordon, cantered past the stands for the Newmarket Stakes, he was greeted with unaccustomed merriment by the hard-headed professionals who form 80 per cent of the crowd at Newmarket except on Guineas and Cesarewitch day and regard racing as a very serious business.

Pinza had met with an accident to his shoulder after getting rid of his rider one morning on Newmarket Heath, and could not be trained for the Two Thousand Guineas and, judging by his appearance, Bertie had been able to give him very little work before this belated appearance. Normally a very deep-bodied colt, he looked enormous on that day, more like a candidate for the fatstock show than a racehorse.

I expected him to blow up at the Bushes, but he was cantering over the opposition all the way and won by four lengths. He blew fairly hard as he stood in the winning enclosure, and with Derby Day only a fortnight away it seemed that Bertie would have his work cut out to get him fighting fit on the great day.

Fred Darling lay dying at Beckhampton, but Gordon visited him almost daily to inform him how the horse he had bred was faring. Ill though he was, Fred gave the man who had served him so well his final orders: 'Go down to Newmarket twice or three times a week and ride him a strong gallop.' Gordon had never failed to carry out the guv'nor's instructions, and with the full co-operation of Mr Jack Clayton and Norman Bertie Pinza shed his superfluous flesh, and arrived at Epsom trained to the hour. He was still heavier than any of his opponents, but that was the way he was built.

As he was such a big heavy colt, and his three successes were over the straight flat courses at Doncaster and Newmarket, I doubted whether he would act at Epsom, and when I met Gordon at Hurst Park on the Saturday before the Epsom meeting I said to him: 'I bet you wish the Derby was going to be run at Newmarket this year'; to which he replied with unaccustomed vehemence; 'I wouldn't care a bugger where they ran it; I'm telling you, Pinza will win the Derby.'

M. Boussac: a battle royal

The Marcel Boussac empire – Steve v. Ramus – No electric spurs – The writing on the wall – English horses lack stamina – Airborne wins 1946 Derby and St Leger – Alycidon, a great stayer, puts us back on the map again.

It took M. Marcel Boussac thirty years to build up the greatest equine empire in the history of the Turf, but in only three years between 1957 and 1960 it crumbled, and eleven years later there is no sign of a revival in its fortunes. Fresnay le Buffard, his magnificent stud in Normandy, has produced its quota of foals, but whereas in the halcyon days during and after World War II its products swept the board in England and France, carrying the orange jacket and grey cap, it is now a rarity for one of M. Boussac's horses to be good enough to compete in a classic race.

My first introduction to the colours which were to become the most famous in the world was in 1921. George Stern was his trainer as well as his jockey, which meant that this internationally famous rider, who won our Derby on Sunstar, could no longer ride in this country, where a man cannot hold a jockey's and trainer's licence at the same time.

Stern won the first French Derby I ever saw, in 1922 on M. Boussac's Ramus, beating Steve on Kefalin by a short head, having given his mount an awful hiding which Ramus never forgot. Kefalin, on the other hand, tenderly ridden by Steve Donoghue, went on to carry Steve to victory in the Grand Prix, in which he beat Ramus, who was again given a thrashing. Stern had been a great jockey, but years of good living had sapped his vitality, and the only way he could now fully extend his mount was by hitting it as hard as he could with an extra long whip.

M. Boussac sent Ramus over to run in the following year's Goodwood Cup and engaged Steve to ride him. Ramus had by this time turned savage, and would not go near a starting gate, and M. Boussac chose the Goodwood Cup for him as this was (and still is) the only race started by a flag. There were only three runners, the other two being Triumph, ridden by Joe Childs, and Bucks Hussar, the mount of Brownie Carslake. Both the opposing jockeys knew that Ramus would not start unless he were given a lead, and they were determined not to give him one. After a long struggle Steve had been able to induce Ramus to do a gallop on the day preceding the race, but Ramus knew the difference between an exercise gallop and a race, and he still had memories of Stern's whip. M. Boussac, of course, knew nothing about it, but Ramus' stable lad offered Steve a pair of spurs attached to an electric battery, and informed him that without this contraption he had no chance of making Ramus start. Steve told the lad where he could put his electric spurs.

There ensued the most prolonged struggle between horse and rider ever seen on a racecourse, and Steve knew that if Ramus got rid of him he might eat him before help arrived. A rodeo had nothing on this fight between Steve and Ramus, as Ramus was up to every trick, rearing and coming down on stiff legs, bucking, and going down on his knees in an endeavour to shift Steve. When all these tricks failed he turned his head to try to bite Steve in the leg. The fight went on for exactly twenty-five minutes, but Steve won. Or did he? Ramus finally agreed to start, but Joe and Brownie lagged behind, and with nothing to lead him Ramus stuck his toes in after going a few strides, and that was that.

The great days of the Boussac empire began with Charlie Elliott and ended with Rae Johnstone. Charlie did not speak one word of French when he moved to France, and M. Boussac always maintained that he spoke no English, though I should not have liked to make a derogatory remark about one of his famous horses in his hearing in my own tongue. However, from the word go, a perfect understanding developed between owner and jockey, which only goes to prove that actions speak louder than words. Charlie was at an advantage in that the opposition in France, except for Frank O'Neill, was far less formidable than it was in England.

The Germans encouraged racing in France during World War II as they thought it might make the Parisians less hostile to them, and also because all French bloodstock would fall into their hands when they had gone through the formality of disposing of Great Britain, Russia and the United States. Apart from stealing Pharis, and commandeering Corrida, then a brood mare, for some chore during the German retreat through the Falaise Gap from which she never returned, they did not molest M. Boussac's racing and breeding establishments.

'Jacko' Doyasbere, a charming young Basque who became very popular with the English jockeys after the war, was Mr. Boussac's stable jockey, but as soon as Paris was liberated in 1945 the French tycoon contacted Charlie Elliott, and the partnership was resumed where it had left off five years earlier.

The Rowley Mile course at Newmarket reopened in the autumn of that year and M. Boussac sent over Priam to run in the Champion Stakes, the first French runner in this country since the spring of 1940 when the same owner's Djebel had won the Two Thousand Guineas having won the Middle Park Stakes the previous autumn. Priam was regarded as being no more than the fifth or sixth best horse in M. Boussac's stable, and as England was represented by Court Martial, who had beaten Dante by a neck in the Two Thousand Guineas and finished third to him in the Derby, few people gave Priam much of a chance. But in a desperate finish, in which for over a furlong the two horses galloped stride for stride, Court Martial beat Priam by the shortest of heads, Cliff Richards having ridden a finish worthy of his elder brother Gordon on Lord Astor's colt.

That race was the writing on the wall. If the humble Priam could run Court Martial to an inch or two, what would such as

Caracalla, Ardan and Marsyas do to our horses in 1946?

At the end of World War I English horses were immeasurably superior to the French, but after the Second World War the boot was on the other leg. For five years there had been no long-distance races in England worthy of the name, and even the Gold Cup had been decided over two miles of the July Course, which provided no real test of stamina. On the other hand there had been plenty of races for fast, quick-maturing horses. Breeders therefore had mated their mares with the fastest stallions to which they could secure a nomination, to meet the demand for precocious animals. The result was that when racing got back to normal British bloodstock was bankrupt of stamina. Even the mighty little Hyperion had been mated with sprinting mares so that for several years he appeared unable to sire offspring capable of staying one and a half miles. Over any distance in excess of a mile, our horses were impotent when up against the stayers sent over by M. Boussac and other French owners, and humiliation followed humiliation.

The best horse from overseas to run in this country in 1946 was M. Boussac's Caracalla, by Tourbillon out of Astronomie, one of the most successful brood mares of all time. He had not long recovered from some ailment and his trainer, Semblat, had had to hurry his preparation for our Gold Cup, but he won like the great horse he was reputed to be—and was followed home by two more French-trained horses in Chanteur and Basileus. The English horses were completely outclassed. It was the same story in the Queen Alexandra Stakes, won at a canter by Marsyas, a six-year-old half-brother to Caracalla, by the dual Gold Cup winner Trimdon. And Priam won the Hardwicke Stakes from the three-year-old Anwar, to whom he was conceding 33 lb.

Sayani, of whom I shall have more to say anon, won the Jersey Stakes. M. Boussac's five-year-old Ardan had won our Coronation Cup, but fortunately for us there were no French horses in either the Derby or the St Leger, for the simple reason that when the nominations for these races were due France was still under German occupation and it seemed as if the war might continue for years to come.

Caracalla proceeded to win the Prix de l'Arc de Triomphe by a neck from Prince Chevalier, winner of that year's French Derby. Some idea of the strength of the Boussac stable may be gleaned from the fact that Ardan was one of Caracalla's two pacemakers. I had accompanied Charlie Elliott when he flew over to Deauville to win the Prix Kergolay Nirgal, but this was my first visit to Longchamp for over six years and what a thrill it was to be racing there again. I was the only English racing journalist present: how different things are today.

Dick Perryman, who had only recently been granted a trainer's licence, made a brilliant start to his new career by winning the 1945 St Leger with Chamossaire and the 1946 Derby and St Leger with the grey Airborne, Tommy Lowrey being the successful jockey on all three occasions. Chamossaire had been beaten out of sight by Dante in the Derby, and the St Leger, which was run at York for the only time in its history, appeared to be at the latter's mercy, but he went wrong. Airborne was fortunate in having no opposition from France, and although a consistent colt I do not rate him high in the list of Derby winners, as he appeared to be the only stayer in the field. Souverain, narrowly beaten in the French Derby and winner of the Grand Prix, was sent over to contest the King George VI Stakes at Ascot over two miles that autumn and he made Airborne look like a selling plater, while the Irish colt Bright News also finished in front of our Derby and St Leger winner. The following year Souverain was beaten by Marsyas in the French Gold Cup, but won our Gold Cup. Marsyas was lame and could not go to the post.

In 1946 this remarkable old horse won five races in England, including the Goodwood and Doncaster cups. His forelegs were battered and scarred, but unless he was actually lame he would reproduce his form to an ounce. He was a magnificent old warrior, and Trimdon never sired another horse within a stone of him.

The French won our Derby with Pearl Diver in 1947, with My Love in 1948, and after the French horse Amour Drake had been beaten a head by Nimbus in 1949 they won it again in 1950 with Galcador. My Love was bred in France by M. Leon

Volterra, who sold a half-share in him to the Aga Khan whose colours he carried.

I have told this story before but it is worth retelling as never before had Gordon expressed his complete confidence in his Derby mount. He was over fifty, and time was running out, but he had complete faith that Pinza would enable him to realise his only unfulfilled ambition. Pinza, as Gordon had sworn he would do, came round the bends and galloped down the steep hill to Tattenham Corner as if the course had been especially laid out for him, and he entered the straight about four lengths behind the Aga Khan's Shikampur. The latter was still going well for Charlie Smirke, but when Gordon pulled out about two and a half furlongs from home it was all over in a few strides. The Queen's Aureole ran on to finish second, beaten four lengths, and would have won comfortably with Pinza out of the way, but neither he nor anything else had any chance with Gordon's mount, who someone suggested looked more like a Grand National winner than a Derby winner.

Pinza beat Aureole in much the same way in the 'King George', and perhaps this was an even more praiseworthy performance as he had returned very sore from Epsom and Bertie had been able to give him very little work between the two races. He broke down when being prepared for the St Leger. Aureole started a hot favourite for the St Leger, but he didn't get a yard over a mile and a half and he could only finish third to his stable companion Premonition, ridden by Eph Smith. He was however a very good horse over one and a half miles, and as a four-year-old he won the Coronation Cup, Hardwicke Stakes and King George VI and Queen Elizabeth Stakes. To have beaten him twice over one and a half miles with at least 7 lb in hand Pinza must indeed have been a champion.

Three days after Pinza's victory Fred Darling died. He had listened to the race on the wireless, and when Gordon went to see him that evening he told his jockey how happy he was that the horse he had bred should have triumphed where so many had failed. Fred Darling was a hard man but he died happy in the knowledge that his friend, who had served him so loyally, had demonstrated to the world that if the horse was good enough he was as efficient over the Derby course as he was over all the other courses, something which Fred had never doubted for a moment. Sir Gordon has a first-class brain and has always used it to full advantage. Although his reflexes when riding in a race were as rapid as those of any of his rivals his day-to-day life was not governed by his subconscious mind. He is one of the best after-dinner speakers, but though he delivers his sallies as if they have come to him on the spur of the moment and he never refers to his notes, his speeches have been carefully prepared and stored away in his mind.

Although he never contemplated any profession other than that of a jockey till his retirement, when he became a trainer, and a very fine one, I am convinced he would have made a success in any walk of life he might have adopted. Integrity, the will to succeed and a refusal to contemplate failure were his greatest assets. Without them a man may possess great skill but still remain at the foot of the ladder.

Although their backgrounds could hardly have been more different, the Aga Khan and M. Volterra had one character-istic in common—they would buy or sell anything in the world, provided the price was right. I would have given a great deal to be present when the deal over My Love was negotiated. The horse was a lamentable failure in the St Leger, won in great style by the big powerful Black Tarquin, trained by Captain Boyd Rochfort, and ridden by Edgar Britt as stable jockey Harry Carr had broken his leg.

Second to Black Tarquin at Doncaster was a chestnut son of Donatello called Alycidon, carrying the colours of Lord Derby. Quite early in his three-year-old career his trainer Walter Earl and jockey Doug Smith believed that good colt that he was in his classic season, Alycidon would be a far better one after another year. They also believed that the further he had to go the better it would suit him. In other words, here was a colt who might recover our lost prestige as breeders of bloodstock and erase the memory of the humiliations we had suffered in the previous four years at the hands of the French. Alycidon began his four-year-old career by winning the Ormonde Stakes (a mile and three-quarters) at Chester by a length from his pacemaker Benny Lynch, and he went on to win the Corporation Stakes (two and a quarter miles) by twelve lengths from the useful Lake Placid, to whom he was conceding 12 lb. For once in a way the French stayers were very moderate and the Gold Cup was regarded as a match between Black Tarquin, who started at 11/10, and Alycidon at 5/4. Entering the straight Alycidon drew clear and beat the St Leger winner by five lengths, finishing so fresh that I'm sure he wouldn't have minded going round again.

That evening, English racing enthusiasts felt as my French friend had felt all those years ago, when Ksar, the grandsire of Caracalla and Djebel, had trounced the English horses in the Prix de l'Arc de Triomphe. We could hold up our heads once again in the knowledge that we had bred the best stayer in the world. Alycidon won the Goodwood Cup by twelve lengths and the Doncaster Cup by eight lengths. I have no doubt he was the best stayer I've had the good fortune to see in action, and Doug Smith does not believe there has ever been a Cup horse like him or ever will be again. Felicitation could go on galloping till he had ground the opposition to a halt, but he did not possess the acceleration of Alycidon.

Alycidon had put us back on the map as breeders of stayers, but we were a long way from being out of the wood. Although his sire Donatello raced in Italy, except for his unlucky defeat in the Grand Prix, he was English bred and was a great-great-grandson of Pretty Polly.

Charlie Elliott decided that he had lived in France long enough, and for a time M. Boussac agreed that he should continue to ride his runners in England, and that either Doyasbere or Poincelet should ride them in France. These jockeys, however, had other commitments and M. Boussac approached Rae Johnstone, who had been riding with phenomenal success for Dick Carver, Alec Head and Joseph Lieux. Johnstone's reply was that he would ride all the Boussac runners in England and France or there would be no deal. This was a perfectly reasonable attitude for a successful jockey to take as the English races at that time were far more valuable than their French counterparts.

M. Boussac therefore told Elliott that they had come to the parting of the ways, though after Elliott's retirement from the saddle he appointed him as one of his two trainers (Semblat was the other) and Elliott trained Apollonia, who, next to Corrida, was the best filly M. Boussac ever owned.

13 The Colombo Story: Rae Johnstone vindicated

Rae Johnstone arrives as first jockey for Lord Glanely – Hot favourite Colombo finishes third in 1934 Derby – Johnstone, unfairly blamed, gets the sack and returns to France – Mesa, third in 1935 Oaks, another Johnstone failure – Sayani's incredible Cambridgeshire (1946)—better even than Epinard – Johnstone lays Epsom bogey by winning 1947 Oaks on Imprudence and 1948 Derby on My Love – Three Derbys in three weeks.

Charlie Elliott introduced me to Rae Johnstone in Paris in the early thirties. A very successful but somewhat stormy apprenticeship in Australia had been followed by a couple of triumphant seasons in India, and now he was riding winners galore in France. The brothers Pierre and Paul Wertheimer had been responsible for his coming to France where he had been champion jockey two years running. In the autumn of 1933, however, he was offered the job which any jockey in the world would have jumped at. He had previously applied for a licence to ride in England, but it had been turned down. His somewhat murky past in his native land may have been responsible for the Jockey Club taking the view that racing in this country could continue quite happily without him. He was therefore unemployed when the Wertheimer brothers, who had owned the magnificent Epinard, decided to take a chance with him, and they never had cause to regret it. Rae Johnstone brought a new dimension to jockeyship in France, and though his style was somewhat unorthodox it was 100 per cent effective. The crowd nicknamed him 'the Crocodile' on account of his habit of waiting behind the impetuous French jockeys, and then, with split-second timing, swooping down on them and gobbling them up.

The job he was offered was that of first jockey to Lord Glanely, and in nine years out of ten he would have taken some time to make up his mind, as he was riding on the crest of the wave in France, with every chance of being champion jockey for the third time. But as first jockey for Lord Glanely in 1934 he would ride Colombo in all the classics. Outstandingly the best two-year-old of 1933, Colombo was winter favourite for the Derby. Both Steve and Gordon had ridden him as a two-year-old, and Steve believed that he would be engaged to ride him in all his races the following year. He was therefore very indignant when Lord Glanely announced that he had engaged Rae Johnstone as his stable jockey, and he made no secret of his disappointment. Lord Glanely was, of course, perfectly within his rights in engaging Johnstone; Steve had never had a retainer from him and his resentment was childish. It was quite out of character, but the world had not been treating him very kindly and Colombo was the horse who might put him back on top of the world. He had ridden Thrapston as pace-maker to Hyperion and when Weston on Hyperion shouted for him to do so Steve obediently pulled away from the rails and let Hyperion through. So far had the mighty fallen.

Colombo, with Johnstone in the saddle, won the Craven Stakes in a canter and started at 7/2 on for the Two Thousand Guineas. He duly landed the odds, but he did not win as convincingly as I had expected him to do and Rae had to shake him up to beat the French-trained Easton, ridden by Semblat. The latter was subsequently sold to Lord Woolavington, who sent him to Beckhampton, and he became Gordon's mount in the Derby.

Darling also saddled Medieval Knight, who was ridden by Steve. As the two horses were in different ownership it would be incorrect to describe Medieval Knight as a pace-maker, but he had little chance of winning the race and his primary objective was to see to it that there was no dawdling, and who better equipped to carry out this duty than Steve?

12 Italian colt *Ribot* unbeaten winner of sixteen races. Look what he did to our horses in the 1956 'King George' at Ascot, his only race in England

13 *Pinza's* owner, trainer and jockey, Sir Victor Sassoon, Norman Bertie, Sir Gordon Richards

14 M. J. Ternynck leads in *Sea Bird* (Pat Glennon) after winning the 1965 Derby. The only Derby winner in my time to win on the bit

Few Derbys have created more controversy and ill-feeling than the 1934 race, and those who talk through their pocket were obviously biased. Medieval Knight led down the hill followed by Colombo, and the favourite, who had started at the unrealistic price of 11/8, was still pulling hard. Medieval Knight began to tire as he approached Tattenham Corner, and with Windsor Lad and Easton coming up on his outside Johnstone found himself pocketed. To my way of thinking this gave Colombo the breather he so badly needed, and although it cost him approximately three lengths he had time to get his second wind.

Windsor Lad led into the straight, and although both Colombo and Easton made gallant efforts to catch him they never looked like doing so. Colombo headed Easton a furlong out and looked certain to finish second, but he was a very tired horse and Easton beat him by a neck for second place, without troubling Windsor Lad, who won comfortably by a length.

Rae Johnstone was described by some of my colleagues as having ridden a shocking race, but for my own view of the incident I will quote from Johnstone's memoirs, *The Rae Johnstone Story*. 'Among the professional race writers Quintin Gilbey was almost alone in expressing the view that it was lack of stamina that beat Colombo. Quinny wrote: "The interference did Colombo more good than harm—had Johnstone not been forced to check him, he'd have run himself out sooner than he did." '

Thirty-six years later I can still see the field approaching Tattenham Corner and I am just as convinced now as I was then that Rae Johnstone was unjustly blamed for the defeat of a colt who did not stay a mile and a half.

Steve Donoghue, in his memoirs, wrote: 'Had I ridden Colombo he would have won on the bit by many lengths. Had any other English jockey, who knew the course, ridden him he would have won comfortably; had Johnstone called out to me to let him through when I was whacked I would of course have done so.'

Like hell he would! In my opinion Steve's views as expressed in his book were complete nonsense, and I can only imagine

I

that they were those of his ghost writer and that Steve omitted to correct his proofs.

Owners like Lord Rosebery, Lord Derby, Colonel Loder or Lord Astor would have told their jockey's detractors to go to hell, but Lord Glanely listened to and read all the adverse criticism levelled at the unfortunate Johnstone, and gave him the sack. Lord Glanely told Johnstone that another jockey would ride his horses whenever available. His name? Yes, you've guessed it right—Gordon Richards.

Through no fault of his own Johnstone had been a flop in England, but M. Wertheimer welcomed him back to France where he was once again brilliantly successful; although he did not resume riding in France until July he had ridden sixty-two winners by the end of the season. Among his winners for M. Wertheimer was a two-year-old called Mesa who was engaged in the English classics. She fulfilled her first season's promise by winning our One Thousand Guineas by three lengths, and those who thought that Colombo should have won the Derby on the bit began to wonder whether Johnstone was quite the nitwit they had described him as being after the previous year's Derby. Johnstone's reprieve, however, lasted for no more than a month, as after Mesa had finished third in the Oaks, for which she started at 5/4, he was described as being either a villain, who was paid large sums by bookmakers to stop hot favourites, or the most incompetent jockey who had ever ridden round Tattenham Corner.

I had written that no jockey could have won the Derby on Colombo, a non-stayer, but there was no shadow of doubt that Mesa should have won the Oaks, and I wrote that Johnstone had ridden a very injudicious race. Had he pulled round two horses early in the straight, instead of remaining glued to the rails, Mesa would have won comfortably; instead of which she was shut in and did not see daylight till the race was all over.

Rae Johnstone's hopes of ever getting another ride at Epsom, much less of winning the Derby or Oaks, appeared remote, and anyone who prophesied, on the evening of Mesa's defeat, that he would win three Derbys and three races for the Oaks would have been regarded as a suitable case for treatment.

In France, however, Johnstone continued to ride on the crest of the wave, and he was champion jockey for the third time with 102 winners. A memorable race for him was the Grand Prix de Marseille in which he rode the peerless Corrida to victory. This was his first ride for M. Boussac, and in the years to come the partnership was to sweep the board in both France and England.

Between 1935 and the outbreak of war Rae only had an occasional ride in England, his name being permanently associated with the failures of Colombo and Mesa. When France was liberated, Johnstone was soon riding winners again, and in 1945 he won the Prix de l'Arc de Triomphe on Nikellora. I did not see that race, but a French friend described Johnstone's riding of Nikellora as a marvellous piece of jockeyship, and in his opinion Johnstone would have won on any of the first three. M. Boussac started three in that race. They were, of course, coupled for betting purposes, as is the rule in France, and started at 10/1 on.

Aly Khan had a very high opinion of Johnstone, not only as a jockey but as a judge of racing. Rae had at last given up betting, and as happens to most of us when we have no financial interest his judgement improved. No one can watch a race objectively in which he is financially involved, and Aly had such faith in Rae's judgement that on one occasion, after Rae had tipped him a horse to win a race later in the day, Aly promptly bought the horse and engaged Rae to ride it. The horse won by a neck, after which Aly used to refer to Rae as 'the oracle'.

Owner-trainer Joseph Lieux had a marvellous run of success in the years immediately succeeding the war, and Rae rode most of his runners, among them being a lovely colt called Sayani who was sent over to contest the Royal Hunt Cup. Three-year-olds have a poor record in this race and Sayani, who had a big weight, finished unplaced. He was saddled two days later for the Jersey Stakes, which he won ridden by Roger Poincelet as Rae had engagements in France. Ridden by Rae, Sayani next won the important Prix Jacques le Marois at Deauville, the Godolphin Plate at Hurst Park and the Select Stakes at Newmarket. He was sent to Epsom to be trained for the Cambridgeshire in which he had the gigantic weight, for a three-year-old, of 9 stone 4 lb.

Having seen him win at Deauville and three times in England I'd formed a very high opinion of Sayani and had made up my mind to back him for the Cambridgeshire despite the fact that he was carrying a weight under which no three-year-old had proved successful. Unfortunately I allowed myself to be talked out of it. Two very successful Epsom trainers informed me that Sayani had done very little work and was as big as a bull. In their view Joseph Lieux didn't know the first thing about training a racehorse. Rae, however, assured me that Lieux knew what he was about, and that Sayani would be fit enough if he was good enough. I decided to have no bet, and when I couldn't pick Sayani out till the race was half over and he was still a dozen lengths behind the leaders, I was grateful to those Epsom trainers for saving me money.

I subsequently learned from Rae that there had been some jostling in the early stages of the race, as there usually is when a field of thirty-four horses goes to the post, and that Sayani had stumbled so badly after going a hundred yards that Rae thought he had 'gone'. Sayani found another leg, as the jumping people say, but by this time he was virtually out of the race, and in 99 cases out of 100 he would have been. Sayani, however, was no ordinary horse, and despite his misfortunes he succeeded where the mighty Epinard had failed.

I have described this handicap in detail as Sayani's performance bordered on the miraculous. Rae too must be given his share of credit, as many jockeys would either have pulled him up when his chance appeared hopeless, or gone hell-for-leather to make up the lost ground. Rae, however, waited patiently till Sayani had recovered his composure before calling on him for an effort, though his opponents were increasing their lead over him with every stride. Sayani demonstrated beyond doubt that a really great horse can give away both weight and distance.

Although even his most severe critics agreed that Rae had ridden a superb race on Sayani they tempered their praise with 'Wait till he finds himself at Epsom again'. They did not have long to wait, as in 1947 Joseph Lieux booked him to ride the three-year-old filly Imprudence in all her races unless he was required by a stable that retained him. Imprudence won her first race as a three-year-old, beating Pearl Diver, who was still backward; but she had satisfied her connections, and was sent over to run in our One Thousand Guineas, which she won, a trifle cleverly, by a neck from another French-trained filly, Rose O'Lym. Imprudence, who appeared to thrive on racing, won the French One Thousand Guineas sixteen days later. She was ridden by Brethes as Rae was claimed to ride Montenica who finished second to her.

And now for the Oaks. Rae had been the first to admit that he should have won the Oaks on Mesa, and unflappable as he was he must have suffered some qualms as he cantered to the post on yet another hot favourite. The result, however, was never in doubt from a mile from home, at which point Rae decided that the pace was too slow and that he would make the rest of the running himself. Imprudence increased her lead, without Rae having to ask her a question, and won by five lengths.

Imprudence was a daughter of Canot, on whom Rae had split Nearco and Bois Roussel in the Grand Prix, out of Indiscretion. Indiscretion was bred and raced by Lord Rosebery, who sold her to M. Pierre Corbière for 600 guineas. On three occasions she had refused to start and when she did agree to go she couldn't go fast enough to keep herself warm. That a mare with such a record should have a daughter who set up an all-time record by winning the English and French One Thousand Guineas and the English Oaks is a classic example of the glorious uncertainty of racing. The Oaks was run before the Derby that year, but though Pearl Diver had finished second to Imprudence first time out, no one I met, except Brethes, fancied the colt to win the Derby.

A fortnight later Rae won the French Oaks on Montenica, who therefore paid a compliment to Imprudence, who had beaten her with a bit in hand at Longchamp. Fillies are apt to be less consistent than colts, but their form in 1947 was reproduced to a pound. Rae stated in his memoirs that he owed much of his success to watching Harry Wragg, and though he could ride any sort of race it was when bringing his mount with a late run that he excelled. In 1947 he had taken a great fancy to a two-year-old called My Love, and he was sure that the colt would win good races if given time to settle down, which the French jockeys had not allowed him to do. My Love's trainer Richard Carver asked Rae to ride him in the Prix Hocquart, but Rae only consented to do so on the condition that he would ride him in all his races. He could afford to be a little bit independent by this time, and the colt's owner, M. Volterra, agreed to his terms. Richard Carver, a great man with horses, had two other highly promising three-year-olds in his stable in Bey and Royal Drake. Year after year the Prix Hocquart provided a pointer to our Derby, and Rae rode My Love with infinite patience, waiting till the field was well into the short Longchamp straight before moving on him. Immediately he did so My Love accelerated, and went on to beat a high-class field with such authority as to convince Rae that he was a worthy contender for our Derby. It was undoubtedly as the result of Rae's enthusiasm that the Aga Khan purchased a half-share in the horse before he was sent over to Epsom.

The 1948 Derby field was well up to standard. It included Royal Drake (who had beaten My Love in a gallop, though Rae was certain that his mount would prove the better on a racecourse), the Two Thousand Guineas winner My Babu, Black Tarquin, of whom Captain Boyd Rochfort had a high opinion, M. Boussac's Djeddah, Valognes, winner of the Chester Vase, and The Cobbler. In view of his polished display when winning the Prix Hocquart, 100/9 seemed a generous price about My Love and I can only imagine that there were still people who doubted Rae's ability to ride a big winner at Epsom when the pressure was on. (They could argue that anyone who could sit on a horse would have won the Oaks on Imprudence.) Once again Rae rode a waiting race on My Love, and he was well behind Black Tarquin, who was lying seventh when the latter ran wide at Tattenham Corner and took My Babu with him. Royal Drake opened up a lead of several lengths early in the straight but was challenged by My Love, full of running, as they approached the final furlong. The two stable companions had the finish to themselves, My Love beating Royal Drake by one and a half lengths with the Aga Khan's English-trained Noor four lengths away third. The result was a great triumph for M. Volterra, who bred the first two, and for Richard Carver who trained them. Rae had ridden a typical 'Harry Wragg race' on the winner, and had once and for all silenced his critics.

When My Love had first caught Rae's eye as a prospective Derby colt he had never won a race, and he would not, I feel sure, have won a classic had not Rae discovered that he had to be waited with in order to produce his best form.

What a year this was for Rae. He had won a modest race on Bey and was asked to ride him in the French Derby. On the book he appeared to have little chance of beating his stable companions Royal Drake and Turmoil. Royal Drake would have won the Derby by four lengths with My Love out of the way and on the book he looked a good thing, but the race had taken its toll of this far from robust colt and it was asking a lot of him to tackle the best in England and France twice in the space of two weeks. This was the first French Derby to be run at Chantilly since the war. Rae showed his virtuosity on Bey by being in the leading bunch throughout, thereby proving that he could be just as effective when waiting in front as he was when coming from behind. These forcing tactics suited Bey, who won by a length from Tanagrello with Flush Royal a neck away third.

'Make it three Derbys in three weeks,' Aly Khan told Rae when engaging him to ride his father's Nathoo, trained by Frank Butters, in the Irish Derby. The race was not worth a tenth of its value today, though it attracted a fair-class field. There was no stopping Rae this golden summer and Nathoo won by five lengths from Charlie Smirke's mount Star of Gujarath.

The following day he completed the Derby–Grand Prix double on My Love at Longchamp. The winning margin over Flush Royal was one and a half lengths, the same distance as he had between himself and Royal Drake in the Derby. Four years later Flush Royal, who had been in several different stables and was then trained by Jack Fawcus, won the Cesarewitch carrying 8 stone 13 lb.

14 A golden year

*M. Boussac's golden year – Johnstone's great riding –
Galcador wins Derby from Prince Simon – Scratch beats
Tantième in French Derby – 'I fluked it' – Asmena, the
cripple, wins the Oaks – Scratch wins St Leger – The
mighty Ribot – Talma's St Leger – Who backed him? –
No dope test – M. Boussac and Rae Johnstone part
company – Lavandin's Derby – Johnstone's thirtieth and
last classic victory – The end of an era for Marcel Boussac.*

Early in March 1950, accompanied by François de Brignac, I
paid my annual visit to Chantilly on an inspection of M.
Boussac's two stables, named after his famous horses Pharis and
Djebel. On our way to Chantilly from Paris François told me
that he thought that 'the boss', as he always spoke of M.
Boussac, had the strongest team of three-year-olds since he had
become an owner of racehorses thirty years before. He named
Geraphar, Cardinal, Pardal, Galcador and Scratch as all likely
to be up to classic standard. He also owned Corejada, who had
won the Cheveley Park Stakes, proving herself the best two-
year-old filly in 1949. François' optimism did not surprise me as
in the French Free Handicap six of the top nine belonged to M.
Boussac. A tour of inspection of the Boussac stables was an
experience in those days comparable to a visit to the Louvre for
connoisseurs of great pictures.

Over coffee with Semblat at the end of our inspection I was
asked which horse I would choose in the somewhat unlikely
event of M. Boussac offering me the pick of his stable. I chose

Scratch, at which François and Semblat smiled at one another, before François told me that this chestnut son of Pharis was only rated number five by them and that they would be surprised if he proved himself superior to the other four colts I have mentioned.

I had to admit that I was slightly prejudiced in Scratch's favour, having seen him win the Solario Stakes at Sandown the previous autumn when he was ridden by Charlie Elliott, but I went on to say that I thought he had more scope for improvement than any of the other four colts, and that he had an ideal Derby pedigree.

I think that both François and Semblat would have picked Pardal, but would have been well pleased with Geraphar. The latter broke down and did not run as a three-year-old. They were a bit doubtful concerning Galcador's stamina, and their reason for placing Scratch at the bottom of the poll was that they thought he was a trifle outclassed, though at that time none of the horses had done more than half-speed work.

After we had said goodbye to Semblat, François asked me if I would like to see Tantième—a rhetorical question, as M. Dupré's colt had won the Grand Criterium and Prix de la Forêt the previous autumn, and was unanimously regarded as the best two-year-old colt in Europe in 1949. François Mathet, one of the all-time great trainers, is not the most genial of men, and as I only knew him slightly I would not have approached him on my own account with a request to see Tantième, but he and François de Brignac had been brother officers in the cavalry, and he received us with courtesy. Tantième was certainly a sight for sore eyes. A well-grown, all-quality bay, he had obviously gone the right way from two to three years, and even at that early stage of the year had a summer bloom on his coat.

Tantième and Galcador both won first time out as three-year-olds. In neither case was the opposition very strong, but both pleased their connections by the ease of their victories. The races for the French Guineas do not carry the same prestige as their English counterparts, but the 1950 event, in which Tantième and Galcador were in opposition, aroused more than usual interest. I flew over for the race and it was well worth the visit. Tantième started at 6/4 on and beat Galcador by half a length, but the latter had fully extended him, and I was surprised when Rae expressed a doubt as to whether the son of Djebel would ever get much more than a mile, as he did not appear to me to be tiring. Rae, however, blamed himself for coming too soon and thought that had he waited a bit longer he might have won.

Rae won the French One Thousand Guineas on Corejada, but things were not going according to plan. Geraphar had already broken down, and Pardal had been beaten by Fast Fox in the Prix Juigne which he had been thought certain to win. He subsequently finished only third in the Prix Hocquart. This was a bitter blow, as prior to these two defeats M. Boussac and his men believed that Pardal was their best colt. Worse was to follow as Pardal developed knee trouble and could not be trained for the Derby. M. Boussac therefore had to fall back on Galcador for Epsom and the unconsidered Scratch for the French Derby. Cardinal was very strongly fancied for our Two Thousand Guineas, but was injured when entering the plane to take him to England, and Emperor, who was substituted for him and was considered to be well over a stone behind him, ran well enough to suggest that Cardinal would have beaten both Palestine and Prince Simon, who finished first and second separated by a short head.

Rae, however, received some consolation by winning the One Thousand Guineas on M. Jean Ternynck's Camaree, trained by Alexander Lieux, brother of Joseph. Rae was as good a judge of the potentialities of a horse which he had ridden as any jockey of my acquaintance, but he was way out in his reckoning when he assessed Galcador as a miler who might be even better over seven furlongs. Rae Johnstone, Alec Head and other French-based friends showed me much hospitality when I visited France, and I usually entertained them in return on the eve of the Derby. On this occasion Rae informed my other guests and myself that a miracle would be needed if Galcador was to get the Derby trip.

In the paddock he looked a picture, with his lovely Arab

head, peculiar to so many of Djebel's offspring, and his general air of well-being, but to my eyes he looked more like a beautiful polo pony than a prospective Derby winner; being so compact made him look smaller than he really was. Palestine was not in the Derby field, and the American-bred Prince Simon, regarded by Captain Boyd Rochfort as an even better colt than Black Tarquin, was a 2/1 favourite with two French colts, L'Amiral and Vieux Manoir, at 11/2 and 7/1 respectively, and Galcador at 100/9.

The pace was a slow one by Derby standards, and Carr, realising that stamina was Prince Simon's long suit, sent him into a clear lead descending the hill to Tattenham Corner. Rae had intended to hold up Galcador for a short run close home, but realising that Prince Simon would not come back to him he dare not leave Galcador with too much leeway to make up. He therefore challenged sooner than he had intended, and though Galcador took a lead of a length over Prince Simon 100 yards from home, he was tiring, and with Prince Simon plodding on at the same pace there was only a head in it at the finish and I think Prince Simon would have regained the lead in another twenty yards.

Harry Carr was criticised for his riding of Prince Simon, as jockeys nearly always are when they are narrowly beaten in the Derby on a hot favourite, but I could not see that he had done anything wrong, and Captain Boyd Rochfort fully agreed with my views on the race expressed in the following day's *Sporting Chronicle*, and sent a copy of my article to Prince Simon's owner, Mr Woodward, in America.

One of the most fascinating aspects of the Derby is that no two races are alike, though some are more different than others. The 1950 race constituted the supreme paradox in that Prince Simon was beaten by the poverty of the opposition rather than by its merits.

Had there been two or three reasonably good stayers in the field who needed a strong gallop their jockeys would have sent them along with Prince Simon when Harry Carr stepped up the pace seven furlongs from home. Racing alone is a tremendous disadvantage to a lazy stayer like Prince Simon, and had he had something to race with all the way up the straight I doubt whether Galcador would have ever got to him, as his stamina would have run out before Johnstone could pick him up and deliver his challenge.

Galcador's victory completed the greatest double of all for M. Boussac, his Asmena having won the Oaks two days earlier. This was the first time an owner had brought off the double since Signor Ginistrelli won both races with Signorinetta in 1908. On Rae's advice I had backed Asmena at starting price, and when I saw her canter past the stands on the way to the post I prayed that her number would be withdrawn and that she would not come under starter's orders.

So short was her stride that she did not appear to be covering more than a few inches at a time. She had been subject to occasional attacks of rheumatism, but never before had it had such a crippling effect on her. Rae told me that he debated whether to ask the starter's permission to withdraw her, but decided to let her take her chance, informing his colleagues as they lined up: 'I expect I'll have to pull mine up before she falls down.' After watching Asmena gallop with the utmost freedom, and win in great style by a length from another French filly, Plume, ridden by Charlie Elliott, I wondered whether my own aches and pains could be cured by a brisk run, but my medical adviser thought not.

Scratch had won his first two races, but was beaten two lengths by Lacaduv in the Prix Noailles. Following his victory over Galcador in the French Two Thousand Guineas Tantième beat Lacaduv by a length in the Prix Lupin, so M. Dupré's colt did not appear to have much to fear from Scratch in the French Derby. This was Rae's view and he decided that the only chance he had was by saving several lengths, or, to use his own words to me before the race, 'If I can fluke it'. Chantilly is one of the courses in which hugging the rails can more often than not lead to disaster. Time and again the field will remain closely packed until halfway up the straight, and a jockey riding a waiting race 'on the inner' may be confronted by a wall of horses, and not see daylight till it is all over.

Poincelet on Tantième, knowing that he had several pounds

in hand, had no problems, and was not unduly disturbed when
he was taken a length or two wide entering the straight. This
was Rae's heaven-sent opportunity, and he dashed Scratch
through the gap to take a clear lead. After a desperate race the
judge decided (there was no photo in those days) that Scratch
had won by a short head. This was not Poincelet's view, and for
describing the judge as a blind old so-and-so, in the hearing of
the stewards, he was fined approximately fifty pounds. Rae's
riding of Scratch was the finest example of 'fluking a race' I
have ever witnessed, but if it had not come off he would no
doubt have been criticised for going where he had no business
to go. I reckoned that Scratch had covered at least two lengths
less ground than Tantième, and he won by a matter of inches.
No wonder the favourite's connections considered him an unlucky loser.

Scratch could only finish fourth in the Grand Prix, won by
the Baron Guy de Rothschild's Vieux Manoir from his stable
companion Alizier, but he had had a very hard race in the
French Derby and was probably feeling the effects of it. The
Boussac entourage was therefore very hopeful that he would
turn the tables on Vieux Manoir in our St Leger. The English
horses left in the race were extremely moderate, and the race
appeared to be in the nature of a match between the two
Frenchmen. Miel Rosa was started as pace-maker for Vieux
Manoir, but as he failed to do so Laumain, on Vieux Manoir,
wisely went to the front a mile from home. Rae dare not let
such a proved stayer get too far ahead, so he sat on his tail,
hoping that Scratch would still have enough in reserve to beat
him for speed. Both horses were full out a furlong from home,
but Scratch was gaining inch by inch and took the lead close
home to win by a length. This victory rounded off a marvellous
season for M. Boussac, Semblat and Johnstone, but poor
Semblat was not permitted to witness the feats of the horses he
had trained so skilfully when they ran in England. M. Boussac
believed that a trainer's place was in the home, and Semblat
must be the only trainer in the history of racing to top the list
without once setting foot in this country.

Tantième, ridden by Jacko Doyasbere, won the Prix de l'Arc

de Triomphe like the great horse François Mathet had always believed him to be, thereby establishing himself as the best colt of his generation. Scratch finished fourth, and Rae's feat in winning the French Derby on him now seemed even more incredible than it had done at the time. A year later Tantième again won the Prix de l'Arc de Triomphe, proving himself a wonder horse over the one-and-a-half-mile course at Longchamp. He was a bad traveller, and though he won the Queen Elizabeth Stakes at Ascot and the Coronation Cup he never showed his true form in this country. M. Boussac won the St Leger in 1951 for the second year running, with Talma. He had won two small races in France but Rae described him to me as a one-pacer who might win the Queen Alexandra Stakes at Ascot one day. In the paddock at Doncaster he behaved in the most shameful fashion, indicating that his thoughts were far removed from racing. I would not have taken 100/1 about him, but the money continued to pour on him, and he started at 7/1, having been backed down from 100/7. The going was heavy, and knowing that Talma stayed, though he believed him to be lamentably short of speed, Rae rode a most untypical Johnstone race. There was still nearly a mile to go when he set Talma alight and rode for dear life. Passing the post he looked over his shoulder, and to his amazement saw that he had won by ten lengths.

This was one of the most mysterious races in my experience, as although M. Boussac was not so pessimistic about Talma's prospect of success as was his jockey, he betted very little, and this flood of money certainly did not emanate from the stable. Never before or subsequently did Talma run within two stone of the form he displayed when winning the St Leger. His connections were as mystified as were the rest of us, and although I realise that the supposition may appear far-fetched I do not rule out the possibility that someone, not connected with the stable, administered a strong stimulant to Talma. If that is correct it must have been something pretty powerful. In view of Talma's behaviour before the race, and his vast improvement on his previous form, I consider that the stewards were remiss in not ordering a test to be carried out on him.

Most of M. Boussac's best horses (since Ramus) had been

equable animals, but Auriban, a very handsome son of Pharis of great ability, was a tearaway, and would stop at nothing in his determination to get his own way. He was in an ugly mood when he went to the post for the 1952 Prix Hocquart, but Rae humoured him and after it had appeared very doubtful whether he would consent to start he did so and won in the style of a champion.

He started a hot favourite for the French Derby, but from the moment they came under orders it was apparent that he didn't want to know. The starter was patient, but there was a limit to any starter's patience before the introduction of starting stalls, even if the miscreant was carrying the orange jacket and grey cap in a French classic, and Auriban was still backing away when the gate went up. The rest of the field had gone at least fifty yards before Auriban consented to follow them. It must have been a great temptation to go hell-for-leather after them, but Rae was content to make up his ground gradually. Auriban came to grips with the leaders entering the final furlong, and went on to win comfortably. So once again the old adage about horses being unable to give away distance was proved to be a lot of nonsense.

Despite their unprecedented run of success together, M. Boussac and Rae Johnstone had never seen eye to eye, and at no time was there any love lost between them. An owner is, of course, fully entitled to tell his jockey when he is dissatisfied with his riding, but when Rae told me that M. Boussac thought he had ridden an ill-judged race on Auriban I could not believe my ears. I never did discover what he was supposed to have done wrong.

As far back as 1918 M. Boussac had purchased the blood-stock of Mr Duryea, who had won our Derby in 1914 with Durbar II. These horses were not eligible for the General Stud Book. This did not worry M. Boussac in the slightest, though he once described the Jersey Act to me as an absurdity, and I believe that the overwhelming success of his 'half-breds', plus the victories of Quashed in the Oaks and Gold Cup, were partly responsible for its repeal.

M. Boussac's great stallion Tourbillon, sire of Djebel and

many other good horses, was by Ksar out of Durban by Durbar out of Banshee, who was by Irish Lad out of Frizette, from whom so many good horses are descended. One of M. Boussac's shrewdest purchases was Asterus, by Teddy out of Astrella. A top-class racehorse, Asterus, ridden by Charlie Elliott, won the 1927 Royal Hunt Cup under 8 stone 13 lb as well as the Champion Stakes, and became a most successful sire of brood mares. His mares, mated with Tourbillon, Djebel and Pharis, a grandson of Phalaris, were tremendously successful. What, then, went wrong with the Boussac operation?

All sorts of theories have been put forward in explanation of the catastrophic decline of an empire which had seemed indestructible. M. Boussac had experimented with in-breeding, but he only did so on a small scale. The product of what was regarded as an incestuous example of in-breeding was Coronation, winner of the Queen Mary Stakes at Ascot and the Prix de l'Arc de Triomphe.

As the years passed, M. Boussac became less and less inclined to delegate responsibility, and he liked to direct the training of his horses himself. Much of the bad feeling which existed between him and Johnstone stemmed from Rae's conviction that the horses were given too much galloping—'strained rather than trained', as he put it. Even in 1950, the most golden of all the golden years, half a dozen of M. Boussac's best three-year-olds broke down, and Rae attributed a black Ascot to the horses having been over-trained. A horse who is short of a gallop may win; but those who have been given too many have little chance.

A policy of the survival of the fittest may enable a man with an unlimited supply of money and a string of horses to fall back on to enjoy a great season, as M. Boussac did in 1950, but it is a ruthless policy and who knows what adverse effect it may have on posterity?

M. Boussac was no Nero, and he put his long experience and ice-cold brain to the task of rebuilding his empire. His families contained no Blandford blood, and he remedied this by the purchase of stallions descended from Blandford, but they did not 'nick' with the descendants of Tourbillon, Pharis and

Asterus, and the experiment was a failure. I do not pretend to be an authority on genetics and the mechanism of inheritance, but the failure of Djebel's and Pharis' offspring to sire sons and daughters who were within three stone of themselves is not without precedent. Hurry On, a great racehorse, sired horses of the highest quality, but it was not till he was twenty years old that he sired Precipitation, who was to restore the family fortunes as a stallion.

M. Boussac is only a name to those under the age of thirty-five and I am often asked what kind of man he is. I think '*très correct*' best describes him. Always immaculately turned out, he takes life very seriously and racing to him has never been a relaxation. It is in fact just one more business to add to the score of companies of which he is a director.

'*M. Boussac à deux femmes—Mme Boussac et son travail*', the French used to say of him, and in twenty years, in the course of which I interviewed him many dozen times, I never saw him smile. He was, however, courteous and punctilious in supplying me with information concerning the plans for his horses.

I imagine he must have derived great satisfaction from the success of his stable during the golden years, though he never showed any trace of emotion. His face relaxed into a somewhat wintry smile when accepting the congratulations of his fellow owners, but the correspondent who described him as having danced a jig after Scratch won the St Leger must have been looking at someone else. So far as I know he has never had any close friends, his acquaintances being business associates, and I cannot believe that anyone other than Mme Boussac has ever addressed him by his Christian name. Life is a business to M. Marcel Boussac, and business is his life.

In July 1952 M. Boussac and Rae Johnstone parted company, but Rae's services were still in great demand, and in 1954 he won the Prix de l'Arc de Triomphe on Sica Boy. Rae, having won on both Pop Off and Sica Boy, chose to ride the latter in the Grand Prix. Although one of the best judges of a horse's potentialities, he was not infallible, and Sica Boy ran very badly, the race being won by Pop Off, ridden by Freddy Palmer.

K

Rae believed that Sica Boy's running in the Grand Prix had been too bad to be true and he stuck to him in the Prix de l'Arc de Triomphe after he had won the French St Leger in which Pop Off finished last. It was apparent once again that this gruelling race at the end of June, nearly two miles long, had imposed too great a strain on the winner. Sica Boy had been given an easy race in the Grand Prix when Rae realised he had no chance of winning. There have been many better fields for the Arc de Triomphe, but in winning the race convincingly Sica Boy proved himself the best horse around at that time. His victory gave Rae particular satisfaction as if he had not severed his connection with the Boussac stable he would have been on one of the 'also rans'.

In 1956 Rae won the Derby for the third time. The horse was Lavandin, in the colours of his old patron M. Pierre Wertheimer, and trained by the brilliant young Alec Head, who was also training at that time with great success for Aly Khan.

Roger Poincelet was riding as first jockey for M. Wertheimer that year, but he had ridden a very ill-judged race on Lavandin in the Prix Hocquart. Alec Head was so dissatisfied with his riding that with the assistance of Peter O'Sullevan he persuaded M. Wertheimer to replace him in the Derby, and put up Rae Johnstone, who had served him so well in the past. Poincelet was a brilliant jockey and he, Jacko Doyasbere and Yves St Martin were the best French riders of the past fifty years; but about once or twice a season Poincelet would ride like a novice and he had done so in the Prix Hocquart.

Rae has described how on the eve of the Derby he, Alec Head, Frank Vogel and Peter O'Sullevan dined with me and that our confidence in Lavandin was ebbing when we met that evening. The horse did not have the best of forelegs and that morning he had given Alec heart failure by moving somewhat feelingly after his morning exercise. The bandages he always wore were not just ornaments. The three-year-olds were far from being a vintage crop and the betting was very open, Lavandin starting favourite at 7/1. Derby Day was a wet one as it so often is but Lavandin's connections consoled themselves

with the knowledge that every drop that fell would ease conditions underfoot for those doubtful forelegs. As usual, Rae
gave his mount plenty of time to settle down, and at the top of
the hill he was lying about twelfth and a long way behind the
leaders. No matter how good a jockey may be he depends to
some extent on luck and this particularly applies in the Derby.
The luck was on Rae's side on Lavandin as an opening appeared
near the rails running down to Tattenham Corner which saved
him several lengths. Even so he was half a dozen lengths behind Pirate King who was the same distance behind Monterey
entering the straight.

But the leaders came back to him, as Rae was sure they would
do, and Lavandin had his race won entering the final furlong.
Rae eased him in the last fifty yards and Montaval, also trained
in France, was catching him fast at the finish. The judge called
for a photo but no one had any doubt that Lavandin had won.

We had fought our way back almost to equality with France
in the eleven years since the war ended, but 1956 was a disastrous year for us. Not only were the first two in the Derby
trained in France, but the third horse, Roistar, was trained in
Ireland. The first three in the Oaks, Sicarelle, Janiari and
Yasmin, were all trained in France, as they had been in 1954
when Rae won on Sun Cap from Altana and Philante.

M. Boussac won the 1956 Gold Cup with Macip, trained by
Charlie Elliott and ridden by Serge Boullenger, from two more
French horses, Bewitched and Clichy. This was the last great
race that M. Boussac was to win in England. He had won the
1954 Gold Cup with Elpenor, also trained by Elliott, who beat
another French horse, Silex, by a short head. Baron Guy de
Rothschild's Tropique won the Coronation Cup and the
Eclipse Stakes of 1956 while the Italian four-year-old Ribot won
the King George VI and Queen Elizabeth Stakes. Ribot won
the Prix de l'Arc de Triomphe two years running, and his
record of sixteen victories without defeat may never be surpassed. I am inclined to believe that Sea Bird, in the form he
was in when he won our Derby and the Prix de l'Arc de
Triomphe, might have beaten him, but whereas Ribot bore the
heat and burden of the day for three seasons Sea Bird was re-

tired to the stud, with indecent haste, at the end of a far from strenuous three-year-old career. At stud, Ribot has sired horses in his own likeness. Sea Bird has yet to do so.

I watched Ribot's first Arc de Triomphe with Charlie Elliott, and as the field ran down the hill about half a mile from home, Charlie exclaimed: 'Look at Camici's feet!' Ribot was pulling his Italian jockey out of the saddle, and he was leaning back in an endeavour to restrain him, in contrast to the other jockeys who had all begun to niggle, push and scrub. What a horse!

Lavandin was Rae's third Derby winner and his thirtieth and final classic winner, an astonishing record rendered all the more remarkable by the inauspicious start to his classic career twenty-two years earlier. It must also be remembered that he did not ride for five years during the war.

Of his three Derby winners, he was reasonably confident that My Love would win, he did not fancy Galcador, and though he was very hopeful about Lavandin he was a little doubtful how his forelegs would react to the Epsom gradients. The Derby mount about whom he was most confident, however, did not run, and a dejected Rae watched the 1955 Derby from the stands. Lady Ursula Vernon, daughter of the Duke of Westminster, had bought a mare called Sakountala from M. Boussac when she was in foal to Djebel. She named the foal Hugh Lupus and sent him to be trained by Hubert Hartigan in Ireland. Hartigan died at the end of Hugh Lupus' two-year-old career and Lady Ursula left her colt with Lenehan, formerly assistant trainer to Hartigan. Ridden by Rae, Hugh Lupus won the Railway Plate by eight lengths and Rae was engaged to ride him in all his races as a three-year-old. It was intended to run him in the Two Thousand Guineas, but Hugh Lupus declined to board the plane for Newmarket. He was therefore started for the far less valuable Irish Two Thousand Guineas which he won at a canter by four lengths.

Hugh Lupus travelled by boat to England for the Derby and he looked in magnificent shape when he arrived at Epsom. The English-trained colts, apart from Alice Lady Derby's Acropolis, an own brother to Alycidon, were very moderate, and Acropolis had had his preparation disrupted when he was jarred up on the very firm going. It was feared that he might not be 100 per cent fit. Rae thought that a mile and a half might be rather further than Hugh Lupus' best distance, but was encouraged by the fact that he had won the Derby on another son of Djebel, Galcador, whom he had thought had little chance of getting the trip. It was in Hugh Lupus' favour that he was a very handy horse, with the perfect action of his sire, Djebel. Such horses take far less out of themselves than do those who are less tractable. Rae knew that he could put him anywhere and produce him at the moment he considered the time for action had arrived. A hard-pulling horse, like Colombo, will not win a Derby unless he gets every yard of the distance, but Hugh Lupus was so co-operative that he would be 'free-wheeling' all the way down the hill.

On the day before the Derby, Rae rode Hugh Lupus round Tattenham Corner and he went like a dream, but he jumped the road at the intersection of the courses, landing awkwardly. To the relief of his connections he pulled up apparently sound, but later in the day, when Lenehan visited his box, the horse was in pain and was found to have injured his near foreleg. So there was no Derby for Rae that year, and he was heartbroken at the spectacle of the Irish-trained Panaslipper running Madame Volterra's Phil Drake to one and a half lengths, as in the Irish Two Thousand Guineas Hugh Lupus had beaten him out of sight. Hugh Lupus recovered in time to run in the Irish Derby, but Lenehan had been unable to give him an orthodox preparation. Panaslipper beat him by two lengths. Rae believed, however, that but for his mishap Hugh Lupus would have won both the English and Irish Derbys. As a four-year-old Hugh Lupus was trained by Noel Murless and won five races, including the Hardwicke Stakes and the Champion Stakes.

Madame Volterra's Phil Drake, very astutely ridden by Freddy Palmer, put up a remarkable performance to win the Derby of 1955. Still green, the lanky son of the Grand Prix winner Admiral Drake had no idea how to gallop downhill, and in my description of the race I compared his descent to Tattenham Corner to that of an old gentleman negotiating a steep flight of stairs. Wisely, Palmer did not attempt to hurry him, and rounding Tattenham Corner I made him twenty-first of the twenty-three runners, and approximately fifteen lengths behind the leaders. As the result, however, of Palmer's patience he had taken nothing out of himself and when he got into top gear he galloped past his opponents as if they were so many trees, to win by a length and a half. The Derby had brought the backward Phil Drake on by at least 10 lb, and he beat a much stronger field for the Grand Prix just as convincingly as he had won at Epsom. Once again, however, the big Longchamp race had taken all the stuffing out of the winner, and Phil Drake was only a shadow of his former self when he came over to run for the King George VI and Queen Elizabeth Stakes. This race provided a thrilling finish between Vimy, trained by Alec Head and ridden by Poincelet, and Acropolis, ridden by Doug Smith. Acropolis would have been a comfortable winner with Vimy out of the way, thereby demonstrating that he would in all probability have won the Derby had George Colling been able to give him an orthodox preparation.

Serge Boullenger succeeded Rae Johnstone as first jockey for M. Boussac in 1953, and with Semblat in charge of the Ecurie Pharis, and Elliott installed at the Ecurie Djebel, there was as yet no sign that the fortunes of this vast empire were on the brink of a decline. Boullenger was a very good rider indeed and topped the list on several occasions in France. He was inclined to overdo his waiting tactics, but he made all the running when winning our 1956 Gold Cup on M. Boussac's Macip, trained by Elliott. Unfortunately he put on several stone when engaged in his military service, which was responsible for his retirement when still in his mid twenties. Nineteen-fifty-four was a highly successful year for M. Boussac as he won the French Derby with Philiu and the French Oaks with Apollonia. But in 1957 the rot set in and it was not till 1969 that Crepellana's victory in the French Oaks provided M. Boussac with his first classic winner for thirteen years. Present indications are that her success is unlikely to be supplemented in the near future.

15 Doug and Scobie: worthy champions

Doug Smith learns in a hard school — Two fine races by a small boy on a big horse — Doug's long losing run — Hypericum bolts, but wins sensational Guineas in the royal colours — Eph and Doug beat one another in the Oaks — Doug triumphs by other jockeys' mistakes — Wins 1958 Two Thousand Guineas on Pall Mall and 1959 One Thousand Guineas on Petite Etoile — Lester picks the wrong one — That man from Wagga-Wagga — Scobie Breasley wins the 1964 Derby on Santa Claus and gets the sack — Meld, the best filly in my time, coughs her way to victory in the 1955 St Leger.

Since the retirement of Sir Gordon Richards, midway through the 1954 season, there have been only three champion jockeys —Doug Smith (five times), Scobie Breasley (four times) and Lester Piggott (eight times).

Doug's brother Eph, his senior by two years, was already established as a successful apprentice, and Gordon Richards had been champion jockey five times when Doug had his first ride in public in 1931, after only five months in a racing stable. The Smith brothers were apprenticed to Major Sneyd, an unlovable character without a spark of human kindness. He was, however, a first-rate teacher, and three small boys, entrusted to his tender care at his stable at Sparshold near Wantage, became famous jockeys. Eph and Doug had learned to ride as soon as they could walk, but Joe Mercer, whose elder brother Manny had been apprenticed to George Colling, had no previous experience with horses.

As the deeds of Doug Smith, Scobie Breasley and Lester Piggott are still fresh in the memories of all racing enthusiasts I am not going to deal in great detail with their careers. All three men have been worthy champions, in their totally different styles, and a credit to their profession. Despite the strong challenge of Geoff Lewis I expect Lester to retain the championship for at least another five years.

Doug can be said to have taken up where Sir Gordon left off. These two champions had many characteristics in common, one of them being that, unlike so many jockeys, they put their employers' interests before their own. No straighter and more highly respected jockeys have ever ridden on Newmarket Heath, and throughout their long careers there was never a breath of scandal associated with their names. Successful men in all professions are the target of the mudslingers, but not even the most nasty-minded scandalmonger could invent a plausible story to the detriment of either Gordon or Doug.

In his early days, Doug was one of the lightest apprentices of his time, and when he rode his first winner he weighed only 4 stone 11 lb, approximately a stone lighter than Gordon was when he broke his duck. An apprentice has to ride several winners before he makes much impression on the seasoned writers, but I remember making a favourable note of Doug's riding when he was still a very small boy. What impressed me about him most was his skilful riding of several big horses, who appeared to be unsuitable mounts for so small a boy.

He still had several years of his apprenticeship to run when he caught the eyes of leading owners, among them being Sir Alfred Butt. This very astute owner suggested to his trainer Frank Butters that he should engage Doug to ride the stable's lightweights. Sir Alfred had sent his horses to be trained by Butters after Frank got the sack from Stanley House, and it was largely the success of these horses which influenced the Aga Khan into appointing Butters as his trainer when he fell out with Dick Dawson.

Like many intelligent apprentices Doug moulded his style of

riding and tactics on Harry Wragg, and by studying his every move when riding in a big race he became one of the best judges of pace in the country. Freddy Fox was his mentor and father confessor, and the senior jockey and the young apprentice became great friends. How different was Doug's life during his apprenticeship from that of Gordon Richards, who in Marty Hartigan had a master of wisdom and understanding to whom he could bring the problems which confront all teenagers. While Hartigan thought the world of Gordon, Sneyd regarded a successful apprentice merely as a medium for supplementing his own income. Freddy Fox was therefore the first professional racing man to whom Doug felt he could turn for advice. The Smith brothers certainly learnt the hard way, but the fact that they triumphed over hardships testifies to their determination to succeed and is not a recommendation of Sneyd's methods. It was not Sneyd's fault that he had few horses on which to give his apprentices public experience. It was, however, in his own interests to move heaven and earth to secure them good rides from other stables, as a successful apprentice in those days was a valuable asset.

Although I had watched Doug's riding with interest, he had ridden a number of winners, including one for my brother Geoffrey, before I appreciated him at his true worth. The occasion was the Liverpool summer meeting, when he rode the Aga Khan's Sind to victory in the St George Stakes and Atlantic Cup on consecutive days. Sind was a very big strong colt, and the last mount one would have chosen for a featherweight boy round the sharp Liverpool track; but Doug had no difficulty in negotiating the bends and in fully extending his big mount when he reached the straight.

I remember remarking to a colleague as we left the stands after Sind's second victory: 'That boy will be a champion one day.'

I only wish all my prognostications had been so accurate. Doug was the only jockey apart from Gordon Richards for whom Frank Butters had any time, and he therefore participated in most of the gallops. This aroused the indignation of Charlie Smirke, who was retained by the Aga Khan, but it was

Butters who decided *who* should ride *what*, and as the stable usually had several runners in the important races this created a certain amount of ill-feeling.

No matter how successful a jockey may be, a time will come when nothing goes right, and the string of losers grows longer and longer. I travelled with Doug from Warwick to Manchester for the November Handicap meeting of 1938, and over our tea he told me that he had ridden 112 consecutive losers and he doubted whether he would ever ride another winner. I told him not to talk nonsense and said I was sure he would break his losing sequence before we left Manchester. I was relieved that he did not ask me 'On what?' as I did not know the name of one of his mounts; but sure enough, my prophecy, although born of wishful thinking, was fulfilled on the very next day.

He had been engaged to ride a horse with an outstanding chance, but at the last moment its owner decided he would prefer it to be ridden by a jockey with a shorter losing sequence. This seemed to be the last straw to Doug as from the jockeys' stand he watched it win by ten lengths. He was, however, asked to ride a horse called Guest in a selling handicap later in the day. The horse was not fancied, but Doug set out to make all the running on him, and he emerged from the Manchester fog alone in his glory to win by eight lengths. Never again did Doug experience such a long losing run, and if he had it would not have shaken his confidence in himself.

Doug was a versatile rider but he was seen at his best at Newmarket. In the accuracy with which he would time his challenge over the wide open spaces he reminded me of Brownie Carslake, though neither in build nor in style of riding did they bear the slightest resemblance to one another.

I saw Doug ride in many hundreds of races at Newmarket, but I cannot recall his ever losing a race there that he should have won. For a jockey who was five times champion, he did not enjoy great success in the classics, but two of his victories were in the royal colours. At the end of the Second World War Doug was riding as first jockey for Captain Boyd Rochfort. Both Joe Childs and Rufus Beasley, who had ridden with such success for the Freemason Lodge Stable, had retired, and Doug, still in his early twenties and weighing seven stone, was chosen for this responsible post—which carried with it the honour of riding for King George VI.

The King's Hypericum, by Hyperion, had proved herself a pretty good two-year-old, but she was very excitable and had an extremely light mouth. She was a difficult filly to train and an even more difficult one to ride; on one occasion she reared up with Doug and fell on the road when he was riding her back to her stable after early-morning work. By a miracle neither horse nor rider was injured. Once she was started in a race she was as good as gold, but she had only to see a starting gate to charge it, head down. Many horses disliked the gate with its thick strands of rope and refused to go near it, but Hypericum seemed bent on demolishing it.

Neolight, trained by Fred Darling and ridden by Gordon Richards, had been unbeaten in six races as a two-year-old. She was at odds on for the 1946 One Thousand Guineas, with Hypericum second favourite. The King's filly behaved herself reasonably well in the preliminaries but immediately the starter called in the runners she made a bee-line for the gate and Doug was shot from the saddle like a stone from a catapult. Her mission completed, Hypericum cantered down the course, taking nothing out of herself, but the bookmakers thought it was unlikely she would be caught on that wide expanse of heath in time for her to take part in the race, and knocked her out to 100/6. In point of fact her escapade proved far more disadvantageous to her opponents than to Hypericum, as while she was enjoying herself the others were fretting and fuming for twenty-five minutes at the start. She eventually allowed herself to be caught in the car park.

Neolight's supporters complained that had Hypericum not been carrying the royal colours the race would have been started without her. I will not comment on this view, but I am thankful that the introduction of starting stalls has precluded the possibility of another such incident. At the second attempt Captain Allison pulled the lever when Hypericum was still well short of the gate. She was, however, on the move and lost no ground. No filly could have put up a more workmanlike display and she beat Neolight by one and a half lengths. The favourite had become very worked up during the long delay and may not have given her true running. One way and another, it must be admitted, Hypericum was a very lucky winner.

The King was not at Newmarket, but Princess Elizabeth was present to welcome Doug and Hypericum in the winning enclosure. Hypericum's victory, in such dramatic circumstances, kindled the young Princess's enthusiasm for racing. During her reign Her Majesty has been leading owner in 1954 with £40,993 and in 1957 with £62,211.

I do not think Hypericum stayed one and a half miles, but I hope Doug will forgive me for saying that he did not give her much chance to do so in the Oaks. In the same way that Charlie Elliott on Flamingo and Gordon Richards on Sunny Trace cut one another's throats in the 1928 Derby, Eph on Lord Rosebery's Iona and Doug on Hypericum appeared to think they had only each other to beat in the Oaks. Hypericum was beaten early in the straight, while Iona had nothing in reserve when Harry Wragg loomed up on Sir Alfred Butt's Steady Aim who treated her as Felstead had treated Flamingo eighteen years earlier.

If Captain Allison had been less patient Doug would not have won the 1946 One Thousand Guineas and if Harry Carr picked the right one he would not have won the 1958 Two Thousand Guineas on Pall Mall, also in the royal colours. Captain Boyd Rochfort trained the American-bred colt Bald Eagle as well as Pall Mall, and in their gallops Bald Eagle had given the impression that he could pick up Pall Mall and carry him. When a stable jockey has to choose between two horses, and one of them belongs to the reigning monarch, all things being equal he would choose the one in the royal colours.

Bald Eagle's superiority, however, was so pronounced that Carr had no alternative but to ride him, leaving Pall Mall for Doug.

Pall Mall had performed without much distinction in the Two Thousand Guineas Trial Stakes at Kempton, which was run in very heavy going, but it was not appreciated at that time that he had to have it 'right on top' to be seen at his best.

Captain Boyd Rochfort had a very high opinion of Bald Eagle, and hoped that he would succeed where Prince Simon had failed so narrowly eight years earlier.

Unfortunately, Bald Eagle was to prove one of those infuriating horses who are lions at home but lambs in public, and he declined to exert himself in the Two Thousand Guineas. A month later in the Derby Harry Carr told me that Bald Eagle was cantering over the opposition at Tattenham Corner, but from that point on he didn't want to know.

The going at Newmarket was as firm as it had been soft at Kempton, and Pall Mall, with his light action, was a different horse. In a thrilling finish Doug on Pall Mall beat his brother Eph on Mr Jim Joel's Major Portion by half a length. Unlike Pall Mall, Major Portion was not happy on the firm going. I can only assume that Bald Eagle hated racing in England as he proved himself a champion on his return to the States, winning the Washington International two years running.

Doug's victory on Petite Etoile in the 1959 One Thousand Guineas was also 'by kind permission' of another jockey. Despite the fact that Aly Khan's filly had won the Free Handicap Lester Piggott chose to ride Collyria; and Doug therefore 'copped' for the ride on the grey filly, who in company with Sun Chariot and Meld were the three best fillies over one and a half miles in my lifetime. Petite Etoile was still on the upgrade when the One Thousand Guineas was run, and Doug had to ride for his life to win by a length from Mr Jakey Astor's Rosalba, with Paraguana, also in the colours of Aly Khan, four lengths away third.

Ridden by Lester Piggott, Petite Etoile won the Oaks by three lengths from the favourite Cantelo, who was to beat the colts in the St Leger. On the previous day Cantelo had been beaten by Collyria in the Park Hill Stakes, so the 1959 fillies must have been a bit out of the ordinary.

Doug's only other classic success was on Our Babu in the 1955 Two Thousand Guineas. Owned by Mr David Robinson and trained by Geoffrey Brooke, Our Babu triumphed in a terrific finish by a neck from Scobie Breasley's mount Tamerlaine, with the French colt Klairon a short head away third.

In fifteen years Doug rode 465 winners for Geoffrey Brooke's stable, and following the combination of Smith and Brooke became a popular form of wagering. The horses were always doing their best, and as it was not a betting stable they often started at longer odds than expected. Trainer and jockey were the best of friends, and during their long association I never heard of their having a difference of opinion.

Doug was also retained for a number of years by Harry Peacock, for whom he rode many winners, including Marmaduke Jinks in the Lincoln Handicap of 1937. Here again a very real affection existed between trainer and jockey. Harry Wragg retired at the end of 1946 and Doug was asked to succeed him as first jockey to Stanley House. It was a big decision to make, but after due consideration he accepted it, and in the course of eighteen years he rode 350 winners for the stable, a large proportion of them in the colours of Lord Derby. As I have said before, the best horse he ever rode was Alycidon, but the Stanley House stud was in a decline and Lord Derby won few big races in the post-war years. I shall, however, always think that Swallow Tail was an unlucky loser of the 1949 Derby, won by Nimbus, and had not Amour Drake beaten him a head for second place Doug would have won the race on an objection.

Doug was the stable jockey every trainer dreams about—a highly competent rider, straight as a die, who never asked permission to ride a horse from another stable when his own stable had one engaged in the same race, no matter how forlorn its chance might be.

Shortly after I began this book I was asked what I considered the most unlikely event which had come to pass on the Turf in my time. Without a moment's hesitation I answered 'Scobie'. Pressed to enlarge on this monosyllabic reply I went on to say that I thought that the stingiest bookmaker would have been happy to lay you 10,000/1 against a man from Wagga-Wagga, who had already toyed with the idea of retiring, arriving in this country for the first time at the age of thirty-seven and becoming champion jockey on four occasions.

The feat becomes even more surprising when we remember that following two reasonably successful seasons he decided to

ride no more in England. Fortunately for racing in this country
he changed his mind. It would be hard to imagine two jockeys
more dissimilar in style and tactics than Sir Gordon and Scobie,
but Sir Gordon, with the full approval of his owners, engaged
Scobie as his stable jockey in 1957. The partnership was not
broken until Scobie's retirement from the saddle at the end of
1968.

When Scobie was champion jockey for the first time in 1957
he was only the second Australian to be champion, his predecessor being Frank Wootton, who was leading rider from 1910
to 1912 inclusive.

Scobie came over to ride for the Druid's Lodge Stable when
that delightful personality and first-class trainer Noel Cannon
trained for Mr J. A. Dewar and Mr Jack Olding; but his
first classic success was on Mr Ley On's Ki Ming, trained by
Michael Beary, in the 1951 Two Thousand Guineas. By the
sprinter Ballyogan, Ki Ming had no pretensions to stay the
Derby distance, and his subsequent performances revealed that
he was at his best over six furlongs. The Derby that year was
won by Arctic Prince, trained by Willie Stephenson and ridden
by the hurdle-race rider Charlie Spares for Mr Joseph Mc-
Grath. This was far from being a vintage year, but Arctic
Prince was probably a pretty good colt. Unfortunately he broke
down when contesting the King George and Queen Elizabeth
Stakes and could not run again. Stephenson is one of our most
versatile trainers: he also saddled Oxo to win the 1959 Grand
National. Scobie's next classic victory was in the 1954 One
Thousand Guineas on Festoon in the colours of Mr J. A.
Dewar. Festoon, who beat Lester Piggott's mount Big Berry by
two lengths, was one of the loveliest fillies I have ever seen, but
she was by Fair Trial, few of whose stock stayed one and a half
miles, and Festoon was no exception.

Scobie had to wait ten years for his next classic winner, but
as it was in the Derby it was well worth waiting for. On the
strength of his runaway victory in the National Stakes Santa
Claus, who was by the 1945 St Leger winner Chamossaire, a
far from fashionable stallion, was made winter favourite for the
Derby, and after he had outclassed a moderate field for the

Irish Two Thousand Guineas he became a red-hot favourite at 15/8. As I have stressed before, some Derbys are more different than others and the 1964 Derby was peculiar in that never before have I seen the rider of the favourite lie so far out of his ground. The heavily backed second favourite Oncydium was beaten soon after reaching the straight, and with Santa Claus not even in the TV picture it seemed as if we were in for an old-fashioned turn-up for the books; the most likely one to do it appeared to be Mr Charles Engelhard's Indiana.

We were prepared to see Santa Claus one of the backmarkers at the top of the hill, but we expected to see him make up ground descending the hill to Tattenham Corner. But Scobie continued to hold him tight by the head and he was one of the last to enter the straight. When Scobie eventually picked him up Santa Claus fairly ate up the ground, though Scobie had to ride him hard to get within hail of Indiana, who still held a lead of several lengths approaching the last furlong. When he met the rising ground, however, Santa Claus increased his stride and swept by Indiana to win by a length.

Santa Claus was owned in partnership by Mr J. Ismay, whose colours he carried, and Mrs Darby Rogers, and was trained by the latter's son Mick, who had trained Hard Ridden, the 1958 Derby winner. I rate Santa Claus among the half-dozen best post-war Derby winners. Ridden by stable-lad Burke, who only had an occasional ride in public but had ridden him in the Irish Two Thousand Guineas, Santa Claus won the Irish Derby in a canter. I regard his defeat by the French colt Nasram, in a field of four for the King George VI and Queen Elizabeth Stakes, as a fluke. Burke was unfamiliar with the Ascot course and left him with too much to do. Ridden by Jimmy Lindley, he returned to his best form when finishing second to Prince Royal in the Prix de l'Arc de Triomphe.

As Scobie was not asked to ride Santa Claus again following his victory in the Derby, I assume that the colt's connections were dissatisfied with his riding at Epsom, though he rode him exactly as he had planned to do. He knew that Santa Claus would have all too much finishing speed for his opponents, provided he came down the hill without discomfort. He did not have the best of joints, and Scobie was taking no chances. Had he ridden him hell-for-leather down the hill he might have jarred himself, in which case he most certainly would not have won the Irish Derby.

Scobie's only other classic success was on Lady Zia Wernher's Charlottown, trained by Gordon Smyth, in the 1966 Derby.

Even those who had found fault with Scobie's riding of Santa Claus agreed that he rode a lovely race on the son of Charlottesville and the immortal Meld. On Santa Claus Scobie had challenged on the outside, but he hugged the rails throughout on Charlottown, thereby saving a length or more on all his opponents. Pretendre, ridden by the young jockey Paul Cook and trained by Sir Jack Jarvis, appeared to be going the better of the two 150 yards from home, but Scobie still had a little bit up his sleeve and Charlottown won a thrilling race by a neck. I had napped and backed the second, and would have drawn my money and received a pat on the back from my editor had not the fifty-two-year-old from Wagga-Wagga excelled himself. Steve in his hey day could not have done it better.

As a judge of pace Scobie has had no superior in my time, and though I have often thought he had left it too late I cannot recall his actually doing so on more than a couple of occasions, and even then I wasn't sure. I watched Scobie ride brilliant races on almost every racecourse in this country and on a couple of occasions at Longchamp, but if he excelled on any one course more than another it was at Brighton.

Like all Australians Scobie loved the rails, but at Brighton he usually made his effort towards the centre of the course where the ground is more level than it is near the rails. Gordon Richards, who for years appeared almost unbeatable on the switchback course, employed the same tactics. I have lost count of the number of times I have seen two horses battling it out when from out of the blue has come Scobie, with his mount perfectly balanced, to beat them both. Scobie may not have been Steve's equal as a horseman, but he had his delicacy of touch and only used his whip as a last resort when all the other aids had failed. Like Steve, he refrained from punishing his mounts when he realised that they had no more to give, and

L

this acceptance of what he knew to be inevitable, though it may not have appeared so from the stands, occasionally evoked the displeasure of backers.

Meld, whom I regard as the best filly I have had the pleasure of watching, had several children who bore little resemblance to their illustrious mother before she gave birth to Charlottown. Trained by Captain Boyd Rochfort, Meld split a pastern early in her two-year-old career and did not make her début till the autumn when she gave promise of being a champion. Her first race as a three-year-old was in the One Thousand Guineas where she stayed on well to beat Lord Rosebery's Aberlady by two lengths. This was a good workmanlike performance though the opposition was of no great account. Her trainer, however, realising that she would be a stone better with another half mile to travel, thought she was sure to win the Oaks; and *how* she won it. Taking the lead early in the straight she galloped right away from her opponents to beat Ark Royal by six lengths with Reel In three lengths away third. I have no doubt that Meld's performance was the best I have seen in this race, because Ark Royal, in all her races confined to her own sex, proved herself as superior to them as Meld was to her, and would have won nine races out of ten for the Oaks.

In the autumn of 1955 our stables were subjected to one of the worst coughing epidemics in living memory, and all but two of Captain Boyd Rochfort's string were afflicted by the time of the St Leger. Fortunately, one of the two immune was Meld, but she coughed on the morning of the race and was sickening for the complaint when she went to the post. Harry Carr told me that he knew she was not herself from the moment the race started, and only her great courage carried her through. Lester Piggott, rider of Miss Dorothy Paget's Nucleus, lodged an objection but this was quickly overruled. The luckless Acropolis developed the cough three days before the race was run. Had he and Meld met when both were at the top of their form we might have seen a splendid race.

Comparisons between horses of different generations are a matter of pure conjecture, and I have no doubt that many good judges consider that Sun Chariot or Petite Etoile have just as good or better claims to be considered the best filly of the past fifty years. Neither Meld nor Sun Chariot remained in training as four-year-olds, but both fillies defeated the best colts around at the time in the St Leger, Sun Chariot beating the Derby winner Watling Street by five lengths. Petite Etoile, on the other hand, beat the subsequent St Leger winner Cantelo by three lengths in the Oaks, and the following year she defeated the previous year's Derby winner Parthia in the Coronation Cup, going on to win the race again as a five-year-old.

16 Charlie Smirke and Windsor Lad

Charlie Smirke warned off – Inhuman sentence on an inno-cent man – Hubert Allison, a good starter but an unreliable witness – Welcome Gift, a bad starter, who got jockeys into trouble in India – Marcus Marsh buys Windsor Lad for a maharajah for 1,300 guineas – 'The best horse that ever lived,' said Charlie Smirke.

As a man's sins, real or imaginary, are more entertaining than his virtues, Charlie Smirke's five-year suspension will be dis-cussed when his four Derby victories and other feats of excep-tional skill as a jockey are no more than entries in the record books.

This is, of course, grossly unfair, but while human nature re-mains as it is mouths will continue to water when some racon-teur treats us to a juicy piece of scandal, while a hand will be raised to the mouth to conceal a yawn if he follows it up with details of the month's good deed.

Charlie Smirke talked too much for his own good, but on the one occasion when his career depended on his own eloquence he was tongue-tied, and his silence was interpreted as an admission of guilt. Varied versions of the scandal of Charlie and Welcome Gift have been told a thousand times and I am only raking it up again forty-three years later because I believe that my version establishes Charlie's innocence beyond any shadow of doubt.

The two-year-old, Welcome Gift, was an 11/4-on chance left at the post in a race at Gatwick in 1928. I was present at Gatwick that day, and though I cannot vouch for what happened at the start I do know that he was as firm as a rock in the market, which he most certainly would not have been had any bookmaker had an inkling that Charlie was going to pull him up at the start. The local stewards, however, were not satisfied with Charlie's explanation; they referred the matter to the stewards of the Jockey Club, who withdrew Charlie's licence after hearing the evidence of the starter, Captain Allison, and another jockey, Kenny Robertson.

What evidence of value midget jockey Robertson could provide, I cannot imagine. He was a nice little chap, and at the age of forty weighed little more than six stone, but it was surely not his business to give evidence against a fellow jockey in such a vital matter, and most improper of the stewards to allow him to do so. The only occasion when a jockey should be allowed to testify is in the case of an objection or when there is an accusation of foul riding; even then his evidence should be taken with several grains of salt as should have been the evidence of Captain Allison.

Hubert Allison was a good starter, and a more upright man has never pulled a lever, but to describe him as obstinate would be an understatement. If he got an idea into his head nothing in heaven or earth would induce him to change his mind. He was a close friend of my brother Geoffrey, and through him I knew Allison quite well.

I have never told the following story before but I think it demonstrates what a hopelessly unreliable witness Allison could be. In the same fateful year of 1928, Felix Leach junior trained a four-year-old called Doch-an-doris. He had proved himself one of the best sprinters in the country the previous year, winning the King's Stand Stakes at Ascot among other good races. As a four-year-old, however, he was turning out an expensive failure. He was a very quick beginner and had won all his races by opening up a lead and defying his opponents to catch him. He was still as fast out of the gate as ever, but had developed the infuriating habit of dropping his bit when called upon to resist the challenge of his rivals close home.

In my presence Felix told his brother Chubb, who always

rode him, to adopt different tactics in a race at Sandown the following day. The new plan was to steady him at the start, and give him plenty of time to settle down, hoping that as the result of not having had to exert himself in the early stages Doch-and-doris would go through with his effort. At the same time Felix instructed me to put £100 on him to win, which may or may not have been the entire stable commission.

The new tactics were a failure. Deprived of his greatest asset, his initial speed, Doch-an-doris sulked and never got within hail of the leaders, finishing well down the course. That evening Geoffrey rang me up to say that Allison was dining with him and had told him that Chubb Leach had made no attempt to get away on Doch-an-doris, whom he described as 'a shocking non-trier'.

I asked to speak to Allison and told him that I had put £100 on Doch-an-doris for the trainer. He replied: 'You were the dupe, in case they were had up.' I pointed out at £100 I was a rather expensive dupe, but nothing would convince him that Chubb Leach had made any attempt to win the race. I can only assume that had the stewards enquired into the running of Doch-an-doris Allison would have given the same damning evidence he gave in the case of Welcome Gift.

At the end of that season Doch-an-doris was gelded, and the veterinary surgeon reported that only one of his testicles had dropped; the other was wedged where it would give him severe pain if he fully extended himself. As a gelding Doch-an-doris developed a renewed zest for racing and won several races.

I believe that provided a horse is well treated he enjoys racing, which to him is a normal function, as is jumping fences, and nine times out of ten those who take a dislike to racing have either been ill-treated or are suffering from some physical disability. Racehorses have long memories, though they are not particularly intelligent animals by reason of the fact that for generations human beings have done all their thinking for them and have directed all their activities.

I don't know who or what it was that gave Welcome Gift his aversion for the starting gate, but ridden by Bobby Dick in his only other race in England he behaved very badly at the start and lost several lengths. The opposition, however, was weak, and he made up the lost ground and won. He was sold to Mr Shantidas Askuran, a wealthy Hindu, for £3,000, a big sum in those days for a horse destined to race in India. Welcome Gift would not go near the starting gate when he arrived in Bombay, where at that time I was a Stipendiary Steward with the Western India Turf Club. I have never seen a horse so determined not to start, and he would not have done so at all if the starter, Colin Gulilland, had not vowed that he would make Welcome Gift start or die in the attempt. He and the stable jockey Bill Bowley displayed monumental patience with this obstinate horse, and eventually it was rewarded. Having jumped off without giving the slightest trouble he proved himself the good horse we knew him to be and won two races.

But Colin's triumph was short-lived, as when Welcome Gift was sent to race in Calcutta under a different starter he was as mulish as ever and got several jockeys into trouble, including Rae Johnstone. Back in Bombay, Welcome Gift wouldn't consent to start even for Gulilland. And this, mark you, was the horse Smirke was supposed to have prevented from starting and on account of which he was deprived of his livelihood for five years. Had he been sentenced for that period it would have been a savage punishment, but what he got was worse: he was merely informed that his licence was withdrawn. For inhumanity, the indeterminate sentence is on a par with the Chinese water torture. On the first of every January for five years Charlie Smirke applied for his licence: year after year he was turned down, and given no intimation as to when, if ever, he would be allowed to ride again. Finally, in October 1933, it was restored.

Such an experience would have broken the spirit of 999 out of every 1,000 young men—but not Charlie's. He emerged from the ordeal unscathed. Such was his confidence that although his first winner had at least seven pounds in hand, Charlie contrived for it to win by only a head. His services were soon in demand again, and watching him riding and listening to his views on all and sundry it was hard to believe that he had not been riding winners every day of the week for the past five years instead of eating his heart out in the wilderness.

I have been told by those who knew old man Dick Wootton and his sons Stanley and Frank in their riding days that if Stanley had not become too heavy to ride on the flat before he was out of his teens he might have rivalled his famous brother, who was one of the all-time greats (though he too became too heavy to ride on the flat when still in his early twenties). Stanley, who served with distinction in World War I and was awarded the Military Cross, set up as a trainer at Epsom as soon as peace was declared. Although horses trained by him won a vast number of races and earned him large sums of money in bets it was as a trainer of apprentices that he will be always remembered.

The most famous of these was Charlie Smirke, who rode his first winner at Derby in April 1922 at the age of sixteen; in 1924 he rode seventy-eight winners and in 1925 he rode his first big winner excluding those of some important handicaps—Mr James de Rothschild's Reine Lumière in the Grand Prix de Paris, the race in which both Steve Donoghue and Fred Bullock were seriously injured. Most of Stanley Wootton's apprentices were Cockneys, recruited from working-class homes, Staff Ingham being the only one to make the grade from a middle-class background. Staff, one of our leading trainers for many years, might have been as successful as Smirke had he not stood six feet in his stockings at the age of seventeen. He was only fourteen when he won the Royal Hunt Cup for King George V on Weathervane. The stewards knew that the youthful Smirke betted in the same way they knew that his buddy Elliott betted. It is, however, well-nigh impossible to obtain proof that a jockey bets as no bookmaker would accept a wager from him except through a third party. The stewards were out to get Smirke and Elliott, but I am not for one moment suggesting that they had Smirke's betting in mind when they warned him off on the evidence of the starter.

A steward who sat on the inquiry told me years afterwards that Smirke put up no defence, but neither he nor his colleagues appreciated that this unaccustomed silence was a result of Charlie's being so overawed that he lost the power of speech. It was certainly ironical that a man who had the reputation for being too garrulous and self-assured should have been struck dumb when it really mattered.

It may be asked why, if he was innocent, was he so nervous? To be arraigned before the stewards of the Jockey Club is a terrifying experience in any circumstances, in addition to which Smirke was well aware that they were gunning for him on account of his betting. The stewards have a great sense of occasion, and the atmosphere is guaranteed to strike terror into the staunchest heart. I was once interrogated by the stewards at Newmarket in connection with an article I had written, and though I was not in the dock as Smirke was, I was scared stiff. They were most polite to me, but I had to pass my tongue across my parched lips before I could reply, and when the words came I did not recognise my own voice. I was not being accused of any felony, but I had an awful feeling of guilt.

Charlie Smirke had his faults and his enemies, one of the most formidable being himself. I take my hat off to him, however, for his courage in the face of adversity, and for his determination that when his reprieve came he would be mentally and physically capable of carrying on where he left off. A disqualified person is not allowed in the precincts of a racing stable or on ground used for the training of racehorses. What a temptation it must have been to say 'To hell with it' as January succeeded January and he was still warned off, a social pariah in the eyes of the racing world.

Stanley Wootton was a strict disciplinarian, and as a teacher of jockeyship has never had an equal. His apprentices did not need to copy a senior jockey; they did what the guv'nor told them and in no time were riding winners in his cerise jacket and straw sleeves. He had forty horses of his own, but once his boys had ridden a few winners in his colours their services were in demand by trainers over the length and breadth of the country. Every boy was told 'get the rails and stick there', and if one of them won a race having gone the long way round he was 'for it'. Arthur Wragg, Bobby Dick, Pat Donoghue, Marshall, Caldwell, Carroll, Turtle, Cordell and McGee are just a few names that come to mind.

At the time his licence was withdrawn Charlie Smirke had recently been appointed first jockey to the Aga Khan, a tremendous responsibility for so young a jockey, but one which left him quite unmoved. Never for one moment in his career did he have the slightest doubt that he could carry out the job in hand.

His colossal self-confidence was sometimes construed as conceit, but I regarded him as having the courage of his convictions. He believed himself to be the best jockey of all time and he may well have been. Marcus Marsh, the one trainer with whom Charlie was always on the best of terms, had no doubt he was the best jockey and in his delightfully entertaining autobiography *Racing with the Gods* he wrote: 'Charlie could ride work on a horse he had never seen in his life before, and could come back and tell you just about everything you could possibly want to know about him.'

Charlie rode only two winners in what was left of the 1933 season after his licence had been restored, but Marcus Marsh, son of the man who trained Persimmon, Diamond Jubilee and Minoru for King Edward VII, had seen enough to satisfy himself he was the same old Charlie, bursting with confidence and determined to reinstate himself as the best jockey in the world.

In 1931 Marcus had been commissioned by the Maharajah of Rijpipla, whom I shall henceforth refer to as Pip, as he was known to all his friends, to buy him a yearling. Marcus, a splendid judge of horses of all ages, secured one of the biggest bargains ever when he gave 1,300 guineas for a bay colt by Blandford out of Resplendent.

Bred by Mr Dan Sullevan, he was not an outstandingly good-looking colt, but Marcus appreciated his tremendous potentialities even at this early stage. He was called Windsor Lad on account of the fact that Pip lived at Old Windsor, where he entertained lavishly. Windsor Lad was still unfurnished when, ridden by Fred Lane, he won the Criterion Stakes by a short head from Bright Bird in October. Pip was good enough to advise me to have a small bet on him, and he started at the nice price of 100/8.

The official handicapper, however, was not particularly im-

pressed with him and gave him only 8 stone 3 lb in the Free
Handicap, 18 lb less than Colombo. Windsor Lad wintered well
but he was still unfurnished when he won the Chester Vase, in
which he was ridden by Freddy Fox as Charlie Smirke could
not do the weight. I had wondered whether such a big long-
striding horse would be suited by the Chester course, but he
came round the turns without the slightest difficulty, a good
omen for his prospects at Epsom. The following week, ridden
by Charlie Smirke, Windsor Lad won the Newmarket Stakes
(a mile and a quarter) in great style from Lord Rosebery's
Flamenco.

When a backward three-year-old starts to improve in the
spring of the year an ugly duckling can mature into a beautiful
swan in the space of a couple of weeks, and Windsor Lad had
filled out and let down into a real racehorse when Marcus un-
boxed him at Epsom. The big frame was now filled with a
lovely picture.

I have described the 1933 Derby when writing about
Colombo, and it only remains for me to say that Marcus Marsh
and Charlie Smirke agree with my view that Colombo did not
stay one and a half miles and that he could never have beaten
Windsor Lad over that distance. I was a member of Pip's
celebration party at the Savoy on the evening of Windsor Lad's
victory, and watched the film of the race with Charlie Smirke.
It was not till he acted as commentator that I fully appreciated
how easily Windsor Lad had won. Like so many good horses
Windsor Lad was disinclined to exert himself when he had nothing to race with, and Charlie told me that had he pushed him
out he would have won by three or four lengths. If he had done
so Rae Johnsone would not have been accused of throwing the
race away, while even Steve's ghost writer would have thought
twice before he wrote that if Steve or any English jockey had
ridden Colombo he would have won unchallenged.

On the strength of his Derby victory, with at least 7 lb in
hand, Windsor Lad looked a certainty for the Eclipse Stakes,
as he would have won just as convincingly had the Derby been
over ten furlongs. The 1933 Derby field was undoubtedly one
of the best to go to the post between the wars. In the Eclipse

Stakes Windsor Lad was meeting older horses for the first time, but they had accomplished nothing which suggested they could beat the 1933 Derby winner. There is, however, no such thing as a certainty in racing, and Windsor Lad could only finish third. As he dismounted Charlie apologised, saying it was the worst race he had ever ridden.

He had hugged the rails as he had been taught to do by Stanley Wootton, though there was no need to save the odd length on a horse which both he and Marcus believed to have 10 lb in hand. Had he pulled to the outside, early in the straight, Windsor Lad would have won by as far as Charlie deemed necessary, instead of which he found himself shut in a box from which it would have defied the genius of Houdini to extricate himself. When an opening eventually appeared King Salmon and Umidwar were uncatchable; but Windsor Lad was magnificent in defeat, and fifty yards past the winning post he was well clear. If the race had been over the Derby distance he would have won on the bit.

After this defeat Pip sold Windsor Lad to Mr Martin Benson for £50,000, one of the conditions of the sale being that he remained with Marcus Marsh. Five years later Mr Benson paid £60,000 for Nearco as a sire. Windsor Lad won the Great Yorkshire Stakes, a race which has now been superseded by the Great Voltigeur Stakes, in a hack canter. So superior was he to his contemporaries by this time that the St Leger appeared to be a formality for him. So it proved to be, though Tiberius, beaten by two lengths, won the following year's Gold Cup by eight lengths.

Windsor Lad and Easton, first and second in the Derby, met again in the Coronation Cup. There were only four runners, one of which was Windsor Lad's pace-maker. This unfortunate horse, however, could not go fast enough to fulfil his mission, and Windsor Lad went to the front after going three furlongs and stayed there. Easton was a very good horse but was unlucky in being foaled in the same year as a much better one. Windsor Lad's time was the same as when winning the Derby, which was a record. Two years later Charlie Smirke set up a new record on Mahmoud which still stands, though Charlie believes that Windsor Lad could have picked up Mahmoud and carried him, and that goes for Bahram as well.

It had been assumed that Windsor Lad would go for the Gold Cup at Ascot, in which race he would have met the French colt Brantome, who had a tremendous reputation in his own country; but Mr Benson and Marcus Marsh decided on the Rous Memorial Stakes of seven furlongs. A great horse is a good horse over any distance, and though Windsor Lad had not run over a shorter distance than ten furlongs since he was a two-year-old he demonstrated his versatility by winning from the useful Pampas Grass, to whom he was conceding 25 lb.

Windsor Lad's final race was in the Eclipse Stakes, in which he appeared a bigger certainty than in the previous year. Marcus had no doubt that at four years old he had only just reached his peak, but a week before the race he twisted a joint. The swelling subsided but his trainer had only been able to give him a couple of canters before sending him to Sandown.

At no point in the race was Windsor Lad galloping with his usual freedom, but he had headed Fair Trial, much fancied by Marcus' uncle, Fred Darling, two out, when it happened, and a groan went up from the packed stands. He stumbled badly, but recovered, and in a thrilling finish held off the renewed challenge of Fair Trial by half a length. It was obvious when Charlie pulled him up that he had broken down and as he hobbled to the winning enclosure he and Charlie were given an ovation which they richly deserved. Windsor Lad's courage and Charlie's skill in holding him together, a lame horse, through that last dramatic furlong, had prevailed, and all honour to them.

Charlie still has no doubt that Windsor Lad was the best horse that ever lived, and while I would not go quite as far as that I have no doubt that he was a very great one.

Windsor Lad's career as a stallion ended in tragedy. He sired one brilliant horse in the Irish Triple Crown winner Windsor Slipper, who owing to the war raced only in Ireland, where he was supreme. In 1938 Windsor Lad developed sinus trouble from which he never fully recovered, and in 1943 he was put down. Had he not contracted the disease this essentially masculine horse might well have proved himself as great a stallion as he was a racehorse. His daughter Phase was the dam of the Oaks winner Neasham Belle and her son Narrator won the Coronation Cup.

17 The Aga Khan and Aly Khan

Mahmoud wins 1936 Derby in record time – Butters is suspicious of Aly Khan and Charlie Smirke – Butters retires and Marcus Marsh takes over – Gordon Richards and Charlie Smirke see eye to eye for the first and only time – Smirke rides race of his life on Palestine – Aly Khan tries to sell Tulyar but fails to get a bid – He wins Derby, Eclipse Stakes, 'King George' and St Leger the following year – Marcus Marsh, leading trainer in 1952, gets the sack – The Aga Khan's horses go to France – Head v. Smirke – Smirke returns to England – Three great fillies – Aly killed in motor accident.

As the Aga Khan had already engaged Charlie Smirke to ride for him in 1936 he was the obvious choice to ride Bahram in the 1935 St Leger when Freddy Fox was incapacitated on the eve of the race. So within two years of his reinstatement Charlie won a Derby and two St Legers.

Frank Butters was in no way responsible for engaging Smirke and he insisted on his right to decide who should ride which in the probable event of the stable having more than one runner in a race. Sir Alfred Butt had retained Dick Perryman and his Noble King was an impressive winner of the Greenham Stakes in which Mahmoud finished unplaced. The going was very heavy, conditions which Noble King revelled in, and which Mahmoud, who was giving his stable companion a stone, detested.

Smirke could not do the weight on the Aga Khan's Taj

Akbar in the Nonsuch Stakes, now known as the Blue Riband
Stakes, so it hardly needs saying that Butters engaged Gordon
Richards, and this charming little colt with the best of actions
won in good style from Lord Astor's Rhodes Scholar, who later
that season was to prove himself a very good horse indeed up
to one and a quarter miles. With Gordon again in the saddle,
Taj Akbar won the Chester Vase in great style and as Beckhampton had no runner in the Derby, Butters decided that
Gordon must ride him at Epsom.

I watched the race for the Two Thousand Guineas that year
with Aly Khan. Steve Donoghue rode Mahmoud and Smirke
Bala Hissar, who started at the shorter price. Aly, of course, had
backed them both, and was upset when Mahmoud appeared to
be slowly away, though I think that this was Steve's intent.
Neither he nor Butters thought that Mahmoud would stay a
mile, much less a mile and a half, unless he was waited with.
These doubts, concerning Mahmoud's stamina, arose from the
fact that his maternal grand-dam was Mumtaz Mahal, who was
the fastest filly that ever lived but could only stay six furlongs.

Steve, having got Mahmoud to settle down, tracked his more
fancied stable-companion Bala Hissar; but when the latter
dropped away before reaching the Dip Steve found himself in
the lead earlier than he had planned. In a desperately close
finish Lord Astor's Pay Up, ridden by Bobby Dick, beat
Mahmoud by a short head. Aly thought that Steve had ridden
a bad race on Mahmoud, a view with which I disagreed though
I considered him an unlucky loser.

Frank Butters saddled four in the Derby—Taj Akbar (Richards), Noble King (Perryman), Mahmoud (Smirke), and Bala
Hissar (Bobby Jones)—and he fancied them in that order. On
the strength of Taj Akbar's fluent victories at Epsom and
Chester Gordon fancied him more than he had any of his
previous Derby mounts. He started second favourite to Pay Up
at 6/1, Mahmoud being at the generous price of 100/8.

Taj Akbar had to be waited with, and he was one of the last
to enter the straight, with Mahmoud in the middle of the field.
Gordon told me that Taj Akbar was going like a winner, but
two furlongs from home, when he was moving up to challenge

Mahmoud, he caught an almighty bump from a tiring horse which knocked him out of his stride. This left Mahmoud in undisputed command, and he won by three lengths from Taj Akbar, with Thankerton, who was clear entering the straight, third. Thankerton was a son of Manna and that remarkable mare Verdict and had he been ridden with a little more discretion he must have gone very close to winning.

Charlie Smirke rode his customary brainy race on Mahmoud, who had exactly the right conditions for him, with the going as hard as a road and very little grass. Mahmoud, with his feathery action, flew over the ground to set up a new course record of 2 min. 33·8 sec., which still stands. Nijinsky, however, on much slower going, came within a fraction of a second of this time, a truly astonishing performance.

Mahmoud, who was only the third grey horse to win the Derby, was also one of the smaller winners of the race, standing only 15·3 hands. He contracted heel bug in the summer, and as his heels had barely recovered when he went to Doncaster and the distance was some way beyond his best, he did well to finish third in the St Leger to Boswell and Fearless Fox. The winner was owned by Mr William Woodward, trained by Captain Boyd Rochfort and ridden by Rufus Beasley. Boswell remained in training as a four-year-old and won the Eclipse Stakes, but Mahmoud, like all the Aga Khan's Derby winners, was hurried off to stud at the end of his three-year-old career.

At no time was there any love lost between Sir Gordon Richards and Charlie Smirke. The cheeky Cockney extrovert wasn't Gordon's cup of tea, and though many people thought that Charlie's dislike of Gordon was the result of jealousy, I do not agree. I have always attributed it to his inability to comprehend how it was that so much adulation should be bestowed on what he considered the second-best jockey, and a poor second best at that.

So elated was Charlie, who had worn the distinguishing green cap when he beat Gordon in the Aga's first colours, that he was not the most popular member of the weighing room for the next week or two. He had proved himself a good loser, but he did not appreciate that it is just as important to be a good winner.

M

Butters was undoubtedly a great trainer, but his methods did not conform with those of Fred Darling, Marcus Marsh, Noel Murless and Captain Boyd Rochfort, beside whose horses his string looked lean and hungry. Butters and Jack Jarvis believed that 7 lb of superfluous flesh was the equivalent to a 7 lb penalty, and their charges stripped for a race as hard as boards and trained to the hour. A horse of theirs could never be described as 'looking a picture', both men believing that handsome is as handsome does.

No two horses are alike, but the majority will stand up to plenty of work once they are fit. On the other hand one gallop at three-quarter speed can ruin an unfit animal. Physical fitness must be attained by slow work, the slower the better, a fact which is overlooked by some trainers of my acquaintance. These men are delighted when a two-year-old, who is as fat as butter, and is out for an airing, shows great speed before he blows up. Then they can't understand why the next time he runs he finishes down the course.

I cannot recall having seen a horse trained by Sir John Jarvis or Frank Butters run in an unfit condition, though this does not mean that their runners did not often hold plenty of scope for improvement. The records of both men speak for themselves, and their charges kept their form over long periods, proof that they had not been over-trained. A typical example of Butters' skill was provided by a gelding called Near Relation, belonging to Sir Alfred Butt. Butters saddled him to win a three-year-old maiden plate at Lincoln on the opening day of the season, and won the Cesarewitch with him the same year. Although Butters and Jarvis employed similar training methods they were poles apart in character. Sir Jack was an extrovert, a great talker and a highly entertaining companion. The most volatile of men, he would fly off the handle and hurl abuse at his victim, usually his jockey. His anger was short-lived and he never bore a grudge; but when he was in one of his tantrums he could be awe-inspiring, and he would have reached a better understanding with his jockeys by retaining his composure. Two, who shall be nameless, became so rattled that they temporarily lost confidence in themselves, a disastrous thing to happen to a jockey: he who does the wrong thing may still win, but the ditherer is doomed to failure.

Although Sir Jack sometimes, to put it mildly, questioned his jockeys' competence, he never questioned their integrity even if he thought they should have won. In the wartime classics horses trained by him for Lord Rosebery suffered a series of narrow defeats, but he was always the first to congratulate the winners.

Frank Butters was introspective, and behind that open countenance and those steadfast blue eyes there was a deep suspicion of his fellow men. No more upright man ever held a trainer's licence and one only had to be in his company for a few minutes to realise he was incapable of a dishonourable action. On a racecourse he was a man of few words, though when the day's work was done he became an agreeable companion. He had trained in Austria-Hungary before World War I, and was interned there throughout the war. He subsequently trained in Italy, before succeeding George Lambton as Lord Derby's trainer in 1927. He trained four classic winners for Stanley House, but lost his job three years later. In all he trained fifteen classic winners.

His deep-rooted suspicion of jockeys meant that Beary, Smirke, and the others he suspected of betting seldom got to know a horse really well before they rode it in a big race. This antagonised them and for a man of such wide experience he was surprisingly tactless. Smirke was understandably indignant that his loyalty should be questioned. When a man has been warned off for five years he is apt to be somewhat 'prickly', whereas a man who has never been in any sort of trouble would regard a suspicion of his integrity as a joke. Frank Butters did not bet, and though in Aly Khan and Sir Alfred Butt he trained for two of the heaviest punters on the turf he liked to think that he trained for non-gambling owners. At somewhat irregular intervals Aly Khan and Charlie Smirke were on very friendly terms, which infuriated Butters, who thought they were plotting behind his back.

I am often asked if I am in favour of jockeys being allowed to back their own mounts, as they are in the United States. My answer is a thousand times no. In America all betting is on the

Tote and therefore in ready money, so there is no fear of a jockey getting into deep water. In this country all bets of any size are 'on the nod' (as credit bets are called). If a jockey loses it is his own affair so long as he can settle, but it is when he can't settle that he becomes a menace to society.

Let us say he owes £1,000 and is due to ride a hot favourite, who may carry a million pounds of public money. His commission agent and bookmaker see this as a heaven-sent opportunity to touch him for their £1,000 and win several thousand more into the bargain. So they tell him that if the hot favourite gets beaten they will 'knock a monkey off the old', which, in case you don't know, means that if the jockey stops the hot favourite his liability will be reduced by £500.

A jockey with a good job and no financial worries is crazy if he bets. Every time he does so he is committing an offence for which he can be warned off. But one cannot legislate for the compulsive gambler any more than one can for the alcoholic. Those of us who have never felt tempted either to bet in sums which we cannot afford or to drink quantities of alcohol far beyond our capacity cannot appreciate the longing of the addict. We have no reason therefore to feel smug and self-righteous, as there is no great virtue in resisting a temptation that isn't there.

Charlie Smirke had a very high regard for the Aga Khan, as had all the jockeys who rode for him. He would invite them to his villa, to the Ritz, or wherever he might be staying, and talk to them as equals, asking them what they thought of his horses and of the horses they would be likely to meet. In return, he would give them sound advice, drawn from his long experience of life in many parts of the world. He never questioned their integrity, and they never let him down. Smirke's resentment at the suspicion in which he was held by Butters was therefore understandable. He might have a big bet on one of the Aga's horses and encourage Aly to have an even bigger one, but this was no concern of the Aga's trainer.

Charlie was a man of strong loyalties and equally strong dislikes: a man was either a grand fellow or a bastard—it was as simple as that. He would go to the ends of the earth for

Marcus Marsh, but he wouldn't cross the room for Frank Butters. The Aga Khan spent the war years in Switzerland, having disposed of most of his bloodstock. Marcus Marsh spent over four years as a prisoner of war, having joined the Royal Air Force as a rear gunner at the age of thirty-six and been shot down over enemy-occupied territory. Charlie Smirke had seen active service with the Eighth Army in its advance through Sicily to the mainland.

Following the victory of Windsor Lad little had gone right for Marcus, but he was deservedly popular, and within a few months of his release he was training winners at Egerton House, which he had leased from Major Macdonald Buchanan. Needless to say Charlie Smirke was his jockey.

When a man starts his life all over again at the age of forty-two he needs a bit of luck, and Marcus got it in the shape of a far from handsome and unfashionably bred horse called The Bug. Charlie had ridden him in Ireland and advised his owner, Mr Wachman, to send him to be trained by Marcus in England, where there was more money to be won. The Bug proved himself the best sprinter in the country at a time when there were some very fast horses in training. His performance in winning the Wokingham Stakes in a canter at Ascot as a three-year-old with 8 stone 7 lb in the saddle was the best performance I have seen in that race.

In 1949 Frank Butters met with a serious accident when riding his bicycle, sustaining permanent damage to his brain. In the years he trained for the Aga Khan he won all the classics except the One Thousand Guineas, which he had won for Lord Derby with Tide-way. His most sensational achievements were to saddle the first two in the 1936 Derby and four out of the first five in the 1932 St Leger. He trained the winner of the St Leger on five occasions.

The Aga Khan was very grieved at this sad accident to his trainer, who had served him so well, and when I met him racing at Longchamp he was in very low spirits. His studs were no longer producing animals of the class of Blenheim, Bahram and Mahmoud, all of whom he had sold, and he told me that Frank Butters was irreplaceable. He attributed the deterioration of

British bloodstock to the dearth of good stallions, although he was hardly in a position to complain since he had sold three Derby winners himself.

He consulted Gordon Richards and Charlie Smirke as to who should replace Frank Butters. Independently of one another, they both voted for Marcus Marsh. This was probably the only occasion on which they agreed on any subject.

By this time Marcus had collected a useful string of horses at Egerton House; all his owners were personal friends, and though as the Aga Khan's trainer he would have what had long been regarded as the number one job in the racing world, he needed time for reflection before he accepted it. Finally, he decided to do so, though in succeeding Frank Butters he was on a hiding to nothing; if he swept the board in the classics people would say he was only carrying on where Butters left off, while if the horses did not prove up to classic standards, the uninitiated, who form the nucleus of the racing community, would say that he was not up to the job.

In his last season Butters trained a brilliant grey two-year-old colt called Palestine, by Fair Trial out of Una, by Tetratema. He had won six of his seven races, his only defeat being in his final race, the Middle Park Stakes, when with odds of 7/2 laid on him he was well beaten by Masked Light, ridden by Doug Smith. Having had his first race in April he had probably gone over the top.

Gordon Richards had ridden him in all his races except for the National Breeders' Produce Stakes at Sandown in which he was ridden by Charlie Smirke. He had shown tremendous initial speed and it was not till he was headed close home by Masked Light in his final race that he saw another horse.

If he was to stay the mile of the Two Thousand Guineas he must be taught to settle down. Charlie Smirke took him in hand and he was quite a handful. He declined to drop his bit in the Henry VIII Stakes at Hurst Park. Even though he won that race, a mile against second-raters at Hurst Park is a very different pair of shoes to the Rowley Mile and a field of top-class three-year-olds.

Prince Simon was regarded by Captain Boyd Rochfort as the

most promising colt he had ever trained, but by this time Palestine was amenable to restraint, and in the early stages of the race Charlie settled him down and proceeded to ride what was probably the race of his life. Having taken the lead soon after the Bushes he rode Palestine for all he was worth running into the Dip, thereby gaining an invaluable lead. Harry Carr did everything possible on Prince Simon, but the winning post came a yard too soon for him and Palestine secured the verdict by a short head.

It was a wonderful start to Marcus' career as trainer to the Aga Khan, especially since many good judges thought that Palestine would not stay a mile. The promise of such a beginning was not to be fulfilled, but this was not the fault of either Marcus or Charlie—the Aga Khan's studs both in Ireland and Normandy were on the decline.

In the course of my racing career the studs belonging to Lord Derby, M. Boussac and the Aga Khan reached pinnacles of success hitherto undreamed of in the history of the Turf; but although each of them went through these periods when it seemed futile to contest their supremacy, they all declined. So rapid and catastrophic was their fall from grace that in the space of a few short years the produce of families which had reigned supreme were no longer good enough to contest the classics. Success and failure in racing are built on a variety of factors, but I have little doubt there is one common factor contributing to the decline of these three great studs. Hindsight knowledge can make wizards of us all, and it now seems clear that in all three studs speed was neglected to some extent in an endeavour to introduce more stamina.

At the end of the Second World War 80 per cent of Europe's best stayers were owned by M. Boussac, which might be thought a very happy state of affairs for him, though in point of fact it should have been recognised as a red light. If stayers are mated with stayers they breed horses which stay too long in the same place. Studs rise to fame on speed and yet more speed, and though a stud which is producing only short runners must introduce stamina to correct the balance, it must be used very sparingly.

When M. Boussac's stayers were sweeping the board, Stanley

House, in company with every stud in England and Ireland, was producing horses which did not stay a mile and a half. As I have said in a previous chapter, there were no long-distance races worth winning during the war. Can it be that in order to remedy the situation too much stamina was introduced too quickly so that the most important ingredient, the sizzling speed, went flat?

The decline of the Aga Khan's stud began with the sale of Blenheim, Bahram and Mahmoud. I was staying with the Aga in his villa at Deauville shortly after he had sold Blenheim for £30,000, and he told me in confidence that he did so because he thought the stallion was losing his fertility. It was one of the biggest blunders in his long and successful career as an owner-breeder.

The success of his studs had been based on five mares, Uganda, Teresina, Cos and Mumtaz Mahal, all bought for him by George Lambton, and Friar's Daughter, bought for him by Dick Dawson. Blenheim was bred by Lord Carnarvon and purchased as a yearling for 4,100 guineas. Unlike Aly, the Aga was a severely practical man and never allowed sentiment to cloud his judgement. He hoped the Allies would win the war, but in his opinion they could not beat Hitler, and he made his plans accordingly. It sometimes happens that an owner who hopes for the success of his horse, but fears it won't beat another horse in the race owned by a man he doesn't much like, may back the danger and allow his own horse to run for the stake: in the same way the Aga planned for Hitler's success, but prayed he would be proved wrong.

I don't know why he sold Mahmoud, but when I met him in Paris after the war he told me: 'I sold Bahram because I was hard up.' Although lack of communications are an obstacle to monetary transactions in wartime, I would be surprised if the gnomes of Zürich failed to guarantee him three square meals a day so that he had to hock his Triple Crown winner.

Lord Derby sold a number of stallions to the U.S.A., but only when he considered that he had too much of one particular line. Stanley House was a much smaller concern than the studs of M. Boussac and the Aga Khan.

Had the Aga Khan retained his three Derby winners he would not have had to send his best mares to such horses as Tehran and Migoli. Both were good racehorses: next to Sun Chariot, Tehran was the best of the wartime St Leger winners, while Migoli beat Tudor Minstrel in the Eclipse Stakes, and won the Prix de l'Arc de Triomphe from a substandard field when the race was worth a tenth of its present-day value. But neither was in the top class as a stallion.

Aly Khan's expenditure was on such a scale that not even the heir to the richest man in the world could carry on without dipping into capital. His most liquid assets were his mares and in the three years between his father's death and his own he had disposed of one batch of fifty mares and had also negotiated several smaller sales.

Mares are a breeder's capital and their foals are the dividends. The stallions are the stock in which his capital is invested. George Lambton bought very few colts when the Aga Khan gave him that blank cheque at the end of World War I, but the fillies he bought turned out to be worth their weight in gold. Aly was being pressed for money on all sides and at one sale, pictures belonging to him fetched £80,000.

It soon became apparent to Marcus Marsh that the cream was off the milk, and that the majority of the horses he had inherited from Frank Butters were the products of studs which were on the slide. He was not greatly elated when a little colt by Tehran of very ordinary appearance came to be trained by him a month later than the main bunch of yearlings. A May foal, he was so small that it had been decided to give him a little more time in the paddocks at the Gilltown Stud. He was, however, superbly bred on his dam's side, being out of Neocracy, a daughter of Blandford and Athasi and therefore an own sister to the Derby and St Leger winner Trigo. They called him Tulyar. Palestine had been the only colt of his generation within measurable distance of classic form, and though they were all bred in the purple Marcus was quite sure that there was no Windsor Lad among the yearlings which came to be trained by him in 1950.

Tulyar was a nice little fellow, who gave no trouble and

always aimed to please, but it never entered Marcus' head that he would aspire to greater heights than that of winning a few races when the opposition was not too strong. His two-year-old races in 1951 bore this out, his best performance being when winning a mile nursery under top weight at Haydock Park. On this form he looked a good thing for the Horris Hill Stakes at Newbury, but to the disgust of Aly, who had one of his major bets on him, Tulyar was beaten by a horse of no great distinction called H.V.C.

Charlie Smirke was the least depressed of the trio, believing that if he had held him up a little longer Tulyar might have won. Aly, however, was not impressed, and in the course of the winter tried his hardest to flog him for £7,000. Mercifully for him no one would offer more than £5,000, which he didn't think was enough. In the Free Handicap he was given 8 stone 2 lb, 19 lb below the top weight.

As a three-year-old Tulyar was not much bigger than he had been at two, but he showed great improvement on previous form when winning the Henry VIII Stakes first time out at Hurst Park, beating King's Bench, who had won the previous year's Middle Park Stakes. This performance looked even better when King's Bench finished second to the French colt Thunderhead in the Two Thousand Guineas.

Smirke could not do the weight on Tulyar in the Ormonde Stakes at Chester, where he was ridden by Doug Smith. He beat two opponents but did not impress one as a possible, much less a probable, Derby winner. The three-year-olds in 1952 were a poor lot, and Tulyar won the Lingfield Derby Trial Stakes convincingly. As I knew that the horses which finished closest to him were not considered to be within a stone of classic form by their connections I thought that somewhere or other, probably in France, there must be something better than the Aga Khan's colt who even now stood only 15·2½ hands.

Between Lingfield and Epsom Tulyar did everything Marcus asked him to do, and for the first time he appealed to his trainer as a Derby colt. Aly, who had recently been spending even more money than usual, had a fortune on him, and after being on offer at 100/8 twenty-four hours before the race he started at 11/2. This was the most drastic cut in a Derby candidate's price in my experience.

Charlie had discovered at Newbury the previous autumn that Tulyar had only one run and therefore had to be held up, but he struck the front in the Derby earlier than he had intended when those in front dropped away beaten; prepared as usual, however, for all emergencies, when he was challenged by Lester Piggott on Gay Time he took his ground and beat him by three-quarters of a length.

This is a legitimate though borderline manœuvre, consisting of taking your mount close enough to cause an opponent to change his legs, without actually interfering with him. Amateurs are not advised to attempt it. Gay Time slipped up after passing the post, and Lester Piggott returned to the weighing room without horse or saddle. Gay Time was caught by a policeman and Lester was able to weigh-in for second place.

Before his mount was recaptured Lester announced his intention of objecting, which goes to show how narrow the margin is between taking another horse's ground and interfering with him. He was dissuaded, however, by Gay Time's owner Mrs James Rank and trainer Noel Cannon.

Tulyar thrived on racing, and having won the Eclipse Stakes from a substandard field, he again beat Gay Time in the King George VI and Queen Elizabeth Stakes. Charlie Smirke was told that if he could not do the weight Gordon Richards would ride Tulyar in the big Ascot race. This was a challenge which necessitated many hours in the Turkish baths and the most drastic week of wasting that even he had ever undergone. By a superhuman effort he took off 10 lb, and riding on a paper-weight saddle he was only 2 lb overweight. Charlie never believed in winning by a wider margin than necessary, no matter how important the race, but I never saw him ride a cheekier race than he did on Tulyar that day.

Tulyar was an odds-on favourite for the St Leger, and as this was to be his last race of the season Charlie let him stride out to win by three lengths from the handicapper Kingsfold, one of the least distinguished horses that can ever have been the runner-up in an English classic race.

Gay Time was bought as a stallion by the National Stud for £50,000 but was started for several races as a four-year-old in which he carried the Queen's colours. He ran so indifferently that it was evident the National Stud had made a very bad buy. They were lucky in being able to flog him to the Japanese. The price paid was not disclosed, but I would lay a shade of odds that it wasn't £50,000. The Aga Khan announced that Tulyar would remain in training as a five-year-old, but no one took him very seriously, and sure enough it was later announced that the Irish National Stud had bought him for £250,000, over £100,000 more than the Aga had realised from the combined sale of Blenheim, Bahram and Mahmoud. Unlike his predecessors Tulyar was a complete failure as a stallion.

In the course of his three-year-old career Tulyar won £75,173 and largely as a result the Aga Khan was leading owner with £92,518 and Marcus Marsh leading trainer with £92,093. This sum had only once been surpassed—by Joe Lawson, then training at Manton, who won £93,889 in 1931.

Tulyar had a wonderful disposition. Nothing worried him and although he was thought to prefer soft going it was very firm at Epsom and his Derby was one of the roughest I can remember. Charlie Smirke kept Tulyar away from the scrimmaging, but after the race there were hard-luck stories by the dozen. M. Boussac's Marsyad broke his leg, but his jockey Rae Johnstone said no one was to blame.

Neither Marcus nor Charlie considered Tulyar to be in the same class as Windsor Lad, but no horse could do more than win all his races as a three-year-old, beating the best horses that England, France and Ireland could field against him.

The sands were running out, but Marcus Marsh should have won one more classic race for the Aga Khan. Gordon Richards' expertise won him twenty-six jockeys' championships and 4,870 races in all, but I hope he will forgive me for saying that I thought that his judgement was at fault on the Aga Khan's Kerkeb in the Oaks of 1953. Kerkeb was going so well that Gordon dashed her down the hill to take the lead over half a mile from home. She looked all over a winner but the effort left her with nothing in reserve, and Joe Mercer, then an apprentice, brought Lord Astor's Ambiguity with a well-timed late run to beat her by a length. Gordon rode in 21,843 races but this was the only occasion on which I could say with conviction that he lost a race he should have won.

Aly had always been a trifle in awe of Frank Butters, the only man I ever met who was impervious to his charm. Deprived of his greatest asset Aly was much like the rest of us. He knew that the arm-round-the-shoulder, 'dear old boy' technique would cut no ice with Butters, and for perhaps the first and only time in his life he felt frustrated. Both Aly and his father always addressed their trainer as Mr Butters, and in my long association with Aly I cannot remember hearing him address anyone else in this formal manner. Frank Butters and I were fellow guests at the Aga's villa at Deauville on two occasions, and it was apparent that the Aga had a high regard for Butters, both as a man and as a trainer, and in any dispute between his son and his trainer on matters of policy he would have supported Butters.

Marcus Marsh's position was entirely different. He and Aly were close friends: they were of much the same age and of course there was no social barrier between them. Both men had a great zest for life and they had dozens of friends in common. Marcus and his wife, therefore, were as vulnerable to Aly's charm as all the rest of us. We delighted in his company, eagerly accepted his hospitality, and ended up by being at his beck and call.

If Aly had asked Butters if he could have his limit on one of his father's horses, or even on one of his own, Butters would have given him one of his chilling looks, which made one wish one was wearing an overcoat, but Marcus was expected not only to win big races with second-rate horses but to know they were going to win so that Aly could have his limit on.

Had Marcus been less scrupulous he might have lasted longer, as Aly would sooner have lost than been told that the horses were not good enough to bet on. While Tulyar was winning more money than any three-year-old had ever won before, Aly, without saying a word to Marcus or his father, who was a sick man, had arranged for Alec Head and Noel Murless to train the horses the following season.

I had known Aly since his earliest days on the Turf, and his treatment of Marcus Marsh was out of character. I had not seen as much of him in the post-war years as I had done in the thirties, when from time to time he would ask me to back a horse for him. While executing his commission I would more often than not bump into an acquaintance on the same mission, as Aly never gave one any intimation of how many people were engaged in investing his money or the amount involved. It might be imagined that he did not know, but although he was wildly extravagant, and betted like a drunken sailor, I am sure he knew exactly the size of the total commission. He had no idea of the value of money, but like his father he was extremely money-conscious, and woe betide anyone who tried to short-change him.

Charlie Smirke was understandably indignant at Aly's treatment of Marcus Marsh, and they were never again on the same terms as they had been after Charlie won the Grand Prix of 1947 on Avenger. Aly bought this colt quite cheaply, on his own judgement and with the idea of having a gamble on him in a maiden race. It was soon obvious that he had secured a bargain and the decision was to let Avenger take his chance in the Grand Prix. Aly never let a horse run unbacked, and he won over £100,000 on this outsider—a fortune for most backers, but as from time to time Aly was owing the casinos about £200,000 it was no more than just a nice little touch. Of course he paid all his debts in the long run, but in some cases it was a very long one indeed.

Charlie Smirke, after some argument, agreed to go to France and ride the horses trained by Alec Head at Chantilly, but the venture was doomed to failure from the start. Charlie disliked Alec Head, as he would have disliked anyone who had taken over from Marcus. This was of course quite illogical, but Charlie was never very strong on logic. Having arrived in France with a grievance, he declined to co-operate. Although much younger than Charlie, Alec Head would not stand any nonsense from any jockey, no matter how many Derby winners he'd ridden; so from the word go they were at daggers drawn.

A house divided against itself cannot prosper, but Alec and Charlie had their moment of triumph with the Aga Khan's Rose Royale in the One Thousand Guineas of 1957. Second to her, beaten a length, was Aly's Sensualita, a 33/1 chance ridden by Massard. Both fillies were trained by Alec and he and Aly were delighted; but there was no joy on Charlie's face as he rode into the winning enclosure, his expression reminding me of that of Joe Childs after Coronach had run away with him when winning the Derby thirty-one years earlier.

After the race Charlie said nothing would again induce him to ride a horse trained by Alec Head, and the latter said something along the same lines. The outcome was that Massard rode Rose Royale in the Oaks, in which she finished third, as well as all the stable's runners at Ascot. Tora, in the Coronation Stakes, was their only winner, and Aly told me he had one of the worst weeks of his life. Three weeks later the Aga Khan died. Aly replaced Massard with the Australian George Moore at Deauville, and was so impressed with his riding that he engaged him as first jockey on a three-year contract.

Aly Khan grew up with three ambitions—to own the most successful string of racehorses in the world, to win huge sums betting and to make Casanova's exploits appear like those of an elderly gelding. He failed in the first two, but came very close to accomplishing the third. Aly's love live has no place in this book: I will only say that in terms of quantity it was bewildering and in terms of quality superb.

Like all gamblers, he could not visualise failure. The reason he backed horses and gambled in casinos was not that he hoped to supplement his income (with all his faults Aly was never naive) but because he was a compulsive gambler. If there was no racing and no casino within a hundred miles he would bet on flies crawling up the wall if he could find a child (or a grown-up with the mind of a child) to bet against him.

Although all his friends and interests were in the West, his father's action in passing him over in favour of his son Karim was a terrible blow to his pride and on the last occasion on which I was with him for more than a few minutes he was beginning to look middle-aged. We were at Longchamp and I had gone with him and Bettina to inspect the horses before one of the classic trials. The charm remained, but as we talked I felt that some of his zest for living had gone. I do not know whether he had a premonition that he was soon to die, but he had told me years before that he did not want to live to be an old man—and having reached the age of forty-nine I am sure he had not changed his mind.

Life had to be lived at full speed, or it was not worth living; Casanova must not disintegrate into an ageing philanderer. His friends found him an enchanting companion, but he hated his own company; his fame as a lover was widespread, but there is nothing more pathetic than the evening of a great reputation.

When the horses left Marcus Marsh, all except a few went to Chantilly to be trained by Alec Head. Noel Murless took the remainder despite the fact that he already had a stable of seventy horses. Aly was concentrating more and more on the big French races which were increasing in value every year. The English races for the Guineas, however, were still far more valuable and carried greater prestige than their French counterparts, and Guineas Week at Newmarket in 1959 was by far Aly's most successful week as an owner.

One of the horses sent to Murless was a grey filly by Sir Alfred Butt's very good racehorse Petition out of a Bois Roussel mare. She did not appear to be anything out of the ordinary when she arrived at Warren Place, but Noel Murless, as he always does, gave her plenty of time before asking her to exert herself fully.

No great racehorse can have made a less auspicious début than Petite Etoile: in a field of two at Manchester at the end of May 1958 she finished second, beaten eight lengths by Chris, a 4/1-on chance trained by Billy Nevett who was giving her 10 lb. I need hardly say that Lester Piggott did not give her a particularly hard race, and the experience did her so much good that six weeks later she won the Star Stakes at Sandown by five lengths. She was beaten two lengths by a very fast filly called Krakenwake in the Molecomb Stakes at Goodwood, but won her last race as a two-year-old at Sandown at 6/1 on.

18 The Queen and Prince Charles congratulate Sandy Barclay after his victory on Her Majesty's *Hopeful Venture* in the Hardwicke Stakes at Royal Ascot 1968

19 The Royal Procession Ascot 1966

20 Mr. Charles Engelhard's Triple Crown winner *Nijinsky* (Lester Piggott wins the 1970 Derby)

She improved so much in appearance during the winter that Murless began to wonder if she might not be up to classic standards, though as a two-year-old she had never been considered in that light. Lester Piggott rode Short Sentence in the Free Handicap, and as Moore was Aly's jockey in France he rode Petite Etoile. With nine stone in the saddle she fully justified Murless' belief that she was now a very high-class filly by pulverising the opposition.

From his position on Short Sentence, Lester cannot have had a very good view of the race, as to everyone's surprise he elected to ride Collyria in the One Thousand Guineas. I have already described how Doug Smith had to extend Petite Etoile to resist the challenge of Rosalba.

Two days before Petite Etoile's victory Aly Khan's Taboun, trained by Alec Head and ridden by George Moore, had won the Two Thousand Guineas by three lengths. From his early days this son of Tabriz and the Fair Trial mare Queen of Basrah (an ideal Guineas pedigree) had been earmarked by his owner and trainer for the Newmarket classic. To win both the races for the Guineas was something that Aly's father had never accomplished.

The Oaks, of course, was Petite Etoile's next objective, but many people doubted her ability to stay a mile and a half. Cantelo at 7/4 and Mirnaya at 2/1 disputed favouritism, with Petite Etoile at 11/2; but there was only one in it when Lester Piggott gave her her head approaching the last furlong. I have never before or since seen a filly accelerate so rapidly at the end of a race for the Oaks, and she beat Cantelo by three lengths. There was now no doubt in anyone's mind that though our colts were nothing to shout about, Petite Etoile was worthy of comparison with Sceptre, Pretty Polly, Sun Chariot and Meld.

There can be no doubt that she would have won the Derby. Cantelo, whom she beat with 10 lb in hand in the Oaks, beat Fidalgo, second in the Derby, by a length and a half in the St Leger, with the Queen's Pindari three lengths away third and Derby winner Parthia, who started at 13/8 on, a further three-quarters of a length away fourth. While Petite Etoile was a smasher, Collyria and Cantelo were both good enough to win

N

the Oaks in nine years out of ten and at no other time in my experience have we had three such superb fillies in training at the same time.

Petite Etoile's next race was in the Sussex Stakes at Good-wood. She started at 10/1 on and Lester appeared determined to give those that had laid the odds some excitement for their money, holding her so tight by the head that she won by only three-quarters of a length. In the Yorkshire Oaks he again played cat and mouse with his opponents and again she had only three-quarters of a length to spare.

Her final outing was in the Champion Stakes, and in his anxiety that Petite Etoile should not have to exert herself un-duly at the end of a busy season Lester performed a feat I had hitherto regarded as impossible: on the wide open spaces at Newmarket he got shut in in a field of three. He managed to extricate himself in the nick of time, but had to give her a harder race than she would have needed to run if allowed to stride along at her own pace.

In 1959 horses bred by Aly and his father won £100,668—and Aly was leading owner with the same sum. He was the first owner and breeder to win a six-figure sum in the history of the Turf. Since then Mr H. J. Joel, who bred and owned Royal Palace, won £109,883 in 1967, and in 1970 Mr E. P. Taylor, breeder of Nijinsky, was leading breeder with £161,302.

In the last year of his life Aly Khan derived enormous pleas-ure from the triumphs of his wonderful grey filly, and it was his decision to keep her in training as a four-year-old. 'I love that filly,' he said to me as she left the paddock to canter to the post for the Victor Wild Stakes at Kempton on May 7th, 1960. He had a love and understanding of horses which his father lacked, but the only previous occasion on which he had registered any emotion about a horse was some years earlier, when one of his father's horses broke a leg at Longchamp and had to be destroyed. Petite Etoile won that small race at Kempton in a canter and Aly returned to Paris in a happy frame of mind. Six days later he was killed in a motor accident at St Cloud on the outskirts of Paris.

He had only survived his father by three years, and within a few weeks of his death two of his horses of which he had the highest hopes scored notable triumphs. Charlottesville won the French Derby and the Grand Prix, and Sheshoon won our Gold Cup. The horses were ridden in all their races by George Moore. The triumphs of Taboun, Petite Etoile, Charlottesville and Sheshoon gave reason to believe that the Aga Khan's stud was returning to its former glory. This promise was not fulfilled. In the succeeding years the horses were no better than the ones which had cost Marcus Marsh his job. Alec Head had proved himself a great trainer, but he, too, was only human and the man has not yet been born who can turn a congenitally slow horse into a fast one. The young Aga Khan, however, knew nothing about racing and disheartened by his lack of success he sent all his horses to be trained by François Mathet.

18 Lester

Lester Piggott, an infant prodigy – Wins 1951 Eclipse Stakes aged sixteen and Derby on Never-say-die aged nineteen – Loses his licence – 'More sinned against than sinning' – Crepello, a splendid Derby winner – Murless and Piggott complete the double with the Queen's Carrozza in Oaks – A great year for the Queen – Ballymoss pays tribute to Crepello by winning St Leger – A great four-year-old, he wins Coronation Cup, Eclipse Stakes, 'King George', and Prix de l'Arc de Triomphe – Hard Ridden becomes second consecutive Derby winner for Sir Victor Sassoon – Charlie Smirke's fourth and last Derby.

If ever a boy was bred to be a jockey it was Lester Piggott. By top-class National Hunt rider Keith, by Ernie, winner of two Grand Nationals on Jerry M. and Poethlyn, both of whom were carrying 12 stone 7 lb, out of a Rickaby, with several Cannons close up in his pedigree, Lester couldn't miss.

As my readers will have watched him scores of times in the flesh and on TV and will have formed their own opinions on every facet of his riding, I will sum up in just a few words the skills of Lester Piggott, eight times champion jockey, and the greatest rider in the world.

No feat of jockeyship ever performed by any man, alive or dead, could not have been carried out equally well, and in nine cases out of ten a damn sight better, by Lester Piggott.

I read somewhere that he would be an even greater jockey if he let his leathers down a couple of holes. Can anyone seriously maintain that at the age of thirty-six Lester does not know the length of leather which suits him best?

I know he has long legs, and if he was going to ride round Aintree, which his grandfather did with such skill, I have no doubt he would ride half a dozen holes longer, but as he is able to maintain perfect control when perched like a pea on a drum, he would be crazy to ride any other way. The advantage of riding so short is that it places all the jockey's weight on the horse's shoulders, and only the saddle, which in Lester's case often weighs scarcely a pound, rests on the horse's back.

I maintain that more nonsense is talked about racing than any other subject, but I am told this is not so and that I only think so because I have some knowledge of racing but am profoundly ignorant about everything else. That isn't true, but I am always ready to give the opposition a hearing.

Since Lester ceased to be at loggerheads with the Establishment he has made fewer mistakes than any of his predecessors. I confess that I thought he was ill-advised to leave Noel Murless, and when he promptly missed out on a Two Thousand Guineas, a One Thousand Guineas, a Derby and a 'King George', not to mention the thick end of 10 per cent of £250,000, I wouldn't have been surprised if he'd thrown himself off the Post Office Tower, but before the end of the season he had won an Irish Derby and a St Leger, and now, four years later, he is well in pocket as the result of being able to pick and choose his mounts.

It is said by alliteration addicts that 'Lester loves lolly'. Who doesn't? Money isn't everything, but nothing's anything without it, if you get my meaning. Lester earns a stack, but if you're the champ you would be out of your mind if you didn't cash in on it. Rod Laver, Cassius Clay and Tony Jacklin may not earn much more than Lester, but I'll lay a shade of odds that they manage to keep more.

When I can't sleep at night I start calculating Lester's bill for surtax. It doesn't send me to sleep, but I get a nice warm glow contemplating how lucky I am not to have to pay taxes on the same level as Lester does. He is criticised for not being a big spender. It's his money, and having earned it as the result of denying himself food and drink, without which the rest of us would die, I see no reason why he should spend it entertaining hangers-on and layabouts.

Lester's attractive wife Susan and two daughters live very simply in an unpretentious house at Newmarket, but from the middle of March till well into November Lester is away every weekend riding on the Continent. It is as an international rider that he reigns supreme. No man has ever ridden so many winners in so many different countries, and in all of them he is acknowledged as the champion. Our prestige does not stand all that high in the rest of the world, but no matter where you go they will tell you that Lester Piggott, an Englishman, is the greatest rider in the world.

The 'Lester only does it for lolly' brigade should cast their minds back and remember that Lester rode over hurdles. He didn't need the money and he certainly didn't get much unless the owner had had the Bank of England on a horse which obliged and had shown his appreciation in a tangible manner.

My favourite Lester Piggott story concerns an owner who liked to bet. Four times his horse ran and four times his unfortunate 'stopping' jockey told the same story: he could have 'trotted up'. The big day arrived when the horse's remaining back teeth were no longer in danger, and Lester was engaged to ride him. But on reaching the rails the owner found his horse was an even-money chance. Having returned to the paddock as fast as his legs would carry him he informed his trainer: 'Not today.' The good man, who believed in falling in with his owners' wishes whenever possible, appeared ill-at-ease as he answered: 'Lester's a funny boy, guv'nor, and I'm afraid he'll say the horse has to go forward, and bugger the price.' This is exactly what Lester did say. The race was run, and the horse was beaten on its merits. Lester did not stop as he passed the disconsolate owner after dismounting, but glancing over his shoulder as he approached the weighing-room he remarked: 'He wouldn't have needed much —— ' (a seven-letter word) 'stopping.'

Susan Piggott is a daughter of my old friend Sam Armstrong, and like her father she always gives me the impression that there are matters of great urgency needing her immediate attention.

I would like to bet that neither Sam nor Susan has ever missed a trick in their lives, and I am quite sure that if the astronauts had found a man on the moon he would now have a few horses in training with Sam Armstrong at Newmarket. When Sam had a large school of apprentices Susan ran the show, and a first-class show it was.

Sam has trained for all and sundry, the richest being the Maharajah of Baroda, a well-meaning, friendly little man, but lacking the polish of the majority of the Indian princes. Realising that with the end of the British Raj he would be stripped of most of his wealth he spent money like water and paid a record sum for an own brother to Dante, which he called Sayajirao. This much-publicised purchase did not please those who were to become his masters in India and they made it very clear that they considered that 28,000 guineas was too much to pay for a yearling when the peasants were begging for rice. Sayajirao, trained by Sam and ridden by Edgar Britt, won the St Leger. Sam also trained My Babu, a half-brother to Sayani, by Djebel, who was ridden by Smirke to win the Two Thousand Guineas. The Maharajah and Sam employed both Britt and Smirke. The two men hated the sight of one another, but this didn't worry Sam so long as they carried out their jobs to his satisfaction.

After 'wonder boy' Piggott had won the 1951 Eclipse Stakes at the age of sixteen on Mystery IX for Madame Esmond, her son-in-law Baron Geoffrey de Waldner, who had won the Derby with Pearl Diver, asked me if I thought that a sixteen-year-old boy had ever before ridden such a brilliant race as Lester had done on Mystery IX, who was trained by Percy Carter at Chantilly.

I replied that neither of us had seen Frank Wootton, but I fully agreed that the infant prodigy had ridden a super race. Mystery IX was by Tehran, and next to Tulyar he was the best horse sired by the Aga Khan's wartime St Leger winner to run in this country.

Lester was certainly an infant prodigy, but those who described him as having an old head on young shoulders were talking nonsense. When I first interviewed him at the age of fourteen or fifteen he did not strike me as being precocious, rather the reverse, but in his middle thirties he still shuts up like a clam when he sees a journalist approaching with an inquiring look on his face.

On and off a horse Lester has always been two entirely different people, and in his young days the difference was more pronounced than it is today, when, if he chooses, he can be quite articulate. Throughout his teens, and I have not forgotten that he won the Derby at the age of eighteen, Lester was young for his age. Had he not been he would not have been continually in trouble. With greater mental maturity he would have realised that the quickest way to the top is not through the stewards' room.

The greatest mistake a young man can make, and I speak from experience as I made it myself, is to underrate those in authority. I don't know who marked his card, but Lester was definitely under the impression that the stewards were a bunch of incompetent old women and he would emerge grinning from an interview with them. He seldom smiles, and at thirty-six he doesn't do much grinning either.

At the age of fourteen he had bags of self-confidence and displayed flashes of brilliance, but a race such as he rode on Mystery IX would be followed by one which revealed that he still had a great deal to learn. These substandard performances became fewer and fewer with the passing of the years, but they still persisted till he was well into his twenties, by which time he was riding as first jockey to Noel Murless.

By and large, his faults were those of over-emphasis, the result of his overwhelming anxiety to win. Jockeys are sometimes accused of not trying hard enough, but Lester would have run into far less trouble had his desire to win been tempered with more discretion. Rules counted for nothing and no holds were barred when Lester saw an opening, or perhaps I should say what he hoped might become an opening, with a little not so gentle persuasion.

Cautions and short periods of suspension did not worry Lester in the slightest, and one didn't need to be a mind reader to realise that he was saying to himself: 'Silly old bastards. I'll

show them.' If he had known as much as most boys of his age
he would have realised that it was only a matter of time before
'the silly old bastards' would tire of censures and short periods
of suspension, and would throw the book at him.

He was eighteen years of age when he won the Derby in 1954
on Mr R. S. Clark's Never-say-die; none the worse for the race
the son of Nasrullah was saddled for the King Edward VII
Stakes at Ascot, which I, for one, thought he was sure to win.

It was without any question one of the roughest races I have
ever seen, and had the patrol camera been in operation at the
time I have little doubt that the stewards would have had all
the jockeys on the mat and not only Lester.

I watched the race from the press stand, from which I have
watched many hundreds of races, but there were so many 'inci-
dents' that I should have hated to adjudicate at the subsequent
enquiry. It had appeared to me that each and every jockey had
contributed his share to what might easily have ended in a
tragedy, and while I am not saying that Lester was blameless I
formed the opinion that he was more sinned against than
sinning.

Rashleigh, ridden by Gordon Richards, was the winner,
while Never-say-die was unplaced, so whatever sin Lester may
have committed it had not done him much good. The stewards
lodged an objection to Rashleigh, but before hearing any evidence they withdrew it.

The reason for their strange behaviour has never been di-
vulged and all we were ever told was that the stewards had
taken notice of Piggott's dangerous and erratic riding both
that season and in previous seasons, and that in spite of con-
tinuous warnings he continued to show complete disregard for
the Rules of Racing and for the safety of other jockeys. They
went on to say that before any application for a renewal of
Piggott's licence could be entertained, he must be attached to
some trainer, other than his father, for a period of six months.
So the rider of the Derby winner became a stable boy again.

Jack Jarvis was chosen to instruct Lester in how to confine
himself to the straight and narrow path. An acquaintance who
spent much of his time writing to magistrates to chide them for

their leniency expressed the view that Lester's period of correction should have been spent with Major Sneyd. I pointed out that while Lester might have been a naughty boy he had not, so far as I had heard, committed a murder.

Lester's chief punishment lay in his missing the ride on Never-say-die in the St Leger. Few classic winners have started their three-year-old careers in a less auspicious fashion. On the fourth day of the flat-racing season at Liverpool he was well beaten by Tudor Honey, who was giving him 5 lb. His two-year-old career had been that of just an ordinary colt who might win a race or two in modest company. The official handicapper shared this view and gave him 18 lb less than the top weight, The Pie King, in the Free Handicap. He was well fancied for this race with 8 stone 3 lb, but never showed with a chance. His only other outing prior to the Derby was in the Newmarket Stakes in which he finished third to Elopement and Golden God.

On all form therefore Never-say-die did not appear to possess a 100/1 chance in the Derby, but his very experienced trainer, Joe Lawson, then seventy-three years of age, knew that the extra distance would be all in his favour, while he attributed his defeat in the Newmarket Stakes to the very slow pace at which the race was run. In the weeks prior to the Derby Never-say-die improved out of all knowledge, both in appearance and in his work, and having engaged Lester Piggott to ride him Lawson was something more than mildly hopeful.

There were doubts whether Darius, winner of the Two Thousand Guineas, would get the trip and the race appeared wide open with the French-trained Ferriol and North-Country-trained Rowston Manor joint favourites at 5/1. Never-say-die was a 33/1 chance, but his success was assured a long way from home. The Queen's Landau, by Big Game out of Sun Chariot, was one of the leaders at Tattenham Corner, but this colt of royal blood did not stay any better than his sire had done, and was beaten two furlongs from home. It was at this point that Lester challenged on Never-say-die and he drew away to win most convincingly by two lengths from Arabian Night with Darius a neck away third.

He was an even better horse when he ran in the St Leger, and

Charlie Smirke, substituting for Lester, has never had an easier winning ride. Never-say-die's maternal grand-dam was Galatea, trained by Joe Lawson for Mr Clark to win the One Thousand Guineas and Oaks in 1939. She was ridden in both races by Bobby Jones, a delightful character who was never appreciated at his true worth. Before he succeeded Alec Taylor in 1928 Joe Lawson had been assistant trainer to the Master of Manton for many years, but the last occasion he had been associated with a Derby winner was in 1910 when Lemberg won in the colours of Mr 'Fairie' Cox. Lawson moved to Newmarket when Manton was sold to George Todd after the Second World War.

In 1957, three years after his success on Never-say-die, Lester Piggott, now first jockey to Noel Murless, won the Derby on Crepello for Sir Victor Sassoon. Sir Victor had spent vast sums of money over a long period in an endeavour to win the Derby, and Crepello's success was therefore very popular—and not just because he started the hottest favourite of any Derby winner since Bahram twenty-two years earlier.

Crepello had won the Two Thousand Guineas and Murless had no doubt that he would prove himself 10 lb better over the Derby course. A glance at his pedigree confirmed this, as he was by Donatello out of Crepuscule, by that great stayer and sire of stayers Mieuxce, winner of the French Derby and Grand Prix. Crepuscule was a most successful brood mare, and was the dam of Sir Victor Sassoon's Honeylight, who won the 1956 One Thousand Guineas ridden by Edgar Britt and trained by Charlie Elsey.

Crepello was a big powerful chestnut colt and it was a fine feat on the part of Noel Murless to get him forward enough to win the Guineas over a distance well short of his best, and yet leave sufficient on him so that he would arrive at his peak on Derby Day. Lester's considerate handling of him in his races as a two-year-old, and again in the Guineas, contributed to his well-being.

Like most big colts Crepello preferred some give in the ground, but though the going was on the firm side at Epsom he was always pulling over his rivals. As the field ran down to Tattenham Corner, Crepello was lying fourth, but it was obvious that he could take the lead as soon as Lester was prepared to let out a few inches of rein. In the straight the Irish-trained Ballymoss was the only possible danger, but Crepello swept by him with contemptuous ease to win by one and a half lengths. Pipe of Peace, Sir Gordon Richard's first runner in the Derby as a trainer, was a length away third.

At that time Crepello was unquestionably the best Derby winner since the end of World War II, though it was not until the autumn that we could appreciate that in Ballymoss he had beaten a colt of the highest class.

Unfortunately Crepello was unsound, and he never ran again. He was due to run in the King George VI and Queen Elizabeth Stakes, but when Noel Murless found that the going was heavy he decided to withdraw him. A huge crowd had gone to Ascot to see Crepello and there was widespread disappointment when it was announced an hour before the race that he would not be saddled.

Derby week of 1957 was to be the most memorable week in the careers of Noel Murless and Lester Piggott, as two days later they won the Oaks with Carrozza in the colours of Her Majesty the Queen. Leased to the Queen by the National Stud, Carrozza was by Sir Eric Ohlson's wartime Derby winner Dante out of Calash, an own sister to Sun Chariot. She was not a big filly, and though I do not place her among the best winners of the Oaks, she had a heart as big as herself.

No one who was present at Epsom that day will ever forget how having struck the front with two furlongs to go, she held a clear lead 100 yards from home. There was not a top hat still on its owner's head and a tremendous cheer went up in recognition of the first royal victory at Epsom for forty-eight years; but our jubilation turned to dismay as something in green was seen to be catching her hand over fist.

Fortunately, Lester Piggott had continued to ride for his life and he redoubled his efforts as the 'thing in green', with her jockey riding like a demon, drew up to him. You could have heard a pin drop as these two gallant fillies passed the post, inseparable as far as the human eye was concerned. The minutes seemed like hours before 'First Number One' was an-

nounced over the loudspeaker—a winner by a short head from
Mr Joseph McGrath's Silken Glider, whose jockey Jimmy
Eddery had done everything humanly possible, and whose
mount would probably have won in another stride.

The judge, Mr Hancock, must have thanked his lucky stars
that he could leave the decision to the camera. If he had had to
decide the result himself I think he must have given a dead heat;
but even so the morons, who believe that the royal colours are
always given the benefit of the doubt, would have accused him
of favouritism, especially in view of the fact that Mr McGrath
had served in the Irish Republican Army during 'the troubles'.

But, thank heavens, there was the photograph for all to see,
with the tip of Carrozza's nose protruding beyond that of Silken
Glider. At the end of the season the Queen was leading owner
with £62,212. Noel Murless was leading trainer with £116,898.
Champion jockey was Scobie Breasley with 173 winners. Lester
Piggott was third with 122 winners. Breasley, Hide, Piggott,
Doug Smith, Manny Mercer and Carr all topped the century.
I think I am right in saying that this was the only year in the
history of the Turf in which six jockeys rode more than a hundred
winners.

In Almeria, by Alycidon out of the Hyperion mare Avila and
trained by Captain Boyd Rochfort, the Queen owned an even
better filly than her Oaks winner. Backward, Almeria did not
make her début till the Lingfield Oaks Trial in which she ran
with such promise that she started a hot favourite for the
Ribblesdale Stakes at Ascot, which she won by five lengths; she
went on to win the Bentinck Stakes at Goodwood, the Yorkshire
Oaks and the Parkhill Stakes. If she had been in the St Leger I
am sure she would have given Ballymoss plenty to do.

As Crepello broke down in the course of his preparation for
the St Leger it is possible that Murless' much criticised action
in withdrawing him from the King George VI and Queen
Elizabeth Stakes saved backers a great deal of money, as it is
quite on the cards he would have broken down in the Ascot
race. In the absence of Crepello the race probably needed less
winning than usual. The winner was Montaval, who had
finished second in the previous year's Derby to Lavandin.

After the Derby Ballymoss went from strength to strength. Ridden by T. P. Burns he won the Irish Derby and then the St Leger. Vincent O'Brien feared that the going at Doncaster, after heavy overnight rain, would prove too heavy for Ballymoss, and he went out in the betting from 4/1 to 8/1. The Town Moor is renowned for its drying properties, and following a morning of bright sunshine and a strong wind the going was only a fraction on the soft side of perfect. Ballymoss was always galloping freely and took the lead early in the straight. Court Harwell and Brioche challenged him strongly close to home but he never looked like being caught.

Burns met with an accident, and Scobie Breasley rode Ballymoss in all his races as a four-year-old. Good horse that he was as a three-year-old he was an even better one when winning the Coronation Cup, Eclipse Stakes, King George VI and Queen Elizabeth Stakes and Prix de l'Arc de Triomphe. Scobie Breasley was a deceptive rider in that he could fully extend a responsive horse by squeezing it with his knees and legs, but in all his races as a four-year-old Ballymoss gave the impression that he could have pulled out quite a bit more had the occasion demanded.

Bella Paola, owned by M. François Dupré and trained by Mathet, had won our One Thousand Guineas and Oaks in a common canter, and was certainly one of the best French fillies to run in this country in my time. Her connections thought she was sure to beat Ballymoss in the Prix de l'Arc de Triomphe, but she was not concerned with the finish. Her jockey complained that she had been badly interfered with while making the bend into the straight. There had been a lot of crowding, and I did not see the incident myself, but his complaints were obviously justified as she was sent over to run in the Champion Stakes and won easily.

Crepello and Ballymoss were undoubtedly the best horses to finish first and second in the Derby in the past fifty years. At that time I regarded Crepello as the best Derby winner I had seen. Since then, however, Sea Bird and Nijinsky have left us spellbound, and it is with some reluctance that I now place Crepello only third.

Having achieved his ambition with Crepello in 1957 Sir Victor Sassoon won the Derby the following year with Hard Ridden. Although he won by five lengths, while Crepello had only one and a half lengths to spare over Ballymoss, I do not think that Hard Ridden was within a stone of his predecessor. After Alcide's victories at Chester and in the Lingfield Derby Trial Stakes, which he won by twelve lengths, Sir Humphrey de Trafford's son of Alycidon looked a racing certainty, but a week before the Derby he injured himself and could not run. Harry Carr told me that he thought Alcide strained a stomach muscle when he ducked to avoid the heels of a horse who was playing up on the gallops; it was not till many years later that I heard it suggested that Alcide had been got at.

Without Alcide they were a poor lot and there was little incentive to try to retrieve the money I had lost over Alcide in ante-post bets. Two French horses, Wallaby and Noelor, started favourite and second favourite, the latter jointly with the ungenerous Bald Eagle, a poor substitute for Alcide.

Few Derbys have created less interest, as it was impossible to make out a convincing case for any of the twenty runners. Although Charlie Smirke had been engaged to ride the Irish-trained Hard Ridden, not many of us gave him a second thought. He had cost Sir Victor only 270 guineas, and the only reason he bought him was because he was by his own horse Hard Sauce. This was the very reason why so few people would entertain the idea of Hard Ridden winning the Derby. Hard Sauce was a successful sprinter, but he had never won over more than six furlongs.

It is possible that Hard Sauce might have got a longer distance as he was by M. Boussac's Ardan, winner of the French Derby, Prix de l'Arc de Triomphe and our Coronation Cup. His dam Toute Belle was bred by Leon Volterra. She was not a very distinguished mare and there was not a single bid for her when she came up for sale at Newmarket. Before sending her home again it was decided to have her covered by Hard Sauce and that's how the 1958 Derby winner came to be born.

Looking back over the years I sometimes think that if I had gone into a particular race more thoroughly and made a more

exhaustive study of the pedigrees I might have tipped and
backed the winner; but that does not apply to Hard Ridden. At
fifty-one Charlie Smirke was still as full of self-confidence as
ever, but even though Hard Ridden would have the advantage
of his jockeyship he could not make out much of a case for him.
His mount had won the Irish Two Thousand Guineas, but the
race did not appear to have required much winning, and in any
case the extra distance would not be to his advantage. However, if he had been hot favourite Charlie could not have ridden
him with greater expertise, and he was suited by the unusually
slow pace at which the race was run.

He was in the centre of the field entering the straight, but
eagle-eyed Charlie saw a gap near the rails, and he was through
it in a flash. From that point there was no danger to Hard
Ridden, who increased his lead to five lengths over another
Irish-trained horse, Paddy's Point, ridden by National Hunt
jockey Willie Robinson, who six years later won the Grand
National on Team Spirit. Trained by young Mick Rogers,
Hard Ridden was the first Irish-trained horse to win the Derby
since Orby fifty-one years earlier.

Hard Ridden made no show behind Ballymoss in the King
George and Queen Elizabeth Stakes, and did not run again.
Although this seemed an undistinguished field several of its
members went on to higher things. Wallaby won the Gold Cup
the following year, beating Alcide, though the latter turned the
tables in the 'King George'. Nagami won the Italian Premio
Jockey Club, while Bald Eagle and Amerigo distinguished
themselves in the U.S.A.

At 270 guineas Hard Ridden was not the cheapest Derby
winner of the past fifty years. The distinction belongs to April
the Fifth, so-called because he was born on that date way back
in 1929. He was sold to dissolve a partnership and bought by
Mr Sidney McGregor, one of the part-owners, for 200 guineas.

Mr McGregor did not believe in pampering horses, and April
the Fifth was turned out till he was sent to Epsom in January,
with a coat several inches long, to be trained by Tom Walls.
Mr McGregor told Tom he could have a half-share in him if he
would train him for nothing and that the horse would carry

Tom's colours if he was good enough to run in a race. April the Fifth was a cheap horse, but even so he cost ten times more than his dam Sold Again, who on one occasion was actually given away.

April the Fifth was not even the cheapest horse in that strangest of all Derby in 1932, as Lord Rosebery had given only 170 guineas for Miracle, who finished third. Men pay hundreds or thousands of pounds for yearlings without owning a horse good enough to run in a classic race, but the first and third in that Derby cost 370 guineas between them. Nothing delights the racing world more than the victory of the little man over the big battalions, so April the Fifth's was one of the most popular, especially at Epsom, which had not turned out a Derby winner for ninety-two years. Tom Walls was a big man in the world of the theatre, but he was a little man compared with the Aga Khan in the world of racing. The Aga's Dastur had looked all over a winner till Fred Lane brought the comedian's horse to beat him by a length.

Hard Ridden was Charlie Smirke's last classic success; his record stands at two in the Two Thousand Guineas, one in the One Thousand, four in the Derby and four in the St Leger, a formidable achievement when one takes into account the fact that he was warned off for five years and did not ride in England throughout the war. Eleven years is a big slice out of a man's life. Throughout his career he had severe weight problems, and he was the only jockey I know who performed the prodigious feats of weight reduction without impairing his health.

Sir Humphrey de Trafford's atrocious luck with Alcide in 1958 changed with a vengeance the following year when he won the Derby with Parthia. The 1959 winner was not within a stone of Alcide, who was undoubtedly one of the best colts to run in this country since the war.

Parthia won the Dee Stakes and the Lingfield Derby Trial Stakes, after being ridden for dear life in both races. In the Derby, however, he put up a very smooth display, and well ridden by Harry Carr he won by a length and a half from Fidalgo, ridden by Carr's son-in-law Joe Mercer. First and second had the race between them a long way from home, but

o

the Baron Guy de Rothschild's Shantung finished like a train and would have beaten them both with a little further to go. Early in the race Shantung had collided so hard with a horse who had stumbled that his jockey Palmer thought he had broken his leg, but as Shantung seemed to be none the worse he set off in pursuit of the rest of the field which was getting smaller in the distance.

I have seen a number of horses (Parth in 1923 and Solario in 1925, to mention just two) who have made up a lot of ground in the Derby, but none as much as Shantung, who must have been 150 or 200 yards behind the leaders by the time Palmer got him going again.

Parthia's victory was tremendously popular. Sir Humphrey de Trafford, in his young days a highly competent amateur rider, had rendered splendid service to racing over the years as a steward of the Jockey Club. He has friends in every walk of life and is as popular with the jockeys as he is with his fellow members of the Jockey Club.

Captain Boyd Rochfort was one of the most competent and highly respected trainers in the history of racing. A wonderful trainer of stayers, this was the first time he had saddled the winner of the Derby. It was also a first Derby for Harry Carr, though he had come within a head of winning on Prince Simon, and was also second on the Queen's Aureole. One of the soundest jockeys, Carr was first jockey to Freemason Lodge, which meant that he rode for King George VI and for the Queen from 1947 till his retirement in 1964.

Noel Murless broke all records in 1959, winning £145,727 for his patrons. Thirty-two of his horses won sixty-three races. Among them was a handsome two-year-old son of Aureole and the Bois Roussel mare Edie Kelly, called St Paddy, bred by his owner Sir Victor Sassoon. Noel gave him plenty of time and he did not make his début till the Acomb Stakes at the York August meeting. Someone must have been impressed by what they had seen him do on Newmarket Heath, as I do not think it was stable money which was responsible for his starting favourite. He was still backward, and Lester Piggott accepted the situation some way from home.

St Paddy's only other appearance was in the Royal Lodge Stakes at Ascot. His race had done him a power of good and he was the best-looking two-year-old colt I had seen that season. After he had cruised home by five lengths he was made winter favourite for the Derby. I can't imagine why anyone should want to back a horse in September for a race the following June, but ante-post prices create a talking point for the winter months when our courses are under six inches of snow, or only the tops of the fences are visible above the floods, and the clerks of the courses have told us that there is some slight doubt as to whether racing will be possible.

St Paddy looked magnificent when I spent a night with Noel and Gwen Murless in March, but it was evident that he would not be at his best in the Guineas. Noel, however, decided to run him as part of his preparation for the Derby. The race brought him on at least ten pounds, and he won the Dante Stakes at York in a canter.

My own view was that he would finish second in the Derby as I had been greatly impressed by the victory of Angers in the Prix Hocquart (a mile and a half) in which he accounted for a better field than St Paddy had beaten at York.

Topography is not my strong subject, and I can give no explanation of why the horses should disappear from view for about 100 yards on the descent to Tattenham Corner so that only the jockeys' caps are visible. It was here that Angers fell, and it was here that seven horses fell two years later. I looked in vain for him as the field entered the straight, and I was still looking when St Paddy drew clear two furlongs from home and went on to win easily from the Irish-trained Alcaeus, ridden by Scobie Breasley.

Poor Angers had broken a fetlock, and no sooner had his jockey, Gerard Thibœuf, returned than I was summoned to the stewards' room. Thibœuf did not speak a word of English and I was to act as interpreter.

My French was adequate to carry on a somewhat technical conversation with the gynaecologist when my son was born in Paris, and it has served me in good stead on countless evenings in Montmartre and Montparnasse, but I was doubtful whether

I would be able to cope with an accusation of dangerous riding, or (who knows?) attempted murder. Fortunately Thibœuf, a pleasant soft-spoken man, said it was a pure accident and no-one was to blame. He even went so far as to say that Angers was not going well when his fetlock snapped.

Mme Strassburger, owner of Angers, was eighty years old, and although she was distressed by the fatal accident to her colt she accepted it as one of the fortunes of war. She was the recipient of widespread sympathy. Two days later her Paimpont was beaten a head by Never-too-late in the Oaks. Yet another French filly, Imberline, was two lengths away third. Although trained in France, Never-too-late, who had previously won the One Thousand Guineas, was 100 per cent English bred, being by Never-say-die out of Gloria Nicky, a daughter of Alycidon. Poincelet got into all sorts of trouble on Never-too-late and in extricating her he crossed Imberline. The latter's owner, Baron Guy de Rothschild, told Poincelet exactly what he thought of him, in my presence, and if Imberline had finished second he would have objected and probably got the race.

The big handsome St Paddy needed a lot of work, and having been let down after the Derby he was not fully wound up when surprisingly beaten by Lord Sefton's Kipling in the Gordon Stakes at Goodwood. He won the Great Voltigeur Sweepstakes by three-quarters of a length from Apostle, and then went on to take the St Leger from the Irish-trained Die Hard by three lengths, the same margin as when he won the Derby.

St Paddy was a good average Derby and St Leger winner, but I do not put him in the same class as Crepello. I may be doing him an injustice, but I gained the impression that he was a smashing good horse against inferior opposition who would not pull out much under pressure.

This view was borne out when he was a four-year-old. He looked a world-beater when breaking the course record in the Eclipse Stakes, but the French-trained Right Royal, ridden by Poincelet, cut him down to size in the King George VI and Queen Elizabeth Stakes. Right Royal, a son of Owen Tudor, was one of the best French-trained horses to run over here since the last war, and St Paddy seemed to lose interest when he realised that he was up against a better horse than himself. St Paddy won the Jockey Club Stakes, but was well beaten in the Champion Stakes by a second-class French three-year-old called Bobar II. St Paddy may not have been too genuine, but he was a generous provider: in his three seasons he won £97,000 in stakes.

A pile-up. Noel Murless beats all records

Poincelet doesn't bother and Psidium comes from nowhere to win 1961 Derby — The nobblers fix Pinturischio — Solera wins One Thousand Guineas and Oaks — Bill Rickaby — The great Derby pile-up—seven fall — Larkspur the winner — Relko's Derby in 1963 — Was he doped? — Stewards' enquiry lasts for months — Ragusa triumphs for Paddy Prendergast — Noel Murless and Lester Piggott part company — George Moore takes over and wins 1967 Guineas and Derby for Jim Joel — Noel Murless breaks all records — Sea Bird, the greatest of them all, wins Derby and Prix de l'Arc de Triomphe — Nijinsky's year.

Any trainer will tell you that if a jockey loses confidence in a horse the horse will lose confidence in itself. There are, however, exceptions to every rule in racing, and there have been occasions when a horse has run the race of his life although his jockey didn't think he had a cat in hell's chance, and just didn't bother.

This, I am sure, is part of the explanation for Psidium's victory in the 1961 Derby. On none of his form as a two-year-old (when he had some very hard races) or as a three-year-old did he seem within a stone of being a Derby colt. No one was more aware of this than Roger Poincelet, as one of Psidium's least impressive performances was in the Prix Daru at Longchamp when Mrs Arpad Plesch's colt was ridden by Lester Piggott. Incidentally, Poincelet was the seventh jockey to team up with Psidium.

After the Prix Daru I asked Lester Piggott his opinion of the winner Moutiers, and was told: 'Not much, he didn't finish far enough in front of my fellow to be any good.' Moutiers started favourite for the Derby, but made no show.

Psidium was last of the twenty-nine runners for the first half-mile, Poincelet giving the impression that his mind was on something else. On the run down to Tattenham Corner he was still not bothering. I must confess I didn't pick him out again till well inside the last furlong when he was galloping past opponents as if they were standing still. There remained three or four in front of him but by this time he was the only one galloping, and he beat Mme Volterra's Dicta Drake by two lengths with Pardao a neck away third.

Several factors contributed to his success. First and foremost he reacted kindly to Poincelet's 'don't give a damn' tactics; he had been subjected to a number of hard races and it was a pleasant change to be allowed to amble along at his leisure for the first mile. The field was a very moderate one by Derby standards, and the fast pace at which the early stages were run left every horse, bar Psidium, stone cold a furlong from home. Last but not least, the going was very firm and Psidium and Pardao were both by Pardal, whose stock cannot have it too hard.

From the previous autumn they had been shouting from the roof-tops at Newmarket the name Pinturischio, a bay colt by Pinza out of the Italian mare Napalina Da Murano. He did not run as a two-year-old, but when I stayed with Noel Murless the following spring he made no secret of his hopes concerning this handsome well-grown colt. Noel is never one to become wildly enthusiastic about a horse that has never run, and as we left his box he said: 'We shall know more about him after the Wood Ditton.'

On the opening day of the Craven meeting at Newmarket Aurelius won the Craven Stakes, and though Mrs Lilley's colt and Pinturischio had not, of course, been tried together I know that in Noel Murless' opinion at that time Pinturischio could pick up Aurelius and carry him. The latter was a nice colt and full of promise, but as yet completely unfurnished. Pinturischio won the Wood Ditton Stakes hard held, and was backed to win a huge sum in the Derby by people from all over the world. The bookmakers reported that never before had there been such an avalanche of money for a Derby colt.

He started at 7/4 for the Two Thousand Guineas, but could only finish fourth. I could see no excuse for him, but comforted myself, having already backed him for the Derby, with the thought that the extra half-mile would be in his favour. The Guineas was won quite easily by the 66/1 chance Rockavon, trained in Scotland by George Boyd and ridden by Stirk, his success constituting the biggest turn-up in my experience of the race. Psidium, who started at 50/1, did not finish in the first ten.

The success of Sweet Solera in the 1961 One Thousand Guineas was far more popular with the locals. Owned by Mrs S. M. Castello, a charming lady who has done much good work for those less fortunate than herself, trained by Reg Day, the doyen of the Newmarket trainers, and ridden by Bill Rickaby, the best-liked jockey of my time, Sweet Solera's success was a happy termination to a hitherto disappointing week. She was given an ovation, but it was a mere whisper compared with that which greeted her victory in the Oaks.

I've never met anyone who had an unkind word to say about Bill Rickaby, a gentleman in the truest sense of the word. There are some men in my life who I know are incapable of a mean action and Bill Rickaby is one of them. He and his wife Bridget, a daughter of the King's trainer William Jarvis and sister of Ryan, have been for years the most popular couple living in Newmarket or within miles of it. If Bill had been prepared to push himself forward and ring up trainers asking for mounts he would have ridden even more winners than he did, but he wouldn't have been Bill Rickaby.

Millions would be won by the unscrupulous if Pinturischio did not run in the Derby and, sure enough, the nobblers broke into the Warren Place stables and fixed him. Hanging is far too merciful a form of punishment for perpetrators of crimes of this nature. He never ran again as he broke down in the course of his preparation for the St Leger. Psidium also broke down and did not run again after the Derby.

Aurelius went on improving all the season, and ridden by Lester Piggott he was a most impressive winner of the St Leger, beating Bounteous by three-quarters of a length with Dicta Drake and Pardao, who had finished second and third in the Derby, third and fourth. Just Great, who had beaten Aurelius in the Great Voltigeur Sweepstakes and was much fancied by Staff Ingham, reared up at the start and was hopelessly left.

The 1962 Derby will go down in history as the Derby of disaster, as at almost the same spot six furlongs from home where Angers had broken his fetlock, seven of the twenty-two runners fell. By a miracle no one was killed, and only one horse, King Canute, was so badly injured that he had to be destroyed. The stewards found that there was no evidence of rough riding, but regretted that so many horses which had no right to be in the field were started. I see no way, beyond appealing to the good sense of owners, to eliminate the million-to-one chances. If any arbitrary pruning had been carried out the previous year Psidium would have been one of the first to go, and in the 1962 Derby Larkspur's credentials were not inspiring. He had been a doubtful starter until the Friday before the race, having developed a thorough-pin, a distension of the tendon sheath covering the hock, and stable jockey Pat Glennon, who had won on him at Leopardstown, elected to ride his stable companion Sebring. Breasley was approached but had been claimed for Prince d'Amour, so Vincent O'Brien engaged the Australian Neville Sellwood, who had succeeded George Moore as first jockey to Alec Head.

My description of what happened was pieced together long after the race. All I or any other journalist knew was that something had gone down and a cavalcade of horses had fallen over him. Journalists are a heartless lot, and I am afraid that my chief concern lay in my inability to 'get a story', all those involved having been removed to hospital. Apparently Romulus was the first to go; Crossen fell over him and the other five piled up over them. Larkspur nearly fell, but recovered and hit the front two out to win easily from M. Boussac's Arcor, with another French horse Le Cantillen third. Fate's grim irony has seldom been better exemplified than in what happened to Sellwood:

having narrowly escaped being involved in the Derby pile-up, he met his death when riding at Longchamp a year later.

Larkspur was one of the smallest horses to win the Derby, and he was undoubtedly a lucky winner. He subsequently finished unplaced in both the Irish Derby and the St Leger at Doncaster.

Had he not been involved in the pile-up I have little doubt that Major Holliday's Hethersett would have won the Derby. His jockey Harry Carr, who received an injury which kept him out of the saddle for several weeks, can seldom have had an easier winning ride than he had when winning the St Leger on Hethersett. Dick Hern turned out the winner looking a picture, a fine training performance as Hethersett had returned from the Epsom fracas a mass of cuts and bruises and could not run again till the Goodwood meeting, where he ran disappointingly. He won the Great Voltigeur Sweepstakes by a short head from Miralgo with Monterrico third. The same three colts occupied the leading places at Doncaster, though this time Monterrico beat Miralgo.

Hethersett was by Hugh Lupus, whose racing career I have dealt with at some length, out of the Big Game mare Bride Elect, and was bred by his owner. Major Holliday, a dour Yorkshireman, had bred and raced on the very best lines for many years, and when he died in 1968 his stud was the most powerful in this country. His Vaguely Noble had won the Time-form Gold Cup in a canter, and when he came up for sale fetched the unheard-of price of 150,000 guineas though he had no English classic engagements. Trained by Etienne Pollet and ridden by Bill Williamson he beat our Derby winner Sir Ivor by three lengths in the Prix de l'Arc de Triomphe, thereby proving himself cheap at the price.

I was in a clinic in Zürich when the 1963 Derby was run so all I shall say about it is that M. François Dupre's Relko, trained by Mathet and ridden by Yves Saint-Martin, made our own and the Irish colts look very moderate indeed.

This Derby, however, will always be remembered by the fact that the 'all right' was not signalled for several months. A test carried out on Relko revealed some foreign body which mysti-

fied the analysts. The case dragged on and on till the Jockey
Club decided that the 'bodies' were not big enough to have
affected the result and allowed Relko to keep the race.

He was, of course, a hot favourite for the Irish Derby, but he
was obviously in great discomfort when he arrived at the start,
and to the consternation of his ante-post backers his number
was withdrawn and he did not come under starter's orders.
Even if all had been well with him I am not at all sure he would
have won.

A moderate third to him at Epsom had been Ragusa, owned
by Mr Jim Mullion and trained by Paddy Prendergast. By
Ribot, he was a late foal, so late in fact tha the had not reached
his third foaling day when he ran in the Derby. It was to be
expected that if so late a foal could run as well as he had done
in the Derby he would make tremendous improvement in the
forthcoming weeks. And so he did.

His easy victory in the Irish Derby was followed by a four-
length success over Miralgo in the King George VI and Queen
Elizabeth Stakes. This win was facilitated by the breakdown of
Twilight Alley, though I think that in any case Ragusa would
have had too much finishing speed for the Gold Cup winner.
He won the St Leger by six lengths from Star Moss, and as a
four-year-old took the Eclipse Stakes from the Two Thousand
Guineas winner Baldric II.

This year of 1963 was a terrific one for Paddy Prendergast as
he also trained Noblesse, far and away the best filly of her year.
She had won the Timeform Gold Cup the previous autumn by
three lengths, looking all over a future Oaks winner. She did not
run in the One Thousand Guineas, but won the Musidora
Stakes at York by six lengths.

At 11/4 on she was the hottest Epsom Oaks favourite since
Pretty Polly won at 100/8 on in 1904, and she won even more
easily than that great filly had done. Ragusa and Noblesse were
ridden in all their races by the Australian jockey Garnie
Bougoure, who had been sadly underrated until his association
with Prendergast. In 1964 he rode a beautifully judged race to
win the One Thousand Guineas for Paddy on Pourparler,
thereby silencing his detractors who maintained that anyone

who could sit on a horse would have won on Ragusa and Noblesse.

Paddy Prendergast, a delightful character and a great trainer, though the luck has run against him in recent years, was leading trainer in 1963 with £125,294, in 1964 with £128,102 and in 1965 with £75,323. In 1966 Vincent O'Brien topped the list with £123,808, which goes to show what the English trainers have to contend with these days. In 1970 Vincent O'Brien, with Nijinsky and one other horse, won £162,285, but Noel Murless won fifty-three races, value £199,524, to be leading trainer for the eighth time.

In the absence of Santa Claus, who was waiting for the Prix de l'Arc de Triomphe, the 1964 St Leger was one of the most open I can remember and though the winner Indiana started at 100/7 it was a highly satisfactory result as the son of the St Leger winner Sayajirao had finished second to Santa Claus in the Derby. Trained by Jack Watts, and splendidly ridden by Jimmy Lindley, he beat the filly Patti, trained by Prendergast, by a head. This was the first classic race won by Mr Charles Engelhard, a great patron of the British turf, whose colours were to become the most famous in the world in the course of the ensuing six years.

Sea Bird's year was 1965, and when winning the Derby and the Prix de l'Arc de Triomphe I believe him to have been the best horse I have ever seen. No horse in my time has come to Epsom with such credentials, and I have never been so confident that, barring accidents, a horse I had backed and napped would win. He started off the season by winning the Prix Greffulhe by three lengths, and did not run again till the £25,000 Prix Lupin on May 16th. Diatome had meanwhile won the Prix Noailles by two and a half lengths. His trainer Geoffrey Watson had a high opinion of Diatome and expected to see him make a close race of it with Sea Bird in the Prix Lupin; but Sea Bird won as he liked.

I have seen the Derby won, by some wide margins but Sea Bird is the only horse I have seen win without his jockey bothering to pick him up. The winning margin, over Meadow Court, was only two lengths, but if Glennon had asked Sea Bird to race it might have been twenty-two. Good as Sea Bird's performance looked at the time it went on looking better and better all the season.

First of all Diatome ran Reliance, believed by Mathet to be better than Relko, to three-quarters of a length in the French Derby, after which Meadow Court was a most convincing winner of the Irish Derby. Reliance and Diatome reproduced their French Derby running to an ounce in the Grand Prix, proving what good honest horses they were, and on July 4th Sea Bird ran for the £38,000 Grand Prix de St Cloud. Glennon's sole concern seemed to be to reduce Sea Bird's winning margin to the minimum, but, try as he might, he couldn't get it down to less than two and a half lengths.

And so to the Prix de l'Arc de Triomphe. Paddy Prendergast optimistically took him on with Meadow Court, and Staff Ingham and George Todd, even more optimistically, sent over Soderini and Oncidium. Those stalwarts Reliance and Diatome were naturally in the field, and there were some who thought that the sober workmanlike Reliance (if ever a horse lived up to his name if was he) might beat the highly strung Sea Bird.

Sea Bird's performance in the Derby was unique, but Glennon saw to it that it was not spectacular. The Prix de l'Arc de Triomphe was to be his last race so Glennon decided to allow the vast crowd to see what he was really capable of. I believe that Reliance, the winner of the French Derby, Grand Prix and French St Leger was the hell of a horse, and I think that Diatome would have won the French Derby and Grand Prix in four years out of five

The leaders were closely bunched entering the straight, but in the course of half a dozen strides Sea Bird had drawn clear. Extending his lead with every stride he beat Reliance by six lengths with Diatome five lengths away third. I have never seen anything like it before, and I know I never shall again.

There was just one more tribute to be paid to Sea Bird: Diatome, despite his busy season against horses which were just too good for him, was sent to the States, where he won the Washington International.

With no Sea Bird in the field odds of 11/4 had been laid

on Meadow Court in the St Leger, but he was beaten ten lengths by Mr Jakey Astor's Provoke. The going was by far the heaviest I have ever known it at Doncaster and Provoke, all honour to him, was the only member of the field who was not floundering in the mud by the time they reached the straight. Meadow Court was hating the conditions, but he beat the third horse Solstice by five lengths.

In 1966 it was rumoured that Lester Piggott, who for ten years had ridden with fantastic success for Noel Murless, was toying with the idea of riding as a freelance. Matters came to a head when he asked to be released from riding Varinia in the Oaks. I was given to understand he had been offered a very large present by Mr Charles Clore if he won the race on Valoris, trained by Vincent O'Brien, and on form she had an outstanding chance. Varinia's owner Mr Marcus Wickham Boynton agreed to release him, but Noel Murless, there and then, began looking for another jockey for 1967. Valoris duly won the Oaks from Berkeley Springs, with Varinia third. Vincent O'Brien had already won the One Thousand Guineas with Glad Rags, ridden by Paul Cook, to whom Berkeley Springs had also finished second.

The 1966 St Leger produced a great finish between two very good horses. Our final classic race has become so overshadowed by the Prix de l'Arc de Triomphe that I doubt very much whether we shall ever see again a top-class French horse in the field at Doncaster, and even owners of the best English horses find it hard to resist the lure of the infinitely bigger prizes to be won in France.

Nijinsky was in all probability the best horse ever to win the St Leger, but in so doing it is possible that he forfeited the infinitely richer race in France. Charlottown and Sodium were, however, worthy contenders. Sodium had finished fourth to Charlottown in the Derby but, ably ridden by Frankie Durr, had turned the tables on him in the Irish Derby. Scobie Breasley was injured so Lindley substituted for him on Charlottown. As Charlottown was an even-money chance and Sodium was at 7/1 the latter looked by far the better value for money, and knowing that George Todd was very hopeful he would confirm the Irish Derby form I napped Sodium. Neither Frankie Durr nor Jimmy Lindley has ever ridden a better race, and in a thrilling finish Sodium just outstayed the favourite to win by a head.

George Moore's wife had been homesick when her husband was riding with such success for Alec Head's stable at Chantilly, and she was not keen to pack up and leave her home again when George received a letter from Noel Murless, offering him Lester Piggott's job in 1967. However, the quality of the horses which he would ride and the size of his retainer overruled Mrs Moore's objections. Neither she nor her husband can have regretted their acceptance of what I believe to have been the biggest retainer ever paid to a jockey in this country.

At the end of the season thirty-four of the horses trained at Warren Place, most of them ridden by Moore, had won £256,899—£111,172 more than Murless' previous record set up in 1959.

But there was one great race won by Noel that season of which Moore did not ride the winner—the Eclipse Stakes. As he had won the One Thousand Guineas on Mr Boucher's Fleet Moore naturally chose to ride her in the Eclipse Stakes, though Noel was also represented by a good-looking four-year-old called Busted. This son of Crepello and Sans le Sou, by the 'King George' winner Vimy, had been trained in Ireland as a three-year-old and had improved out of all knowledge since coming to Newmarket. He had run once, winning the Coronation Stakes of one and a quarter miles at Sandown very easily. With Moore on Fleet, Busted was a lucky chance mount for Bill Rickaby, and he made the most of it.

Taking the lead entering the final furlong Busted accelerated to beat Great Nephew, previously trained by Jack Jarvis and now trained in France, by two and a half lengths. It was a most scintillating performance and earned Busted the right to be considered the best four-year-old in training. Fleet was fourth. She was not as good as she was beautiful: if she had been she would have been another Pretty Polly.

Although Busted was at a longer price than Fleet his success was very popular as everybody was delighted to see the pink and green colours of Mr Stanhope Joel carried by a top notcher. I've heard it suggested by those with little knowledge of racing that horses in the same stable should be coupled for betting purposes. Why on earth should horses owned by men who may not even know one another and may have entirely different views on betting be treated as one unit? A week later, Busted earned Mr Joel a further £24,389 when, ridden by George Moore, he won the King George VI and Queen Elizabeth Stakes, beating another four-year-old in Salvo by three lengths with Ribocco, who had won the Irish Sweeps Derby and was later to win the St Leger, a neck away third. This was a tremendous performance, and one wondered how he would have fared at weight for age with his stable companion Royal Palace. What an incredible year it was for the Joel cousins, with Royal Palace winning the Two Thousand Guineas and Derby for Mr Jim Joel and Busted winning the Eclipse Stakes and 'King George' for Mr Stanhope Joel. Mr Jim Joel was leading owner with £120,923 and Mr Stanhope Joel was second with £64,120.

Noel Murless believed that if Royal Palace, who like St Paddy had won the Royal Lodge Stakes as a two-year-old, could measure strides with some very fast colts in the Two Thousand Guineas he would most certainly win the Derby, the situation being identical to that of Crepello ten years earlier. Beautifully ridden by Moore, Royal Palace won a thrilling race for the Two Thousand Guineas by a short head from the French colt Taj Dewan. Although the margin was such a narrow one Moore had handled Royal Palace so tenderly that he could only have benefited from the race.

Royal Palace, a son of Ballymoss, was a good Derby winner in 1967, and Mr Engelhard's Ribocco, second to him at Epsom, went on to win the Irish Derby, beating Sucaryl, trained by Murless, by three-quarters of a length. Lester Piggott's decision to ride as a freelance did not seem to be paying off as he had missed riding Royal Palace in the Two Thousand Guineas and Derby and the lovely filly Fleet in the One Thousand Guineas. Lester's win on Ribocco in the Irish Derby and in the Doncaster St Leger brought him some consolation and at Doncaster Ribocco again accounted for a colt trained by

Noel Murless. This time it was Hopeful Venture, owned by the Queen, the best colt to carry the royal colours since his sire Aureole was in training.

There have been few more popular Derby victories than that of Royal Palace, his owner Mr Jim Joel being every man's ideal of what an owner should be. The most human of men and at the same time a highly respected member of the Jockey Club, Jim Joel had proved himself a philosophical loser and now that the luck had changed he was a modest winner.

He was full of praise for his trainer and jockey, though it was he who chose Ballymoss as the husband for his mare Crystal Palace. Fifty-five years earlier his father had won the Derby with Sunstar, who like Royal Palace was bred at the famous Childwick Bury Stud.

As a four-year-old Royal Palace, ridden by Sandy Barclay, who had succeeded Moore now that the latter was back in Australia, won the Eclipse Stakes and the King George VI and Queen Elizabeth Stakes. He broke down some way from home in the Ascot race, and it was a fine performance on the part of so young a jockey to nurse his gallant mount home, virtually on three legs.

When Noel Murless appointed Barclay as his jockey I thought that in asking a boy to do a man's job he was saddling him with too heavy a responsibility. I had seen so many promising boys ruined through being entrusted with jobs for which they were not yet sufficiently mature. Sandy, however, proved himself fully capable of holding his own with senior jockeys in the most exacting circumstances. His first big winner was Caergwrle in the One Thousand Guineas. Gwen Murless' filly was not the easiest of rides and she probably had memories of her terrifying experience in the starting stalls at Goodwood the previous summer. Sandy, however, rode her with all the confidence in the world and she beat Mr Jim Joel's Photo Flash, trained by Tom Waugh, by a length.

Mr Raymond Guest's Sir Ivor was one of the very few Derby winners who, in my opinion, did not stay one and a half miles— or perhaps I should say were better over a shorter distance. He won the Two Thousand Guineas in storming fashion from a

P

very good miler in Petingo, Lester Piggott having held him up for a devastating short run close home.

Lester adopted the same tactics in the 1968 Derby, and Sir Ivor was fortunate in finding that his chief rival Connaught was also a one-and-a-quarter-mile horse, but (at that time at any rate) not quite as good a one as he was. Ridden by Liam Ward Sir Ivor did not get the trip in the Irish Derby and Lester Piggott had the satisfaction of beating his own Guineas and Derby winner on Ribero.

I shall always regard Lester's victory on Sir Ivor as constituting one of the finest examples of jockeyship I have seen in the Derby, and I'm inclined to think that he rode an even more artistic race on him when winning the Washington International. American jockeys do not ride waiting races on their own tracks, which are seldom more than a mile in circumference, and the local Press gave Lester a terrible roasting at which he was legitimately annoyed. I did not see the Maryland race but I have seen the film of it on several occasions and each time I have marvelled at the manner in which Lester conserved his mount's energy for that short run close home, an infinitely more difficult manœuvre on a track like Laurel Park than on one of our English courses.

Mr Engelhard, his trainer Fulke Johnston Houghton and Lester Piggott won the St Leger in 1968 for the second year running, Ribero following in the footsteps of his own brother Ribocco by supplementing his Irish Derby success with a victory at Doncaster. I wonder what the odds are against own brothers winning these two classics again in consecutive years.

The victory of Blakeney in the 1969 Derby was a triumph for one of the less fashionable stables over the big battalions. Arthur Budgett has been a highly successful trainer for many years, but his stable is not composed of fabulously expensive horses, or those bred by owners to whom money is no object. Blakeney was a beautifully made little colt, and his young jockey Ernie Johnson, who had roughly 24 lb dead weight under his saddle, went the shortest way, and was fortunate in finding an opening just when he needed it.

He received paeans of praise for his enterprise, but after he had ridden an identical race on Blakeney in the St Leger and got shut in, he was accused of riding a shocking race. Some critics consider it their right to have it both ways. A jockey needs luck if he is prepared to take a chance in order to save a length or two.

I was very impressed with Blakeney when seeing him finish second in the Lingfield Derby Trial Stakes, and as a result I had a small bet on him. I think, however, that I was lucky to draw my money and that if the race had been rerun the French-trained Prince Regent would have won. His jockey had waited till the race was all over and then made his effort wide of the other runners. Geoff Lewis was substituted for Deforge in the Irish Derby and, beautifully ridden, this big black colt won in handsome style; I am sure he would have won our Derby too had Geoff ridden him.

The triumphs of Triple Crown winner Nijinsky in 1970 are fresh in our memories and require no elaboration from me. Lester Piggott has stated that he was unquestionably the best horse he has ever ridden, and as he is a very good judge and has ridden some of the best horses to run in Britain and on the Continent during the past twenty years, including Crepello, he could not have received higher praise.

I must confess I was not all that impressed by his Derby victory—till I learned the time. Two furlongs from home Lester was riding him hard, and not getting much response, or so it seemed to me, but in the final furlong the French-trained colts Gyr and Stintino cracked, and Nijinsky went away to win convincingly.

And then I saw the time: 2.34.38! I couldn't believe it! He had not beaten Mahmoud's record of 2.33⅘ sec. in 1936, but he'd come mighty close to it on going which I reckon was about four seconds slower. In Mahmoud's year the course was as hard as a hard high road and had very little more grass on it. In 1970 conditions were perfect with lots of grass. Records simply don't get broken on perfect going with plenty of grass on the course.

20 The twelve best

Breasley	Moore	Bahram	Pinza
Bullock	O'Neill	Ballymoss	Ribot
Carslake	Piggott	Crepello	Sea Bird
Donoghue	Richards	Hyperion	Solario
Elliott	Smirke	Meld	Tantième
Johnstone	H. Wragg	Nijinsky	Windsor Lad

These, in my opinion, are the twelve best jockeys and horses who have contributed to our enjoyment in the fifty-one years covered by this book.

Donoghue, Elliott, Gordon Richards, Smirke and Piggott, of the jockeys, and Nijinsky, Sea Bird, Ribot and Windsor Lad of the horses, pick themselves: but I have no doubt that the remaining seven jockeys and eight horses will be hotly disputed.

A short time in the company of the professional element will convince you that racing is a most controversial subject. Nothing is black and nothing is white and no two people are in complete agreement over the myriad shades of grey. Conclusions are largely a matter of interpretation.

The views expressed in this book are those of someone who has studied the activities of men and horses in a lifetime devoted to reportage, and I like to think that my views have remained objective and unclouded with prejudice. It will be noted that the names of both the jockeys and the horses are in alphabetical order. If forty-one years as a Fleet Street journalist have taught me anything it is not to stick my neck out.

I will, however, introduce my readers to a fascinating game I play from time to time. It consists of selecting a race which a leading jockey won, or I think should have won, and then selecting another leading jockey and suggesting how he would have fared if he had been in the saddle. Here goes.

I believe that Sir Gordon Richards would certainly have won the 1934 Eclipse Stakes, in which Charlie Smirke, on Windsor Lad, got shut in. I think Lester Piggott would in all probability have won it, but knowing his preference for keeping his mount covered up as long as possible it is conceivable that he too might have found himself imprisoned with a horse in front of him, another horse on his left, and the rails on his right. I think that both Charlie and Lester would have won the Oaks on Kerkeb, in which Gordon appeared to come too soon, but I think that both Gordon and Charlie would have won the 1969 Prix de l'Arc de Triomphe on Park Top and also the following year's Coronation Cup on the Duke of Devonshire's filly, in both of which races Lester appeared to leave it too late.

On the other hand I do not think Sir Gordon would have won either the Derby or the Washington International on Sir Ivor, but I think he would have won the 1969 St Leger on Ribofilio, beaten by Intermezzo, ridden by Ron Hutchinson. I think you will agree it's a fascinating game.

I am taking it for granted that no one will suggest that I should not have included Steve, the two Charlies and Lester. There have been no finer jockeys in my time, but of course I cannot say how they compare with Tod Sloan, Danny Maher, Frank Wootton, Johnny Reiff and George Stern. When I saw the last-named of these ride in France he was a plump, red-faced shadow of his former self. Some readers may not agree with my inclusion of Scobie Breasley on the grounds that he was inflexible, and rode 90 per cent of his winners from behind. This is true but he never fought with his mount and even the hardest puller seemed willing to co-operate. Scobie was an artist, and no one admired his artistry more than former champion Sir Gordon, for whom he rode for twelve years.

Some jockeys need the big occasion to bring out the best in them but Scobie was as effective on a Monday at Brighton as he was in the Derby or the Prix de l'Arc de Triomphe.

If you include Harry Wragg, some people may ask why not

Joe Childs? The answer is that Joe would only ride one way unless his mount ran away with him, while Harry could ride any kind of race on any sort of horse. He will be remembered in a hundred years' time as the man who brought back sanity to the Derby. When he became a trainer Harry's thirst for knowledge was unquenchable, and his study of methods not previously adopted in this country has played a big part in his becoming one of our most successful trainers. A suitable epitaph to him would be: 'He used his loaf.'

Brownie Carslake is a 'must' in my view, though his total number of winners does not compare with that of the other eleven jockeys. He was a master of his craft with the most perfect sense of balance of them all. Jockeys lack panache because of their size, but one had only to see Brownie mount and canter down to the post to appreciate that here indeed was a great jockey, in the same way that when Wally Hammond walked to the wicket and took guard one knew, instinctively, that one was to be entertained by a master.

Rae Johnstone's inclusion may be received with a hail of criticism from those who still think he should have won the Derby on Colombo (once again may I assure you he shouldn't), and who haven't forgotten Mesa. In my view, however, his inauspicious start to his career in this country makes his subsequent achievements all the more remarkable. I agree he wasn't a stylist, but neither was Sir Gordon Richards—and Rae's record of thirty classic winners may never be beaten. An unknown Australian rider arriving in France is not overwhelmed with demands for his services, and he has to get there the hard way. This Rae did, and in the space of a year or two he was champion jockey with over 100 winners, no mean feat in a country in which for long periods they only race five days a week, the other two being devoted to jumping and trotting.

George Moore may not be everybody's choice, but those who saw him riding in this country in 1967 can be in no doubt that he was a very great jockey. His reputation stands as high in France, where he rode for three seasons with outstanding success for Alec Head, who regards him as one of the all-time greats.

In Australia, George is regarded as the greatest jockey they have yet produced, and when I saw him ride four winners in one afternoon at Randwick I was told it was only news when George did not ride at least a couple of winners.

Frank Bullock and Frank O'Neill are only names to anyone under sixty, but believe me they were tremendous riders. I was admittedly young and inexperienced when I watched them ride but I believe that they would be just as effective in the seventies as they were in the twenties. They were two of the most versatile riders of their day, and though O'Neill may have been a trifle past his best when I first saw him ride in France he rode brilliant races to win the Derby on Spion Kop in 1920 and the Oaks on Straitlace in 1924. His greatest years, however, were before World War I. In France in 1910 he rode 156 winners, in 1911 163 winners, and in 1913 156 winners.

In compiling my two lists I have made repeated revisions, crossing out names and then next day reinserting them and crossing out those which had taken their places. How sad it makes me that I have found no room for Doug Smith, five times champion, or Yves Saint-Martin, the greatest French jockey of all time. Geoff Lewis, now first jockey to Noel Murless, is also knocking at the door. He modelled himself on Sir Gordon Richards and has the same rolling gait. A splendid jockey for the past twelve years, Geoff has become an even better one in the course of the last three.

I haven't forgotten Billy Nevett, the Cock o' the North for so many years, and described by his friend Sir Gordon as the best bald-headed jockey he had ever met. Year in and year out, Jimmy Lindley, Joe Mercer, Edward Hide, Duncan Keith, Frankie Durr and a whole lot more maintain the highest standard of English jockeyship. I would also like to include two more Australians, Bill Williamson and Ron Hutchinson. Their records over here are well known, but it may not be common knowledge that Williamson is regarded in his own country as the next best jockey to George Moore that Australia has produced. Hutchinson is a model of consistency.

I am as certain as one can be about anything in racing that Sea Bird, Nijinsky and Ribot were the three best colts over one and a half miles ever seen on a racecourse anywhere in the world. No colt in my time can be compared to them, and as we must assume that the standard of the thoroughbred is still improving I do not think that any colt before my time can have been their equal.

I believe that Sea Bird's performance when winning the Prix de l'Arc de Triomphe transcends anything accomplished by Nijinsky or Ribot. Phil Bull, in *Racehorses of 1965*, points out that there were five Derby winners in that field of twenty—which he believes to have been the best field ever to contest what is now unanimously regarded as the world's greatest race. Phil goes on to point out that Khalife, who had finished third in the Irish St Leger, couldn't go fast enough to fulfil his mission as pace-maker for Meadow Court.

Jockeys who rode in both the 1965 and 1970 Derbys have expressed the view that the going was only slightly faster on the latter occasion; but Nijinsky's time was almost four seconds faster than Sea Bird's. Had Glennon ridden Sea Bird as hard as Lester had to ride Nijinsky in order to beat Gyr, he would have returned a faster time, but not by as much as four seconds.

A feature of the 1970 Derby was that the field appeared to be going a very modest gallop for the first half-mile, and I assume that because the horses had not been extended before they began the descent to Tattenham Corner the last mile was covered at phenomenal speed. If my theory is correct the days when the jockeys rode like mad for one of the leading positions at the top of the hill are gone for ever; and a good job too.

I regard Gyr and Stintino, second and third respectively to Nijinsky, as being superior to Meadow Court, and I say this in the knowledge that Meadow Court subsequently won the Irish Derby and King George VI and Queen Elizabeth Stakes. Although he was a very plain horse Gyr undoubtedly possessed great ability, but unfortunately he had an impossible temperament. Pollet thought the world of him, and it must be heart-breaking for a trainer to see a horse he knows to be a potential champion work himself up into such a state that by the time the trap flies open he is unable to do himself justice.

As individuals, there was no comparison between Nijinsky and Sea Bird, the former being the loveliest horse I have ever seen. Compared with him, Sea Bird, in appearance, was just another racehorse, though he improved out of all knowledge between the Derby and the Prix de l'Arc de Triomphe, having put on at least three stone in weight.

Standing nearly seventeen hands, Nijinsky was the lord of all he surveyed. In the paddock before the Derby he reminded me of the nineteenth-century actor who in order to enhance his stature is alleged to have insisted that the supporting roles be played by pygmies. There were some good-looking colts in the field for his Derby, but compared with Nijinsky they, too, were pygmies. A rich bay with three white socks, he was so beautifully proportioned that one did not immediately realise how tall he was. It was not, however, till the 'Nijinsky Night' party at the Savoy that I fully appreciated the beauty of his head. On a racecourse one rarely sees a horse head on for more than a second or two, but the film showed a close-up of Nijinsky's head with his ears cocked and his eyes, full of wisdom and understanding, set wide apart in an exceptionally broad forehead.

Nijinsky of the bold outlook was certainly a thing of beauty, and I am sure that in fifty years' time those who were very young when they saw him humble the opposition in his successful quest for the Triple Crown will be telling their grandchildren of the exploits of the most beautiful horse that ever lived.

The difference between the good horse and the great one can be summed up in one word—acceleration. This is the quality which enables a horse to make his rivals look as if they were standing still, and this Nijinsky, Sea Bird and Ribot could do more effectively than all other horses of my time.

I first saw Sea Bird when he won the Prix Lupin, and I was disappointed in his appearance. Had I seen him in a string of horses and not known who he was I certainly would not have picked him out as a potential champion. A tallish chestnut, he was not yet furnished, but having seen what he did to Diatome I said to myself: 'To hell with his looks, he's sure to win the Derby.'

He had not improved much in appearance when he came to Epsom, and several people who had read what I had written about him after the Prix Lupin said: 'I don't think much of your world-beater.'

Sea Bird has been described as half American and half French, but though this is roughly correct it is not generally appreciated that he has Stanley House blood close up in his pedigree, his sire Dan Cupid being by Native Dancer out of Vixenette by Lord Derby's Sickle, an own brother to Hyperion.

By the time the Arc de Triomphe was run Sea Bird had furnished, but even so he was a less imposing individual than was Nijinsky when he ran in that race. He also lacked Nijinsky's composure. Mr Engelhard's colt was always on his toes before a race, and would sweat up quite a bit: but this was merely a token of his well-being and exuberant spirits, and he never gave Lester Piggott a moment's anxiety. Sea Bird, on the other hand, gave Glennon several anxious moments before his races; but once the race had started he gave his jockey his full co-operation.

Should Nijinsky have won the Prix de l'Arc de Triomphe? Should, no; could, yes. Lester Piggott was in no way to blame for his defeat, though had he ridden differently he might have won. Nijinsky had proved himself outstandingly the best colt around in 1970, and Lester was justified in taking the view that all he had to do was to keep out of trouble. He lay rather further out of his ground than usual, but Nijinsky accelerated and got his head in front close home. But, instead of extending his lead as he had done in his previous races we sadly saw that he had shot his bolt, and Sassafars regained the lead to win by a head.

Had Lester suspected that Nijinsky was just that little bit over the hill and gone for an opening near the rails I think he would have won; but it would have meant taking a chance which, in the circumstances, would not have been justified. The leaders ran wide, and there would have been room to drive a bus between them and the rails, but Lester was already committed to making his challenge on the outside of four horses. On the other hand if Lester had waited for an opening near the rails and it had not materialised he would have been roasted alive for taking a chance on a horse that had 10 lb in hand.

As an example of physical achievement Ribot's record of sixteen races without a defeat is unique. I do not know the exact strength of the opposition in thirteen of his races, but I saw him win two Arc de Triomphes and a King George and there was not a horse in any of these races which could extend him. The going at Ascot was fetlock deep, and as the field approached the straight I thought Camici was uneasy, but once Ribot turned for home he accelerated to win by five lengths.

One could not rave about Ribot's looks, but he had two remarkable features—exceptional width between his shoulders and depth through the heart. My knowledge of anatomy does not entitle me to expound on these peculiarities, but it is logical to assume that Ribot derived at least some of his remarkable physique from the fact that his lungs and heart had such wide areas in which to operate. When he entered the winning enclosure it was hard to believe that he had just taken part in a race over one and a half miles.

Those who saw Tantième beaten into third place by Supreme Court and Zucchero in the Festival of Britain Stakes at Ascot may be surprised at his inclusion, but there were valid excuses for that defeat. He hated spending a night away from his stable at Chantilly so Mathet decided to fly him over to Ascot on the morning of the race. Air transport for horses was not as efficient in 1951 as it is today, and flying in a gale poor Tantième was shaken about like a jelly. After such an experience it was a praiseworthy achievement to finish third.

Had the race taken place at Longchamp, where Tantième won the Grand Criterium, Prix de la Forêt, French Guineas and two Arc de Triomphes, I am sure he would have won in a canter. His two victories in Europe's greatest race were superb performances, and when winning the Queen Elizabeth Stakes at Ascot as a three-year-old he beat Coronation, winner of the previous year's Arc de Triomphe.

Few people racing today saw Solario pulverise the Two Thousand Guineas and Derby winner Manna in the Ascot Derby, win the St Leger in a canter, the Coronation Cup by fifteen lengths, and the Gold Cup on three legs, but you can take it from he he was the hell of a horse; and if you're still in doubt, ask Reg Day.

I think that in the preceding chapters I have established a

case for the inclusion of the remaining six horses. There are, of course, a number of horses knocking at the door, and the exclusion of such as Blue Peter, Caracalla, Alycidon and his son Alcide, Petite Etoile, Fairway, Levmoss and Right Royal make me wish that I had decided on the top twenty rather than on the top twelve. I have found room for only one horse from Stanley House—Hyperion, an obvious choice, but Fairway and Alycidon have strong claims for inclusion. Alycidon was, I believe, the best stayer this country has produced in my time, but he was not a classic winner and his inclusion would have meant the exclusion of Bahram, winner of the Triple Crown. Blue Peter was one of the best Derby winners between the wars, and only the intervention of World War II prevented his winning the Triple Crown. He would have remained in training as a four-year-old, and what a Cup horse he might have been!

Alcide's accident prevented his winning the Derby, and he made hacks of his opponents in the St Leger as he had done in the Derby Trial Stakes at Lingfield. With the possible exception of Pharis, who did not run in this country and is therefore not eligible for inclusion, Caracalla was the best horse M. Boussac ever owned. I did not see him win the Grand Prix, but I did see him win our Gold Cup and the Prix de l'Arc de Triomphe, in which he defeated a very good French Derby winner in Prince Chevalier. Levmoss, like Caracalla, completed the Gold Cup–Arc de Triomphe Double, but good horse though he undoubtedly was I thought he was lucky to beat Park Top, and I do not rate him quite as highly as I do Caracalla.

Petite Etoile was in my original list, but is excluded on account of the fact that she needed fast going to be seen at her best and was nothing like so effective when the ground was soft.

It will be appreciated that at least a dozen more horses are separated by no more than short heads, so if your choice does not coincide with mine we may be at variance only by a matter of inches. A champion, no matter if he has two legs or four, can only beat those who were around at the same time as himself. He cannot beat those who came before him any more than he can beat the champions of later years.

Index